A Jacana book

They're Burning the Churches

The final dramatic events that scuttled apartheid

Patrick Noonan

The publication of this
book was supported
by the Foundation
for Human Rights

First published in 2003 by Jacana
5 St Peter Rd
Bellevue
2198
South Africa

ISBN 1-919931-46-5

Cover design by Disturbance
disturb@mweb.co.za

Printed by Fishwicks, Durban

See a complete list of Jacana titles at www.jacana.co.za

Contents

Acknowledgements

I would like to thank Jacana Media for making this book possible: Maggie Davey, publishing director, took the risk; Ruth Friedland, the editor, pulled it off and happily gave me no peace; and Angela McClelland, marketing manager, was there to explain the journey to me when necessary. I would also like to thank Barbara Ludman whose invisible hand strongly influenced the final product.

I'm deeply grateful to Sister Henrietta Riordan OP, Dr Teboho Maitse of the Gender Commission, Irish writer, Dolores Walshe (*Where the Trees Weep*) and South African author Karel Schoeman (*The Promised Land*), for the warm encouragement they gave me over the years to complete this work.

I am very indebted to Missionary of Africa Father Sean O'Leary for shoving wheels under this project. His serious suggestions helped to produce this book.

May I thank Father Geoff Moselane (Anglican), Khekhethi Makhudu (formerly SABC), Tom Manthata, Hugh Lewin (both formerly of the Truth and Reconciliation Commission), Francis Don Mokhesi (deceased) and Theresa Machabane Ramashamole (both of the Sharpeville Six), Sarah Crowe (formerly PRO of the Catholic Bishops) and Ashley Green-Thompson (formerly of the Justice and Peace section of the SACBC) and bible specialist John Maneschj MCCJ for inspecting, checking and correcting the manuscript during its long period in gestation. I am grateful to Brian Currin of Lawyers for Human Rights for advising me on an earlier draft of the manuscript, and Bonaventure Hinwood OFM for editing a later draft of the same. My gratitude to Ntsikelelo Manzi for sharing with me his pioneering research paper "Youth in Politics of Resistance in the Vaal, 1980-1990", Vista University, and Thami ka Plaatjie (Secretary General of the PAC) for background information on some of the townships.

I am grateful to fellow Franciscans Robert Stewart and Vumile Nogemane for their valued support, and to Ashley Tillek for the generous availability of La Verna Retreat Centre when I needed space and silence in the preparation of this book. Thank you, Friar Evanie Turner, for bearing with me and phone calls and messages and mayhem in the months leading up to the publication. I am indebted to Allister Sparks, former editor of the *Rand Daily Mail*, for his interest and suggestions. May I thank also the willing victims who typed my scripts when they appeared at different times, in different places and under very different circumstances, using battered typewriters, nice typewriters, electronic typewriters, other people's typewriters, their employers' computers, and even sometimes their own. They are: Imelda O'Luanaigh (my younger sister); Marie Clerkin (my eldest sister); Sister Angela Murphy MSHR; Sister "Maletsatsi" Day" MSHR; Bernice Mohale; Isabel Seady; Madintja Makara; Astrid Te Vaarwerk; Sue Rugg; Constance Nonyana; Thora Walter (deceased); Kitty Garde; Moira Tuthill; Wendy Fung and Caroline da Silva.

I am also indebted to the following people for their valuable help in preparing this book: Moss Chikane MP; former activist and advocate Gcina Malindi; Minister of Defence Mosiuoa Lekota; former activists and contributors Esau Ralitsela; David Mphuthi; Thabiso Ratsomo; Magouws Motau; Aupa Mofokeng; Doctor Malinga; Edith Connie Lethlake; Aupa Tsoabisi; Teboho Khumalo; Lipontso Phate; Pitso Ratibisi; Jacob Ramagole; Julia Matsoho; Bishop Johannes Ntepe; Shaka Radebe; Zanele Dlungwana MEC; Cosmas Thokoa; Simon Nkoli (deceased); Shele Papane; Reverend Gift Moerane; Monica Katrakilis; Kedibone Mogotsi; Monica Fouche; "Chippa" Motubasi and Duma Kumalo.

Covering as much as it does, I'm perfectly sure that readers will find inaccuracies and lacunae in these pages. Given the sheer power, drama and emotion of the times there will be – there must be – different and equally important interpretations of individual events and situations mentioned here. In the interests of the story I would be happy to be informed of these. I have, where possible, tried to cross check and correct any errors. Indeed, many stories still remain to be told.

Dedication

*To my mother and to the memory of my
father, and to my extended family.
To the people who promoted the spirituality
of Justice and Peace: the Vaal Ministers
Solidarity Group, the South African Council
of Churches, the South African Catholic
Bishops' Conference, to diocesan and parish
Justice and Peace formations, to Young
Christian Workers and Students, to trade
unionists, to the Detainees' Parents Support
Committee and all who by their brave
commitment to change, powerfully
contributed to turning South Africa into
a new human experience.*

Foreword

They're Burning the Churches is a book that should be read by those
who claim that apartheid was not so bad; that we should forget the past
and look into the future so that we may become reconciled. Father
Patrick's book is a first-hand account of what happened in the black
townships of the Vaal Triangle during the turbulent decade from the mid
eighties to the birth of democracy.

Tyrants and their underlings often blame churchmen for their
troubles. Archbishops Denis Hurley and Desmond Tutu, Dr Beyers
Naudé and Archbishop Manas Butelezi, together with other high-profile
clerics in the South African Council of Churches, played an important
role in the struggle for freedom, particularly in the 1980s. They were not
alone. There were many other priests, ministers, imams, rabbis and
pastors who were well known to the oppressed in the black communities
which these clerics served. They were also unknown to the vast majority
of white South Africans but were carefully watched by the security
police because they were part of the enemy no less dangerous than the
"terrorists" and "agitators". The apartheid state believed that by putting
the blame on the Friar they would get rid of all of them.

The clergy provided asylum for the oppressed, allowed their churches,
mosques, temples, synagogues and halls to be used for meetings where
inflammatory speeches were made. They attended their trials, gave
assistance to the widows and children of those who had been killed or
put on trial or indefinitely detained. They invited journalists from within
and outside the country to report on shootings, torture and acts of
revenge committed by vigilantes in collaboration with the police.

Father Patrick Noonan was in Sebokeng, part of the Vaal Triangle, on
3 September 1984 when the struggle took a new turn. He was not only
a spectator that day but a vital eyewitness to the tragic events, and a
shepherd to his community.

Thousands marched peacefully towards the local council's offices to protest against an increase of the rent for their houses. They declared that they would not pay it. The police shot with live ammunition, killed some and wounded many more. In the surrounding townships including Sharpeville and Boipatong the council's properties, particularly their beer halls, were destroyed. The apartheid-supporting councillors' shops and homes went up in flames. Community leaders, including priests, were detained under the Terrorism Act. Bishop Tutu's personal assistant, Tom Matata, and three leaders of the United Democratic Front were among these detainees. Charges of treason, murder, terrorism, arson and public violence were brought.

Father Patrick was involved in the lives of the people in their few moments of joy and in their prolonged times of sorrow. He attended funerals at which more were killed and even more seriously injured. He attended the trial of the Sharpeville Six and the Delmas Trial. He speaks of the Boipatong Massacre and the divisions caused by apartheid.

Yet he was there when Popo Molefe, "Terror" Lekota and most of the other victims met some of their tormentors in a football stadium in order to be reconciled.

The book is an important contribution to our recent history, which we, and our children and grandchildren, cannot afford to ignore.

George Bizos SC, Counsel for the Defence in the Delmas and Rivonia Treason Trials

Introduction

Write down all that you see of present happenings – Rev. 1:19

Nine months after my arrival in South Africa, John Knoetze, Chief Director of the Sebokeng Development Board, informed me as we sat in his plush second-floor office: "You don't tell us what to do in our country and we won't tell you what to do in your country" – a reference to the troubles in Northern Ireland. It was on 6 November 1970 that this memorable counsel was delivered with calm, thin-lipped deliberation – more the thoughts of a policeman than an administrator, I felt – and it was offered in the wake of the deportation of Father Peter Shanahan, my predecessor in Evaton township.

Not many years later, Knoetze received favourable government recognition as a thorough, efficient administrator in the black areas south of Johannesburg.

He had effectively "pacified" the townships after the Sharpeville killings in 1960 by overseeing the construction of Sebokeng during the seventies. This township was seen as a model of black housing development, containment and, crucially, contentment.

Thus, understandably, the cumbersome relocation of communities to Sebokeng tended to have a palliative effect on the political aspirations of these communities. But by the early eighties the young people of the new Sebokeng and neighbouring townships were resurrecting old political questions. And there were no political agony aunts to offer solutions. The uprising of Soweto in 1976 and the Black Consciousness Movement were for them the Good News of change. In late 1984, the townships of Bophelong, Boipatong, Sharpeville, Sebokeng and Evaton imploded, and exploded, with far-reaching consequences for South Africa. The country's apartheid structure began to shudder at its foundations, a shuddering and faltering that soon led to its demise in a smoke-filled shower of historical debris. From my perspective as a white township-dweller, the sights and sounds of this period were awesome. At some moment one early township morning, while sitting in a silent sunlit church, it flashed across my mind that this was the stuff of history. And it struck me that many court cases would follow, so it was important that records be kept. I began to write down what I saw and heard. It started as notes on scraps of paper, which graduated to diaries, journals and dispatches. I hid them as they accumulated. It was the sensible thing to do.

Years later, by the time of South Africa's first free elections, publishers were rushing out books in increasing numbers on recent apartheid history. Trawling the bookstores for accurate information on the events that I had witnessed in the Vaal Triangle led me to conclude that there was nothing of value or depth available. And yet it was in the streets, the homes and churches of the Vaal Triangle where arguably the final solution to the scourge of apartheid was hammered into place.

I had stashed away my notes, reminiscences and diaries, and now I began to collect and organise them. The more I read over what I had written in the heat of the upheaval, the more I was amazed at what had happened. I had been privy to the making of a modern-day uprising. And a chance meeting with Father Sean O'Leary (of the Peace and Justice desk of the Southern African Catholic Bishops Conference) prodded me to explore the possibility of publishing.

What had happened was unique in national history. As the world turned its attention to the uprising, church ministers were on the spot, monitoring how the international and local media, the South African government and its opponents were reporting and interpreting events in our neighbourhoods. The situation strongly invited a response. We knew that it was imperative to create channels whereby news, untainted by the powerful apartheid media apparatus, could be spread to the world outside. The churches were determined that government would not win the media war in the ghetto townships.

Since then I have often wondered why this life-changing experience seemed to awaken subconscious memories – impressions – of the subjugation of Ireland in centuries past. Perhaps it was recalling the remark of a British lord in the last century – that the Irish and the

Hottentots were barbarians, uncivilised and incapable of government – that struck a chord, triggered by local events and the social attitudes of so many white people to the dispossessed of South Africa.

My personal experience of forced evictions during the non-violent rent and service boycotts of the eighties among Vaal Triangle residents seemed to trigger a long-dormant consciousness of arbitrary and painful Irish turn-of-the-century eviction scenes. Indeed the word "boycott" (named after Captain Boycott) was coined in Ireland at the timethat Irish peasants decided to "boycott" their political masters as a method of resistance.

The Sharpeville massacre of 1960 both shocked and inspired as it resounded throughout South Africa. In 1976, the Soweto uprising both shocked and again inspired as it spread through most of urban South Africa. The 1984 Vaal uprising, however, was a volcano waiting to explode. Its effects were destined to seep into every city, town, township and *dorpie* of the land, culminating eventually in a new South Africa.

At a post-apartheid thanksgiving function at Mmabatho stadium in November 1996, distinguished human rights advocate George Bizos said to me: "The Vaal Triangle is where the liberation revolution began in earnest." If so, I thought, there must be a story there.

Apart from Johannes Rantete's important initiative *The Third of September*[1] written in the heat of the battle, and Prakash Diar's historical *The Sharpeville Six*[2], nothing of note has been written about the events of 3 September 1984, or indeed about the subsequent turmoil in the Vaal Triangle. The following pages are an inconclusive contribution to the yet untold story of Bophelong, Boipatong, Evaton, Sebokeng and Sharpeville in the 1980s.

I don't pretend that I have written an unbiased history of that period and these places. I would be happy if this book spurs others to delve more thoroughly into the events of those extraordinary times. As Thami ka Plaatjie, Secretary-General of the Pan-Africanist Congress (PAC), told me – as long as the stories of hunting are told by the hunter, the real stories of the hunted will never be told. I have tried, perhaps unsuccessfully, to avoid the emotional neediness of "the self importance of being with the damaged". It is, I'm afraid, the occupational hazard of those who choose to be carers and therapists in this wounded world.

[1] Ravan Press, 1985
[2] McClelland & Stewart, 1990

13

The Vaal Triangle was part of the industrial heartland of South Africa. Five black townships – Sebokeng, Sharpeville, Boipatong, Evaton and Bophelong – housed the workers that made this possible.

These townships kept the factories going so that, bathed in horrific pollution, Vanderbijlpark and Vereeniging became the most prosperous cities in Gauteng if not in the country. Sebokeng, with half a million people, was the largest town – let alone township – in the area. Evaton, established 100 years ago, was next with up to a quarter of a million residents.

The people of these townships were also a close-knit community bonded by decades of feigned submission to white law and order.

In the early eighties the Vaal Triangle, with its booming factories and settled populations, might have seemed the last place for black resistance to grow into fierce anti-government conflict. But the first shots in the final phase of the country's struggle for freedom were fired there – by the police.

This area has intruded on national consciousness in different but powerful ways. Sharpeville survived the infamous massacre of 1960, which saw 69 people killed in police gunfire. After that it became a household name. And one evening in the eighties the township of Bophelong rang out with the sound of police fire which, as if on cue, rang in an uprising the very next morning when the residents of Evaton and Sebokeng marched on the Vaal Triangle centre of apartheid administration at Sebokeng. In 1992, a massacre at Boipatong stalled the delicate negotiations for a new South Africa for at least six months.

The treaty of nearby Vereeniging signed in 1902 brought peace between the Boers and the British. The indigenous peoples were excluded from these deliberations. It was appropriate then that the new constitution uniting the peoples of the country was signed into law in Sharpeville in 2002 before a large gathering of township people.

Part One

The trial that moved the world

Chapter 1

Murder by legal process is immeasurably more dreadful than murder by a brigand. – Dostoyevsky

On Monday, 3 September 1984, a smouldering human rage exploded in a cluster of black townships 40 miles south of Johannesburg, South Africa. The conflagration was sparked off by rent increases proposed by black-run town councils whose members were perceived as collaborators with the apartheid government. At least seventy men, women and children died during the next three months in the violence that spread across the five black townships of Boipatong, Bophelong, Evaton, Sebokeng and Sharpeville.

Kuzwayo Jacob Dlamini, deputy mayor of the area known as the Vaal Triangle and a local councillor in Sharpeville, was among three black township officials killed in mob violence that day. He was approached at his home by a noisy crowd, part of an earlier, much larger crowd which had been dispersed by police with tear gas and rubber bullets. Called on to join them in a march to the administration offices to air their grievances, he produced a gun and began firing, wounding at least one in the crowd. Enraged, the crowd attacked and burnt down his house and car, after which he was felled by stones and finally died from burns inflicted by the attackers.

This was the climax to years of barely disguised public disdain for the government-sponsored town councillors who were seen to be corrupt and lining their pockets at the expense of the community. From this tragic incident emerged the case of the "Sharpeville Six" – five men and one woman who were arrested in the weeks following the killing, tried, convicted and sentenced to hang for having what was called in the judgement "common purpose" with the unknown killers of councillor Dlamini.

Soon the world media wanted to know about the unknown accused. They were:

- Reginald "Jaja" Sefatsa, 32, a fruit and vegetable vendor at a nearby train station, married to Regina, with one daughter.
- Melebo Reid Mokoena, 24, who worked with an engineering firm. He was a trade union member and unmarried.
- Aupa Moses Diniso, 32, a building inspector at Stewarts and Lloyds. A golfer, he was married with two children, a son and a daughter.
- Theresa Machabane Ramashamole, 25, an unmarried waitress at a nearby roadhouse.
- Duma Joseph Kumalo, 26, a student at Sebokeng Teachers Training College.
- Francis Don Mokhesi, 30, a well-known professional footballer, working as a shelf-packer in a supermarket, married with one daughter.

There were orignally eight accused – Christiaan Mokubung and Gideon Mokone were later found not guilty of murder but guilty of public violence, and were sentenced to eight years imprisonment each. They were released after serving five years.

None of the eight accused was known as a political activist.

The trial opened on 23 September 1985, before a judge and two assessors, and was conducted in English and Afrikaans, neither of which was the mother tongue of the accused. Throughout the trial the judge relied on interpreters to render an accurate account of the young prisoners' evidence. Whose voice would he hear, I remember thinking – that of the accused or that of the court interpreters?

From now on the Sharpeville Six were to become familiar with the rarefied sleepy atmosphere of courtrooms, the whirring fans on hot summer afternoons emphasising long pregnant silences during cross-examinations, and the consistent incomprehension of an elderly judge who spoke no African language and had never visited an African township. Although all his legal life Mr Acting Justice Wessel Human had dealt sympathetically with crimes of individual rage and passion, he clearly could not fathom what triggered communal rage and passion.

He appeared incapable of understanding the internal dynamics of life in his country's black townships.

An expert witness told the court that it was "highly probable" that people experience de-individualisation when joining a crowd which sees itself as discriminated against or besieged, and that this leads to diminished responsibility in much the same way as does the consumption of too much alcohol or great emotional stress. A particular event – such as the Vaal riots – triggered what is known as "contagion", marked by the rapid spread of rumours and a mood of anger and impulse.

I was at court for this evidence. It was subsequently rejected in total, prompting a legal expert to remark that "many judges believe that they are impartial and that they administer justice fairly, but they are white judges working within a white system with no experience of black township life, no knowledge of black languages, black aspirations or frustrations."

It was argued that for ordinary people like Theresa Ramashamole, Mokhesi, and millions of others, the daily pervasive realities of living under apartheid, given the powerful social and psychological forces at play, inevitably conspired to draw them into the vortex of political strife. This line of argument was again rejected by the court.

Two months after the trial began, on a hot summer's midday, the trial judge declared before a packed court in a barely audible, gravelly voice: "The result is ... that the accused numbers 1, 2, 3, 4, 7 and 8 are found guilty of the crime of murder ..."

I remember that morning well. Even as the judge disappeared from the courtroom the accused sat dazed for some moments, still facing in his direction. Slowly they looked at one another as if for reassurance and hope, then looked around searching for their families in the crowded courtroom. Their legal counsel, obviously shaken, told them that appeals would be made on their behalf. They must be brave; they must be strong, he said. Meanwhile consternation, anger and indignation swelled the public galleries behind the condemned. Their families and friends straining to get near them, the six Sharpeville prisoners were led away through the waiting cells to a prison van, which took them to Pretoria

Maximum Prison. There they were greeted by noisy, inquisitive death row inmates as they were shown to their cells. Another life had begun. In passing this sentence Judge Human made history and triggered a massive outcry from the international community.

Years later, when it was all over, I visited this place of the slowly dying. I was with ex-detainee Hugh Lewin of the Truth and Reconciliation Commission (TRC) and Duma Kumalo, one of the condemned. The smell was what hit you first: a combination of human sweat, stale cigarette smoke and too little ventilation – the off-loading of tortured souls awaiting execution. "On this corridor," recalled Kumalo with a pained shrug of familiarity, "strong men would cry at night."

The lawyers for the defence, preparing a formal appeal, also launched a campaign to petition for clemency. That campaign would spread worldwide.

In 1986 State President PW Botha refused to intervene. Meanwhile, I brought the case of the Sharpeville Six to the attention of the Catholic Bishops and provided background material for distribution among national conferences of bishops and interested parties throughout the world. I'm sure sister churches were doing the same.

Sharpeville Day, on 21 March, was traditionally the day on which the Sharpeville killings of 1960 were remembered. Joyce Mokhesi, sister of Francis, one of the condemned, spoke about the Sharpeville Six at a meeting of the United Nations Special Committee Against Apartheid.

In early May leave to appeal was granted.

But to digress for a moment. Were the Sharpeville Six the lucky ones? For not all in the Vaal had the benefit of a trial in those days, much less a fair trial. Benedict Moshoke was one of those.

He was arrested at his home in Zone 7, Sebokeng, on 10 October 1986 and brought to Bekkersdal in the Eastern Transvaal for interrogation. The date is important for these were the dread days when the police were hearing more and more orders from above such as "uithaal" (take out), "neutraliseer" (neutralise) and "verwyder" (remove). Moshoke died in mysterious circumstances on 24 March 1987 while still in detention. "If you want to lay a charge you must face me," a security policeman later told his mother.

The matter did not end there. The family was informed that the body had been mislaid. From her home in Sebokeng Mrs Moshoke set off on a lonely search for her son's body. She went to the mortuaries at Pretoria, Witbank, Middelburg and even the "whites only" mortuary at far away Groblersdal – to no avail.

Late one afternoon the police informed her that they had found the remains. A funeral was duly organised at the church at Small Farms. It was a highly political occasion. Police and military "guarded" the services closely. That morning the ageing Mrs Moshoke again met the security policeman who had originally threatened her. He told her, "Jy moet genoeg pap eet want ek sal jou skiet" (you must eat enough porridge because I am going to shoot you). That man was the notorious Barend Strydom, leader of the neo-Nazi group the *Wit Wolwe*, who later went on a racist shooting spree in a busy Pretoria street, deliberately murdering seven black people.

Chapter 2

I am overwhelmed by the thousands of people shouting and waving to me – and I greet you as a friend – PW Botha in the Vaal Triangle, June 1987

Thursday, 4 June 1987

The Sharpeville Six had been on death row for a year and a half when the State President, in a clever political manoeuvre, made a high-profile, stage-managed tour of Vaal townships (which, incidentally, cost the local council R10 000) where he was offered the "freedom" of the rent-boycotting townships by the discredited and manipulated black mayor and town councillors. The trial of the Sharpeville Six, it must be remembered, concerned the killing of the deputy mayor of the region. No reference was made to it during the visit.

A feature of the day was the sight of regular South African army township patrols taking time off to play football with local children, clearly for the benefit of the visiting international media and the comfort of their masters. Government spin doctors loved it. According to a black school inspector, Joseph Makhokolo, farm school children (local schools and various groups refused to be involved) were bussed into Sharpeville to cheer and flag-wave a president they had never known or seen in their young lives. It was a day weeping with contradictions.

Law and Order Minister Adriaan Vlok commented quite innocently (or was it tongue in cheek?), "It is a very wonderful experience for me. How can they receive us like this?" The United States Ambassador, Edward Perkins, who was in Washington at the time, later told me he had a problem explaining this apparently "joyful" reception in the corridors of the Pentagon.

1 December 1987

After waiting for almost two years in the death cells of Pretoria Maximum Security Prison, the accused were informed that their appeal had failed. The five appeal judges found that the accused had had an "intent to murder". Their conviction for murder and subversion was upheld. They were shattered. Their lawyers, from the Johannesburg firm of Ismail Ayob, were seriously concerned.

The churches were involved in the affair, taking positions that were not universally applauded. The South African Catholic Bishops Conference (SACBC) published a plea for commuting all death sentences, especially in the case of the Six, and once again appealed to the State President "to institute the end of every form of apartheid". Unctuously angered, *Business Day* (4 December 1987) declared that the "prelates are talking airily of condoning the necklace" – a system of killing whereby a tyre round a victim's neck was drenched with petrol and set alight – and that by this gesture they "sacrifice their claim to moral leadership".

Ambassador Perkins visited Sharpeville for Sunday Mass, then he met the families of the Six and conveyed to them the concern of his government. Later the Security Branch questioned some young people about this visit – they were especially keen to know if anyone had asked the ambassador for money.

The families met regularly at the church for consultations with their lawyer, to discuss travel arrangements to and from prison, and sometimes for meetings with reporters. The Detainees' Parents Support Committee (DPSC) co-ordinated these meetings.

~

On Thursday, 11 February 1988, a new petition for clemency was sent to the State President. Lawyers for the defence and Father Edward Lennon and I conferred on the advisability of visiting Washington and European capitals, with representatives of the families of the Six, to highlight the case in influential political circles. The Vatican informed the bishops of its "special interest" in the case, and supported local bishops' initiatives in this respect.

On the following Sunday, I attended a prayer service for the Sharpeville Six at the Methodist Church at Sebokeng. The service was well attended and assisted by a number of church ministers. It was important to keep the case before the attention of people.

Later I consulted with the president of the SACBC, Bishop Wilfred Napier, and his vice-president, Bishop Reginald Orsmond of Johannesburg, regarding the proposed visit overseas. After discussion there was consensus that we should meet representatives of key foreign governments here in South Africa at least as a point of departure. (Other prominent South Africans such as Reverend Frank Chikane, head of the South African Council of Churches (SACC), Sheena Duncan of the Black Sash, and civil rights lawyers were also part of these consultations.) After lunch I drove across Johannesburg to the 12th floor offices of the Six's legal team and told them of the morning's deliberations. They accepted the proposal.

That evening Joyce Mokhesi, sister of Francis, and Julia Ramashamole, mother of Theresa, left South Africa for Europe. This and their subsequent journeys to foreign capitals gave the case much valuable exposure.

A few days later Bishop Orsmond, acting president of the SACBC, sent a courier message to the State President requesting a meeting to discuss the case. The bishop's request was declined on the grounds that all legal channels had not yet been exhausted. Meanwhile there were hurried consultations all round as Bishop Napier set up a meeting between the ambassadors of Great Britain, Germany and the United States with myself and advocate Ayob representing the six South Africans – Sefatsa, Mokoena, Diniso, Ramashamole, Kumalo and Mokhesi.

From my journal:

Tuesday, 23 February 1988
I flew to Cape Town this morning with Ismail Ayob who was defending the Sharpeville Six, and for an hour and a half we conferred at the German Embassy with the three foreign representatives. Confidentiality was agreed upon, after which the ambassadors expounded their respective governments' more or less similar positions on the case. The British diplomat appeared to be speaking on behalf of his colleagues, for he clearly took the initiative in our discussions. They were at pains – especially Robin

Renwick of Britain – to indicate that their governments did not have as much clout with the South African administration as is commonly believed. We wondered. Margaret Thatcher and Ronald Reagan are at the zenith of their power, and do not believe in sanctions against South Africa, only in constructive engagement. Surely this is a recipe for friendship with State President PW Botha? Nevertheless, we had useful exchanges with the diplomats that were reported to their respective capitals overseas.

Mr Ayob and I privately agreed before the meeting that if we did not get satisfaction from the Western diplomats we would approach the Japanese. As it happened, we did not need to. The meeting was a reasonable success from our point of view.

Renwick later, in his 1997 book *Unconventional Diplomacy in Southern Africa*, took credit for quietly trying to persuade the Nationalist government not to hang the six Sharpeville youngsters.

Chapter 3

*Moreover, the state-controlled media assisted in promoting
the view that a crowd of black people … was by nature barbaric
and likely to engage in violence* – Truth and Reconciliation
Commission of South Africa Report, 1998

From my journal:
Sunday, 13 March 1988
*I celebrated Mass for the detainees at which an
ex-detainee and member of the Sacred Heart Sodality,
Zanele Dlungwana, shared with the congregation her
experiences of solitary confinement for over a year.
Zanele was detained on the same day, 11 June 1986,
as local church deacon and prominent National Union of
Mineworkers member, Tefo Phate.
She is a paraplegic and by profession a librarian.
She spoke movingly about her programmed humiliation
at Kroonstad prison where she shared a tiny cell and
open toilet with two other detainees.
Zanele recalled an extended period of solitary
confinement: "I still can't stand the sound of keys as
they represent sealing me off into a silent world at 4 p.m.
each day. The only company was birds and the distant
sound of traffic." And at night: "Sleep never came as
the body wasn't tired." She paused to reach for a tissue
as the memory became too strong. The full church fell
into a deep questioning silence as Zanele was wheeled
from the sanctuary. She repeated her message later
at Boipatong Church.*[3]

---

[3] Zanele Dlungwana is now in Parliament and holds a portfolio for the physically challenged.

Monday, 14 March 1988
Even if American prison films hadn't informed me, I now
know what the "slammer" is. It's the clinically clean, cold,
over-polished and sanitised atmosphere of a prison. It is
slamming gates and jingling monster keys echoing through
impersonal corridors. All of which greet the visitor to the
Pretoria Maximum Security Prison en route to visit South
Africans awaiting capital punishment.

For within these precincts, 117 prisoners were to be executed in 1987, often in groups of seven, giving South Africa the distinction of being the hanging capital of the world.

9.00 a.m. This morning I came on my more or less monthly
visit to Francis Mokhesi and Theresa Ramashamole.
Though I had met those from other churches before their
sentencing, I am now allowed to meet only the two
Catholics condemned. And if I wasn't an ordained minister
even this might not be possible.
After the warder, the ever-efficient Sergeant Makhubu –
who escorts all visitors to "non-white" prisoners – had
checked his files for my visit number, he handed me over to
another warder. He in turn led me through the two
remaining steel barred gates to the small upper open-aired
courtyard. Off this courtyard two doors opened into rooms
of eight cubicles – death cell visiting rooms. The guard
smiled as he let me through.
This section of this prison was always under world focus. I
used to wonder what black prison officers thought about
that. How did they feel about working with regularly
decreasing numbers on death row? What did they think
about in the taxi on the way to work on hanging
mornings? Did they tell their wives? Did they talk about it
among themselves? How did they relate to the Sharpeville
Six?
A pane of glass, reinforced by thick iron bars, separates
relatives and the condemned during their last visits.

Conversation is by means of a piped speaker system, fixed to the half-table on both sides of the glass partition, into which one speaks sitting in an uncomfortably crouched position.

Francis was led in by the popular warder Sergeant Mlambo, and greeted me with his usual calm smile tinged with what appeared to be quiet resignation. We spoke in Sesotho (The emotional state of the condemned is not easily accessible to those assured of life tomorrow. There is too much happening in their unreal world, suspended between the here and the hereafter: "I am pulled in two directions" [letter from Francis, July 1988]).

I looked at a person who was somewhat gaunt, with a pasty complexion through lack of sun, whose court appeal had been dismissed and who for two years had bravely tried to cope with the prospect of sudden death by hanging. Domestic affairs certainly engaged his attention – his wife, the children at school, the first communion of his daughter, Mamodise. Over and above these matters, and transcending them, he appeared to be reflecting a lot on the Bible and the life-threatening experiences encountered by Peter and Paul in the Acts of the Apostles and related Bible texts.

When I told him about the Mass and public prayers said for him yesterday, he lit up and talked the strange joy, peace and desire to just simply pray to the Lord that he had experienced on Sunday. In fact, it is not unusual for prisoners, especially those served with the ultimate penalty, to turn to religion to find solace and hope in their situation. The six condemned, all from various Christian traditions, are no exceptions. Enhancing this is the traditional African and Biblical view that sees little division between the supernatural and the everyday details of life. God is present always, often through his children, our ancestors.

The world of Francis "Don" (his pro football nickname)
Mokhesi lies within this broad framework. And more.
Clearly from his letters to me, and in our ensuing
discussions, as well as his meetings with the prison
chaplain for counselling and the sacraments, Francis has
found a Lord with whom he wasn't familiar. A marked
inwardness is evident, profound spiritual insights surfaced
as he wrestles with such themes as the peace of feeling
loved by God, the mysterious will of God in his present
predicament, a death embraced by Christ, resurrection
and future communion with the household of God. Anger
and bitterness seem replaced by a perception that there is
some God-plan working in and through his present
anguish.

Mokhesi was convicted of stoning Dlamini's house, making
petrol bombs on the spot, and ordering the burning of the
house when it was surrounded – a conviction based on
information by a state witness (Johannes "Eyster"
Mongaule) who later, after the trial, admitted that he had
given perjured evidence as a result of repeated assaults by
the police while in detention. Mokhesi, for his part, testified
– supported by his team doctor and football coach – that
he had injured his ankle in a game shortly before the
killing and could not walk without difficulty. He was
nowhere near the Dlamini house, he told the court.
9.45 a.m. I asked him to give my good wishes to the other
four condemned. We closed the visit with prayer. A feeble
parting smile and he was gone.

Later in the day Francis would share some of these moments with his
co-accused, as was customary among them. The corridor in which
prisoners did this was at least fifty metres long. Conversations took
different forms. Some were unconventional. They would shout to one
another from their cells or via linking toilet pipes. The toilet pipe link-
up was done by flushing the toilet, and then soaking up the remaining
water from the bowl and under-pipe with a cloth. Your friend in order to
hear you had made the same preparations. You sent a message to him

secretly about your coming communication: "Hamba Ngasimva/eboshe" (Go to the back area – to the toilet bowl). News-gathering of this type would be done between 5 and 7 p.m.

I made my way down to the condemned women's section, and after a half-hour of very methodical processing I was finally allowed to see Theresa Ramashamole, the only female of the Six.

Theresa – known popularly by her Sotho name, Machabane – was picked up in November 1984, still dressed in her nightgown, and spent several months in solitary confinement before being charged and convicted. Sometimes she got permission to visit her five colleagues in the men's section, where, after exchanging greetings and sharing news, they strengthened one another in spontaneous prayers and hymns.

Theresa was normally high-spirited and talkative, though at times angry at the bizarre fate that had befallen her in the prime of life. She looked forward to meeting her hard-working mother after her overseas journeys to foreign governments on Theresa's behalf. She had always been confident that she would not hang – that justice would eventually be done – to the point of planning for her wedding and joining church groups as soon as she was released. Again, her letters contained much paraphrasing of Biblical passages relevant to her present status as an awaiting-death prisoner.

Like the other five condemned she was aware that much was being said and done on her behalf in the outside world, and wanted the world to know how thankful she was.

From my journal:
10.30 a.m. Theresa was very happy to hear about
yesterday's Mass celebrated for her intentions,
in which I was able to convey to the congregation
her previously written greetings. The prison chaplain,
Monsignor John Magennis, celebrated Mass in her
cell last week. She told me that Sisters Gertrude Ryan
and Francis Sheehy of the Sisters of Mercy had visited
her. The always-present black prison warder noted
my name and address during our meeting, which
again was a non-contact one. Yesterday Theresa

*sent me a card "just to say thank you for everything that
the Church does for us", and asking me to come and see
her as soon as possible. She enjoyed the compliment when
I mentioned that she was putting on weight. Finally we
were reminded that our 40 minutes were up, and our
meeting closed with a prayer and blessing.*

Ramashamole's evidence was that on the morning of the tragedy she
was forced to join a protest march which, when it reached the deceased
councillor's house, was dispersed by police using tear gas and rubber
bullets. A defence witness later testified that she had treated Theresa
Ramashamole who had been struck in the head by a rubber bullet.
Lawyers argued that, as she had been hurt and was in a dazed state,
she would have been in no condition to join the crowd which 15 minutes
later regrouped and attacked Mr Dlamini. She was finally convicted on
the evidence of a single witness who said that during the commotion he
heard her shout, "He [Dlamini] is shooting at us. Let's kill him."

During the trial, evidence was submitted to the court that Theresa
had been tortured in solitary confinement. Electric shocks had been
applied to her nipples.

At the time of the trial, during an altercation with her guards, her arm
had been badly injured. She did not press charges. "I've forgiven him,"
she told me later.

Chapter 4

On the fateful day of September 3 1984, more than thirty people lost their lives. But only four murder charges arose, each of them out of the killing of a community councillor – The Sharpeville Six, Prakash Diar

Tuesday, 15 March 1988

Moments after I departed the Pretoria Maximum Security Prison on Monday, the Sharpeville Six were called to the then head of death row, Major Cronje's, office where a sheriff of the Supreme Court informed them that they would hang on Friday. Their petition to the State President had been refused. I wasn't to know this until the next morning.

A terrible, hopeless sense of resignation – and, they told me later, relief – settled over them as they were led from their old cells to the "waiting cells" section in the middle of a long corridor near the visiting block.

The authorities notified their families of the execution date. On Tuesday the Six were measured for the rope and weighed in order to eliminate any bodily "unpleasantness" as they dangle seconds after the trap door has shot away. Thickness of neck, height and weight were all taken into careful account. "They came and told me I was going to hang on Friday. They measured my neck, weighed me and gave me my number," Theresa said.

> From my journal:
> *8 a.m. Father Kevin Egan, who first heard the news on BBC radio, was, like myself, devastated. He knew the Six from their awaiting-trial days. He broke the news to me. Of course, I had to go to the prison immediately, but first I talked to the prison chaplain. He asked me to delay a while, as he wanted to meet Francis and Theresa*

(Machabane) immediately and bring them the support of Holy Communion. He would do this each morning till the end. In a state of suspended shock I decided to drop into the seminary chapel and ask the Lord how He wanted me to handle the situation when I met Machabane and Francis later that morning. A terrible sinking feeling gripped my guts. I needed time to think. Somehow God's inexplicable purpose had reached a very critical crossroads. On my arrival at the prison, which coincided with that of the case lawyer, Mr Prakash Diar, I recognised shocked and dazed relatives of the five male condemned standing in muted conversation at the side entry point of the male section. Brief greetings and strained smiles were exchanged. Ascertaining that Diar would be going into immediate consultation with his male clients, I slipped down to the uncrowded female section to see Theresa.

After much processing I was ushered into a private visitor's room, a gesture perhaps to a female prisoner nearing early death.

And there she was behind a thick window, smiling bravely, seemingly at peace. When I informed her that further urgent initiatives were being explored on her behalf in the outside world, she betrayed a certain impatience, indicating that she was "ready to go". Previously she told Diar, a Hindu, that Jesus had died for the sins of others, and now she had resigned herself to the same fate. I find it difficult to comprehend fully that I am seated before someone young and vibrant, the average, next-door kid, whose life will be officially terminated in the next few hours for allegedly being part of a highly emotional crowd of over a hundred, some of whom participated in the tragic killing of a prominent discredited local government official.

Since I was the last priest to talk to her in her mother tongue, it was obviously not a time for idle chatter or wasted silences. The image of Christ agonising in the garden of Gethsemane on the eve of his judicial murder came to mind and we talked about it. No, she wouldn't fall asleep like the disciples, but would remain awake in prayer with Him. Besides, He would be with her in daily communion from now until Friday morning at 7 o'clock. Then she would receive Christ in the form of Holy Communion for the last time, twenty minutes before seeing Him face to face. "He who eats My Flesh and drinks My Blood will have life everlasting," she said.

I told her that I hoped that she'd continue to pray for me too, at which she paraphrased St Therese of Lisieux (she had earlier asked for some information on this 19th-century nun who was a doctor of spirituality) who promised to spend her time in heaven doing good on earth. Then poignantly, as the thought struck her, she remarked that she too would be dying at 24 years of age, the age at which St Therese died from tuberculosis. She remarked in total simplicity that like Benedict, the 16th-century Franciscan wonder-worker (the first African canonised, who, according to tradition, by an inspiration of God knew the time of his death), she knew the exact time of her death.

Theresa asked for a rosary, though I was sure she had one. Perhaps she wanted one big enough to be worn around her neck, as is customary in Africa. To be there when the hangman's rope encircled her neck in a few days' time. She also asked for a "scapular of Mary"*, prompted no doubt by the fact that she herself was a former member of the Children of Mary youth association in Sharpeville

At this point we were interrupted, by a white warder who politely excused herself and, with an indulgent smile, asked Theresa for her mother's name, address, and home telephone number. Oh, the chronic insensitivity of it! A touch of the macabre, I remember thinking. Forms had to be filled in; final documentation completed. The hanging

*A piece of cloth worn over the shoulders, of religious or devotional significance – in this case related to Mary mother of Jesus.

procedures were moving into top gear. The South African
prison authorities had by now informed Theresa's mother,
Julia Ramashamole, that she and some relatives could
attend a memorial service held at the prison chapel soon
after the execution. Burial would be private and done by
the authorities of the prison. Later the family would be
informed of the whereabouts of the grave. The warder
departed, content with her information. Theresa seemed
unfazed, but I wondered what was going through her mind.
We continued. She still wanted to talk about spiritual
things. She found it consoling, she said, reflecting on the
Anglican and Catholic Ugandan martyrs when faced with
torture and final execution. Their experience of a strange
joy under hopeless circumstances encouraged her to be
brave. (They were a group of committed Anglican and
Catholic Christians, who faced execution in the last
century rather than submit to the perverted desires of a
powerful chief.)
Later she wondered why they had given her only four
days' notice of the execution, and added almost
immediately and with a brief glint in her eyes, "Tell them
to bring flowers." And then remembered, "But I won't see
them till Sunday," (visiting day) and immediately, "Oh! I
won't be here on Sunday."
All this time the black prison officer had been sitting with
us. Finally, she gently reminded us that our somewhat
extended time was nearly up. We exchanged
understanding glances. We prayed that the Lord would
accompany her from now on, that she'd feel His close
presence, that He would fill her loneliness with His love
and strength.
Just as I was leaving, I met Diar and his assistant, after
their consultation in the male section, arriving to see
Theresa. They reported that their clients, apart from
Mokhesi, were in a state of great anxiety. "It's not
clemency we want, it's justice," the prisoners had told

them. Referring to the contradictory evidence of the state witnesses, the five young people pointed to John 8:17: "It is written in your law that when two witnesses agree, what they say is true."

Diniso had found Romans 8:35 consoling. "Who will separate us from the love of Christ? Will affliction, or hardship … danger or death?"

When I was finally admitted to the all too familiar visiting room of the male condemned, I was greeted with a cacophony of anxious voices as the families and relatives of the five condemned engaged in spirited, hopeless and final leave-taking with their loved ones.

Somebody ushered me into Mokhesi's cubicle – he was half-smiling, calm and composed as usual. It had been my clear impression for some time now that Francis Mokhesi had deliberately worked through the reality of early abrupt death, and had taken the necessary spiritual, cushioning steps to contain his feelings. There was a sense of final relief about him. Yes, even if not a homecoming, at least a perception that his death was not the end, but rather a change – a continuation of life in another sphere perhaps with the living-dead and further – a regular theme of his letters. Our conversation took on the same pattern as earlier with Theresa. Francis seemed in deep concentration half here, half there, oblivious of the heartbreaking din surrounding us. Finally, we prayed a very disturbed prayer, followed by a blessing.

Someone wanted a few last words with him. Visiting time was drawing to a close. I then quickly visited "Jaja", Reid, Aupa and Duma in their cubicles. I prayed with them a prayer for strength, and finally blessed each one.

I hardly noticed the endless security gates opening and closing behind me. I left the prison in a daze, still trying to gather my agitated feelings. Soon, I was winding my way through sunny Pretoria's mid-morning traffic. I was drained and emotionally exhausted.

That night I phoned the Six's lawyer who told me he was preparing papers in an attempt to halt the executions scheduled for Friday. Prakash Diar wouldn't give up.

He worked into the night, and next day a final application for a stay of execution was presented to the Pretoria Supreme Court before trial Judge Wessel Human. Unprecedented national and international interest was focused on the Pretoria court that morning. The public gallery was packed an hour before the court opened. Tense crowds filtered out and onto the streets. Foreign ambassadors including the Vatican delegate were in the public gallery. Foreign and local TV crews clustered around outside the courthouse. For the next two days, riveting courtroom exchanges would lead to life or death for the Sharpeville Six.

Chapter 5

The dangling corpse hung straight and still – Coventry Patmore

A Vereeniging doctor, Kevin O' Hare, appealed on behalf of the Six. He recalls:

> *Apropos my meeting with FW de Klerk [then Minister of Co-operation, Development and Education], I would like to say the following. It took place at the National Party offices in Market Street and was arranged for me by Mario Milani, a town councillor of Vereeniging. I had already expressed to him that I was disgusted about the Sharpeville Six, so Mr de Klerk knew what the purpose of my visit was. He was kind and friendly and my interview was conducted with the utmost courtesy. I told him that I thought the conviction and sentence given the Six was ridiculous, and that the concept of common purpose when applied to a mob was nebulous, to say the least. Mr de Klerk asked me did I know how the Dlamini family had suffered. As it happened, I knew how they had been affected, and proceeded to tell him how on a Saturday afternoon at approximately 2 p.m., when I was locking up the rooms, I heard a noise and found Dlamini's widow under an examination couch wrapped in a blanket in a catatonic state.*
>
> *Mr de Klerk told me that in a case where someone had been sentenced to death, the trial judge had a chance to enter his private opinion (one which was not necessarily justifiable in law), for perusal by the State President when the case came up for clemency. He inferred by that that the judge at the Supreme Court had not added a private*

*addendum to his judgement. As for the appeal, Mr de Klerk
stated that, in his opinion, Mr Justice Botha was a very
capable person. I did ask Mr de Klerk the relevance of a
judge's political opinion when handing down a verdict or
sentence. I then left with the thought that Mr de Klerk had
risen in my opinion but that the system was as bad as
always.*

From my journal:

Thursday, 17 March 1988
*Today, St Patrick's Day, people of the Irish diaspora
celebrated their national identity in clubs and bars
throughout South Africa and the world. For a range of
reasons I have not been part of these annual gatherings –
and certainly not this year, especially today.*
*8.00 a.m.: Theresa asked to visit the other five prisoners.
They prayed and sang hymns together, encouraging one
another. "Giving texts" of consolation is common in some
African cultures. She gave them 2 Tim 4:6, "The hour has
come for me to be sacrificed."*
*2.00 p.m.: Archbishop George Daniel visited Theresa and
Francis. Francis sent his clothes and books home today.
Theresa decided not to send her things home today "but
tomorrow before the execution".*
*3.00 p.m.: In a sensational turn of events, a stay of
execution until 10 April was granted pending lodgement of
an application to re-open the trial on the grounds of
certain irregularities, i.e. that a state witness might have
perjured himself due to police torture. Jubilation, relief,
singing, interviews. Two police vans, tense and eager,
bumped each other as they slowly stalked (old South
African style) a small group of ululating supporters of the
accused around Pretoria's Church Square. Fellow
Franciscans William Slattery and Kevin Egan, with
seminarians, joined in the joy of the moment. At lunch,
journalist Patrick Laurence told me he had never seen
such crowds outside a South African court.*

Prakash Diar, who was earlier carried shoulder high from the court, hurried to the prison across town to inform the condemned of the decision of the court. I drove back to Our Lady of Fatima Church, Sharpeville, a journey of nearly two hours. On the road, thrilled with the outcome, I remember impatiently grappling with the earphones of a walkman to find out what the radio stations were saying about the stay of execution.

In Sharpeville there was great joy and excitement as hooting cars brought people out of their houses and greeted those arriving from work – a deep sense of relief for the time being. I thought it deserved a Mass of thanksgiving! I shared my high spirits with the people.

But parish business soon brought me back to earth – registrations for pre-baptism meetings, youth confirmation classes, a marriage that had taken a downturn, a funeral night vigil, and a few telephone calls, to the backdrop of a choir practice in full swing next door to the church office.

The following day, Friday, the sheriff of the Pretoria Supreme Court did not announce to the world after 7 a.m. that the execution of the Sharpeville Six had taken place as instructed by a Supreme Court decision of December 1985. The first execution day had passed.

Friday, 25 March 1988

I wondered to myself whether we were meeting on borrowed time, as I faced Francis and Theresa through the familiar glass partition exactly a week, almost to the hour, after the execution that did not happen. This meeting wasn't supposed to be. I should have gone to two unadorned graves in a bleak remote graveyard. Francis looked haggard and drawn, and hadn't been sleeping since the stay. He wanted his Sunday Missal returned to him. He had sent it home with his other belongings before the execution date. We talked a little longer and then it was time.

Theresa, too, seemed to be recovering – but slowly – from the convulsive happenings of the previous week. She appeared exhausted, yawning regularly and almost wordless – in a sort of twilight zone, as if she had come back from a near-death experience. The other four accused were probably wrestling with the same trauma. Noting her condition, I didn't force a conversation. She wanted more religious books, and we parted.

Sunday, 29 May 1988

A letter of sympathy from each of the Six was read out (illegally) at the funeral of Granny Makorotsoane, a daily communicant and staunch member of the Sacred Heart Sodality, who regularly trekked to Pretoria to encourage and pray with them.

The Secretary General of the SACC, Bishop Desmond Tutu, appealed unsuccessfully to the State President, PW Botha, to commute the death sentences of the Sharpeville Six. At this stage we were still awaiting a response to an application made the previous month to re-open the trial. We had not long to wait. On 13 June the trial judge refused it, and leave to appeal this decision was also refused. A new date of execution was set for 19 July 1988.

Friday, 1 July 1988

Ten days ago during morning meditation I got an idea that was to lead me to Potchefstroom, south-west of Johannesburg. At Potchefstroom University that morning, Father Edward Lennon, Canon Ben Photolo and I met in private with the rector, Professor Tjaart van der Walt, author of a state-sponsored report on the education boycotts and general unrest in our area in the latter half of 1984. We were thinking that since his somewhat enlightened report (he acknowledged serious corruption in the local administration) had been officially accepted by the government – though belatedly – he was in a position to intercede for the Sharpeville Six in the highest and most influential white circles in the land.

He welcomed us graciously, and over cups of tea we proceeded to analyse the issue in the light of his report. He thanked us for prodding his conscience and, encouraged by our concern, resolved to do everything in his power and at his command to lessen the burden of the condemned. We hoped that he could penetrate the government establishment – if not by the front door at least by the back. The name of Professor Johan Heyns (later assassinated), the moderator of the Nederlandse Gereformeerde Kerk (NGK), was mentioned in relation to this. We were happy with the outcome of this meeting.

40

As we were meeting in Potchefstroom, Ms Mokhesi and Mrs Ramashamole were in Paris for a brief meeting with President Francois Mitterand. The French president had earlier tabled and accepted certain resolutions on the Six at the Toronto and Hanover summits.

The day before, Ruud Gullit, the 1987 European footballer of the year, joined the campaign for clemency for the Sharpeville Six. "Salviamo sei di Sharpeville" (Save the Sharpeville Six), said the AC Milan poster.

The chief justice was petitioned to permit a final appeal to the appellate division in Bloemfontein. This was the last legal channel open to the Six.

The Lekoa mayor, Esau Mahlatsi, then turned down requests to support the "Save the Sharpeville Six" campaign. It was his deputy – Jacob Dlamini – who had been killed and whose death had given rise to this case.

On Tuesday 12 July the Minister of Justice, in an extraordinary move, suspended the executions indefinitely to allow the defence time to pursue a possible appeal to the acting chief justice. This was the first indication that there was serious debate in government circles about this case. In fact, they had discussed a trade-off – to reprieve certain whites earlier convicted of cold-blooded murder and condemned to death.

On the same day, Ms Mokhesi, the sister of Francis Mokhesi, met British Prime Minister Margaret Thatcher, who later said in parliament that if all legal steps failed she would personally appeal to the State President.

On Tuesday 19 July their date of execution expired for the third time. Adjutant Arlow of the prison services could not contain his anger. "Ek sal jou eendag kry," (I'll get you one day) he told Francis Mokhesi.

At the beginning of August, at the church in Sharpeville, the United States Ambassador and his two daughters (I found them washing the dishes) met the families of the Sharpeville Six; he assured them that he had raised the matter with the South African Foreign Minister, the Minister of Law and Order, and Professor Heyns. He told me he had raised points from our last meeting (1987) in the White House in Washington. He was happy with the response he got there.

A few days later I visited Pretoria prison. Francis appeared much brighter that day – something of his old self had returned. The dark swirling clouds of death were diminishing and new life was replacing the shadows of past days. We discussed important family matters. He was delighted to receive a card from his young daughter Mamodise, who was overseas with his sister. He mentioned that he was particularly struck by the previous Sunday's Bible readings, especially the "faith tested like gold" text of Peter 1: 3-8. He said: "I'm no longer really putting my trust in what's happening on mine, or my colleagues' behalf outside. I only trust the power of prayer." His face lit up when he heard that local Catholic primary school children had been praying for him during Mass. "Their prayers have power," he said, "and are listened to by God in a special way."

Theresa, on the other hand, was somewhat subdued. She was looking forward to seeing her mother, who was returning from Europe the next day. She was especially interested when I told her about a recent parish youth discussion on the role of traditional healers and prophets in people's lives. She whispered through the mouthpiece that she was not getting on with her white warder. Knowing that it was complimentary to say so, I suggested that she might be putting on a little weight. I asked Theresa if she was exercising. "No, I'm preparing to leave," she piped up with a smile, "and they'll expect me to have eaten well."

Three days later the Six were placed on the consolidated list, on the grounds that the Minister of Justice was satisfied that their activities endangered the state. These activities included treason, terrorism, sedition and furthering the aims of communism. They were not henceforth to be quoted in South Africa. We did of course continue to quote them at every opportunity in church, the bigger the crowd the better. The Sharpeville Six were now Bible-reading, hymn-singing, faith-filled atheistic communists!

Wednesday, 7 September 1988
Senior advocate Sydney Kentridge, who led the defence at the now infamous Steve Biko inquest 11 years ago, this morning led argument for a re-opening of the case at the Supreme Court, Bloemfontein.

Meanwhile, international protest was in full throat: "Europe begins to boil over the Sharpeville Six" and "Sanctions warning over Sharpeville Six", screamed the press headlines. The European Community was warning South Africa that if the government did not show clemency, apart from recalling ambassadors, other likely punitive measures could include orders to South Africa to make sharp cutbacks in its diplomatic staff in European Community countries, requirements for South Africans to have visas to visit European Community countries, withdrawal of South African Airways landing rights.

The government-funded English language newspaper, *The Citizen*, had been wondering "how the international campaign was orchestrated" and "how a section of the foreign media gave such a false impression of what the case is all about!"

Chapter 6

The day before an execution, Arlow would get the pillowcases from the storeroom, the cases they put around your head when you are hanged – "Jaja" Sefatsa, quoted in *The Sharpeville Six* by Prakash Diar

Monday, 23 November 1988

In the "pot" where prisoners "boiled" before their communal executions – called "the Christmas rush" – informal church services were organised by the inmates themselves, and Bible readings, which were in Afrikaans (for coloureds), and in Zulu, echoed down the long shiny off-white corridor of cells. Verse and chapter were given out earlier so that prisoners could accompany the reader with their own bibles.

Songs or hymns were usually sung, "Hamba Kahle" (Go well) being one of them. Duma Kumalo, one of the Sharpeville Six, introduced *Nkosi Sikelel' iAfrika* (a hymn calling on God to bless Africa) and was promptly transferred to the last cell in the corridor. *Nkosi* was officially banned.

It was customary for those about to be hanged to use up all their remaining money on things such as chicken, sweets, sugar, coffee or cigarettes. These they divided out among their friends. A common final greeting at execution time was "Lefu la hao lea mphedisa" (Your death is a source of life to me). Reginald "Jaja" Sefatsa of the Sharpeville Six had an unimpeded view of those being led away for hanging on their appointed morning. "Nisale kahle bafowethu, Ngeke sife sonke abanye bazo phuma. Nitshele abantu ukuthi sibulawa kanjani." (You won't die all of you, some of you will survive to tell the story outside) they often said, hopelessly, as they passed the remaining cells, chained, eyes wide with fear, on their last long walk down the corridor and up the 52 steps to the gallows.

This well-oiled conveyor belt of death sometimes clanked awkwardly to a halt in the late eighties to let someone off. Among those fortunate few was Duma Kumalo, one of the Sharpeville Six. His last day on death row went like this:

First the bell rang, which meant there were no executions that morning.

7 a.m. Shower, some food and exercise.

8 a.m. Prison inspection by Major Cronje[5].

8.30 a.m. (Outside the prison, BBC correspondent Graham Leach phoned Prakash Diar to inform him that the Sharpeville Six application for appeal had been dismissed. Duma's execution now appeared inevitable.

9.30 a.m. Roll calls at the prison for those wishing to visit the tuck shop.

10.25 a.m. Duma returned with his goods from the tuck shop. He spent the full seven rand, a gift from the prisons department to those who are to hang the next day.

11 a.m. Prisoners are allowed into one another's cells for games such as chess or draughts. Later the prison staff retires for lunch after closing and locking up the section.

11.30 a.m. The Sharpeville Six were brought to see Prakash Diar. Understandably he found it intensely difficult to tell them that the appeal court had refused the application to reopen the case. When the Six, Mokoena, Diniso, Ramashamole, Sefatsa, Kumalo and Mokhesi, heard the news, an icy calm crept over them, deadening their frail, battered feelings. They discussed the possibility of a new petition to the State President. "Where there is life there is hope," someone commented. Duma and Reid Mokoena whispered that they would not sign any new petition to the State President, stating that they would rather die and "be left in the hands of God, who they believe knows the truth, than in the hands of men". All returned to their small soulless cells.

1.30 p.m. The State President reprieved the Sharpeville Six – but no one told them.

1.40 p.m. Meal time. Warders' shifts changed. Sometimes a religious service was held at this point in the day.

[5] Major Cronje was the then head of death row.

5 p.m. The time when inmates could communicate with one another; a type of recreation period while remaining in their cells. It ended at seven o'clock. Then quietness descended on death row. Only echoes remained and later, the sobs of strong men.

(Meanwhile, in the women's section, Sister Gertrude Ryan and a prison chaplain, Father Neville Armstrong, visited Theresa Ramashamole in her cell, where together they celebrated a last Mass using the priest's briefcase as an altar. Theresa was calm throughout.)

6.15 p.m. Duma Kumalo was talking to a friend, Ishmael Mokheti of Soweto, when a passing warder casually informed him that he had just received a presidential reprieve. Duma didn't respond. Sensing this, over his shoulder, from halfway up the corridor, the guard nonchalantly repeated what he had heard. Bewildered, Duma lapsed into an anxious silence. His thoughts racing, he remembered the words on the morning radio news (and the bad news from their lawyer), "Nyewe ya banna ba ba hlano le mosadi e gaotswe ka sehloho, khotleng la dinyewe Bloemfontein" (The trial of the five men and one woman has been kicked out of the Supreme Court in Bloemfontein). He couldn't even contact his Sharpeville co-accused, Jaja Sefatsa, about this news, as his "communication pipe" was a separate fixture. Still dazed, any further conversation with Mokheti was incoherent. He returned to his cell, sat down and stared vacantly at the bleak unadorned wall.

6.30 p.m. While he was still working through his thoughts, the noise and clang of prison keys exploded at his cell door. A prison official walked in and told him to pack his things and follow him. Nothing else. Something began to register. He grabbed two packets of cigarettes and his letters, and left his newly bought groceries for the remaining prisoners.

6.45 p.m. He was led to Major Cronje's office where he was reunited with the four remaining male members of the Sharpeville Six. Kumalo had a cigarette to cool his nerves. Repressed exhilaration seemed to characterise his colleagues. Formally, if reluctantly, the major informed them that they had received a presidential reprieve. Unable to control the primeval emotion pulsing through him, Kumalo burst into uncontrollable laughter. They all, in fact, seem dazed trying to cope with a completely new set of feelings and emotions.

They were led away to another section of the prison, a section where life began again. Where even the drab olive green walls were suddenly friendly with light and hope. But can you reconstruct life after coming through an experience? Can you rise as it were, from the dead? Perhaps so, and the journey of their return from near-death to life had begun.

Chapter 7

Back in Sharpeville, just as I arrived at the parish flat, the phone rang and an agitated Regina Sefatsa, wife of accused Jaja, told me that a reprieve (the first I had heard of it) had been granted. She must have been working through the news of the reprieve for some time for she quickly added that stiff sentences had been imposed on the Six. My heart was thumping. The sentence can be dealt with later, I thought. At least the death and life saga had ended. I was in a state of exhilarated shock.

Eager for clarification, I immediately went to the house of a local church leader for the 8 p.m. TV news. Yes, the news confirmed it. It was really true. It was unbelievable. My mind was churning. We chatted excitedly with neighbours grouped casually outside the four-roomed house, trying to make sense of the day's dramatic news. I remember that the BBC was interviewing Jaja's wife, Regina.

We were still standing around, surrounded by the rich night sounds of the township, when Susan Diniso (wife of Aupa) joined us, clearly under the impression that all had been freed. When the news was broken to her of the severe sentence given her husband, she plunged into a long uncomprehending silence. Someone fetched a chair for her.

Their sentences:

V 3454 Reginald "Jaja" Sefatsa 20 years
V 3455 Malebo Reid Mokoena 18 years
V 3456 Aupa Moses Diniso 18 years
V 3457 Theresa Machabane Ramashamole 18 years
V3458 Duma Joseph Khumalo 25 years
V 3459 Francis "Don" Mokhesi 25 years

After they left death row the Six took up studies in another prison near Johannesburg, where two family visits and two letters a month were permitted. Francis went back to football, and asked his family to bring him a tracksuit, soccer outfit, ball, shoes, shorts and T-shirts. But already South Africa was changing.

Aupa and Duma were released on Wednesday, 10 July 1991. Theresa and Reid (on his 29th birthday) were released on Friday, 13 December 1991. Both were released exactly five years after being sent to death row. Finally Francis and "Jaja" were freed on 26 September 1992.

There ends the saga of the Sharpeville Six. But not really. At the time of writing, the five surviving members (Mokhesi died of a heart attack in 2001) are still recovering from this judicial nightmare.

Oh, there's one last thing. At Groenpunt Prison near Vereeniging just before they were released, Mokhesi and Sefatsa met a prisoner who told them he had actually participated in the killing of Dlamini. "We carried the limp body of the deceased (Dlamini) out to his burning car and put him on top of it. The body kept slipping off the car onto the ground," he confided.

In 1995 South Africa declared the death sentence unconstitutional.

Part Two
Gathering clouds

Chapter 8

I calculated that every 11.5 minutes of that day we had an incident to attend to – Colonel Gerrit Viljoen of the South African Police (SAP)

The Sharpeville Six trial arose out of what had been happening on the township streets from September 1984. But even as far back as 1982 – the incubation period – informal and illegal political meetings were taking place in homes and churches across the Vaal. The momentum only gathered later. For now people with similar social outlooks were finding refreshing solidarity with one another. New political thinking was blowing in the soft breeze. Statements by government that created black town councils were discussed with increasing derision. Anti-apartheid messages coming from Lusaka on the African National Congress's (ANC) underground radio station, Radio Freedom, were listened to with receptive hearts. People looked forward to the annual 8 January address from exile by African National Congress President Oliver Tambo and it was quoted secretly among friends. These friends found themselves coming together more often, as if pulled by an invisible hand.

Not all the major events in the final scramble to scuttle apartheid consisted of pitched street battles and funerals, although there were many – too many – of those. There were also meetings of new organisations, who found the churches safe and convenient venues for organisation and strategy sessions. Simultaneously there was a growing local fusing of political interests, between the Azanian People's Organisation (AZAPO), the United Democratic Front (UDF) and the Congress of South African Students (COSAS).

The churches became sites of political dissent in the Vaal, as well as in other areas. The police saw these meetings as incendiary and would later try to prove that they were the makings of an insurrection, implying that violence had been discussed. While there was no evidence to suggest that violence was mooted as a legitimate solution to the problems of the time, it was true that anxiety, anger and even rage were expressed openly when people came together. The reader is now invited behind the scenes, and into brief contact with the leaders who emerged from the communities of the townships and deftly provided a focus for the widespread frustration of people in the early 1980s.

In 1982 an action committee (see Appendix 1a) was formed in the Vaal Triangle townships which was to have profound repercussions on the future history of the area – and indeed further afield. Later, this committee became the Vaal Action Committee (VAC), a title that enabled it to book venues and guest speakers for meetings. Many house meetings followed this launching, out of which emerged the Vaal Organisation of Women (VOW). Their inaugural meeting was held at the run-down hall at St Francis Xavier Catholic Church, Small Farms, in Evaton. The Vaal women were asserting themselves.

By October 1983 the think-tank and "engine" for a future Vaal Civic Association (VCA) was in place.

A sense of excitement and anticipation in the township was running high at midday of 9 October 1983. Leaflets had been passed from hand to hand announcing the special meeting. I was asked to deliver some boxes of UDF leaflets from a trade union's offices at Emmanuel Church at Zone 14 to Nyolohelo Catholic Church, Zone 12, the venue of the meeting. On leaving the church, I was followed by white members of the Security Branch who stopped me at the corner of Wessels Mota and Makapan Streets. They searched my car. They must have thought I was a courier. They found nothing. I had left my cargo at the church.

It was launch day for the long-awaited VCA interim committee and the launch of the UDF in the Vaal Triangle, and the atmosphere in the township was electric with expectation. It was a highly charged historic meeting that elected Reverend Lord McCamel as chairman. The vice-chairperson of the meeting was Esau Ralitsela[6], the secretary Johnny Motete, the vice-secretary Mike Kgaka, and the treasurer Thabiso Ratsomo.

Among those present were activists Simon Nkoli, Gcina Malindi, and Jerry Tlhopane (all were later to go on trial for treason). Bavumile

[6] Later he became the missing link in the Delmas Treason Trial and thus the most wanted man in South Africa.

Vilakazi (now ambassador to Uganda) represented Zone 3 on the VCA, while Ernest Sotso was the delegate from Boipatong. The air was electric, the message focused. There was a chorus of approval when the representative from Evaton, Teboho Maitse (now a member of the Gender Commission), told the meeting that housing was not a privilege but a right. Curtis Nkondo of the Release Mandela Committee described Bantu Education with graphic imagery. "E tswana le phate ea mahlatsa ha e tshela sefahlehong sa ngwana wa motho e motsho" (It's like vomit poured from an old skin onto the face of an African child). Former COSAS leader Shaka Radebe, who subsequently spent five years on Robben Island, remembers urging the students to go back to their schools and there demand Student Representative Councils (SRCs) immediately, so that the voice of students, and indeed the people at large, could be heard in the area of education.

Soweto leaders Nthato Motlana and Elliot Shabangu of the Soweto Civic Association (SCA) also addressed the community. All of these speakers were detained and interrogated in the following weeks and months.

There was a similar community meeting at the St Cyprian's Anglican Church, Sharpeville, that day.

(Between 1982 and 3 September 1984, a natural networking by highly motivated like-minded people became noticeable. Soon they would be labelled "agitators" by the press and "troublemakers" by the state).

~

In February 1984, in the wake of the founding of the VCA, the Evaton Ratepayers Association (ERA) met with two communities in different venues. The wheels were rolling. The guest speaker was Reverend Lord McCamel from the VCA (See Appendix 1b for details). Discussion was long and earnest, and dealt principally with a plan to boycott the Evaton Town Council celebrations planned for the reopening of Evaton "stadium" near Zone 7, on Sunday, 12 May. The crowd streamed out of the hall singing a chorus to action. The regional authorities were worried.

The town council had proposed a rent increase in the face of growing unemployment. An amalgamation of interests between different groups was now a growing priority in political circles. The new people-driven movements in the Sebokeng area found ready allies in the ERA led by businessman Petrus Mokoena (later to go on trial for treason) of Small Farms. Unity was strength. Meetings multiplied. At Connie Lethlake's home a group of concerned people decided to call a mass meeting of residents on 26 August to discuss the proposed rent increases. This was a watershed decision with huge consequences. Meanwhile the UDF's One-Million-Signature Campaign – a call for people to sign petitions demanding an end to apartheid – was spreading in the townships.

Then a milestone meeting was held on Sunday, 19 August 1984, at St Cyprian's Anglican Church, Sharpeville, concerning the proposed rent and services increases in the Vaal black townships. Years later the keenest minds in the South African apartheid judiciary spent months analysing the details of this meeting. The speakers were later jailed. Their trial with 16 others – called the Delmas Treason Trial – had great historical implications for South Africa. The meeting was addressed by the parish priest, Father Moselane, by Tom Manthata of the Soweto Civic Association, and by the SACC fieldworker Patric Baleka of the Azanian Youth Unity (AYU) and the SCA together with Lazarus More and Aupa Hlomuka of Sebokeng.

Down the street where I ministered (I had been transferred from St Francis Xavier Church, Small Farms, in Evaton, to Our Lady of Fatima Church in Sharpeville a few months earlier), people told me after Mass that morning that they would be attending the 2 p.m. meeting at the Anglican Church. This indicated a strong consciousness of the concerns of the moment. I felt a tension in the township air.

Later in the month, Father Moselane was called to Security Branch headquarters at Vereeniging by Major Theunis Steyn and warned not to go ahead with further rent issue meetings at his church.

It was at this time that Lekoa Town Council chairman Esau Mahlatsi and his town clerk, Nicholas Louw, tried to prevail upon the magistrates of Vereeniging and Vanderbijlpark to ban public meetings in Vaal churches.

Chapter 9

When I came out of the church office to greet the parishioners immediately after Mass on 26 August 1984, I felt a tingle of oddness in the air. The celebratory mood of the people seemed to be evaporating too early. A glance across the church quadrangle to the old hall helped explain. The ERA had called another meeting, this time, I heard later, to discuss leasehold rights to land that had been originally acquired in the area. It was claimed the Sebokeng state authorities wanted to build on it.

Land – the most emotive issue of them all, I thought to myself. The hall was full, jam-packed in fact – people four deep at the entrance. From outside the hall, crowds strained to hear or to see through the open windows. While I was chatting in the yard someone whispered that the Security Branch was parked at the corner of the church precincts watching the hall entrance. A yellow police car passed and a few minutes later returned, observing the crowded churchyard, this time accompanied by a towering police Casspir armoured vehicle that resembled a tank. No wonder there was tension in the air. Most sensed it as they either drifted over to the meeting or moved in the direction of home. Danger hung over the subdued scene. It was a scene I had got used to over the years – as had the people. Soon the police would have the meeting to themselves since most of the non-Evaton churchgoers were departing. But some stayed, drawn by the tense atmosphere and rousing political songs of defiance that accompanied regular sudden ovations in the hall. That was new for the Ratepayers. Ratepayers don't normally sing political songs. They don't normally sing at all unless in their church choirs. Today they were fired up.

In fact, different political groups from around the Vaal Triangle were addressing the ERA that day (See Appendix 1c for details). And I was to learn that this meeting merged with another in the afternoon and was addressed by more emerging community opinion-makers. The stage was set. It was one of those moments peculiar to townships in the 1980s when something new was about to appear out of the swirling mists, but it was too early to be defined. Who could have guessed that it would have come like this? The organisers couldn't have known that every minute of this marathon meeting would be microscopically analysed and airbrushed by future judges, assessors and the best defence teams in the land. By five o' clock the meeting had decided that:

1. A work stayaway would be called for 3 September 1984, in protest against rent increases.
2 Councillors would be asked to resign.
3. If councillors did not resign, their businesses would be boycotted.
4. Buses and taxis were not to operate on that day – ambulances were to be exempted.
5. The Evaton Ratepayers Association was to participate in the above developments.

I believe this meeting now slipped into the annals of national history.

Five days later, on the night of Friday, 31 August, at 8.30 p.m., Captain Theunis Steyn and another white Security Branch officer arrived at the Zone 7, Sebokeng home of popular leader Esau Ralitsela, to try to persuade him to stop the coming Monday's work stayaway. Otherwise he could be charged with sabotage, they told him. Ralitsela replied that he could not interfere with what the community had decided. He was, however, willing to sit down with Lekoa Town Council mayor Esau Mahlatsi and discuss, even on TV, the demands of the community to see what could be done. Steyn replied impatiently that it was not within his competence to arrange such a meeting. Fair enough. But had he taken such an initiative he might have influenced the direction of history.

The next day community leaders in Bophelong (where two people had been shot dead by police the previous day after one of many meetings), Sharpeville, Evaton, Boipatong and Sebokeng declared that Monday's protest march was going ahead.

Speaking from Evaton, local church official Pitso Ratibisi recalls that at about 8 a.m. on Sunday morning he opened the church hall for Esau Ralitsela, Petrus Mokoena and 13 VCA committee members. They were making final preparations for Monday's march. A petition was drafted which was to be handed in at the development board.

That evening, at Sebokeng, Father Lucas Bambezela decided to sleep at Nyolohelo Catholic Church, Zone 12, since it was rumoured that a huge crowd was to converge on it the next morning. (I stayed some of the time in Sharpeville and some of the time in Vereeniging.)

Meanwhile at Zone 11, COSAS were meeting to "strategise and prepare" for the following day's events. That night (Sunday) they stayed expectantly at Sello Hlanyane's place.

And at Bophelong township that afternoon, after a resident's meeting (see Appendix 1d), two people were shot dead in police action. This was the unexpected spark that fuelled the next day's marches. Ntsikelelo Manzi (who made available to me his research paper towards his BA Honours in History called "Youth in politics of Resistance in the Vaal, 1980-1990") later wrote about it, calling it Bloody Monday. The uprising had begun. In this uprising there were to be no arsenals of hidden weapons suddenly appearing on the streets. The only weapons were to be anger, stones and matches. The only guns were in the hands of the South African Police.

Chapter 10

Beware of the risen people – The Rebel by Padraig Pierce

Bloody Monday, 3 September 1984

At 2 a.m. on Monday morning, COSAS activists quietly left their base and fanned out in groups to key pre-planned points such as bus stops and train stations. They hoped to persuade commuters not to go to work that morning.

At the open space between Zone 11 and 12, they stopped a bus of the type especially adapted as a mobile ticket sales unit. Bang! Wham! And screaming shock as they scattered in all directions. It was not a bus. It was a "nyala" or "mellow yellow" vehicle filled to capacity with armed policemen, and followed by a patrol car. Shooting broke out but no one was injured in the encounter. This was confirmation to the police that something serious was afoot. They radioed back to their Vereeniging headquarters that alerted the regional riot control units. Hundreds of residents awoke from uneasy sleep at the sound of gunfire. Peering from curtains behind darkened windows they knew somehow that this was going to be no ordinary day. They wondered about the risks of going to work.

Later I interviewed a few residents across town at Small Farms and added to my diary:

> *8.00 a.m. Residents are already assembling on the church property, the site of the original St Francis Xavier Primary School. At a shop in Residensia, Petrus Mokoena hurriedly buys koki pens and cardboard boxes to help with the making of placards. You can see intensity on people's faces. They are in deep serious conversation. The sun is already high in the sky. There is a strange silence; a silence of the unknowing. Activists are in deep discussion near the hall*

door. People are called into the hall for last-minute instructions concerning the discipline and marshalling of the march. The Security Police are cruising around in their dark-windowed cars. They are clearly anxious as they stop and drive off at different intervals. Always rubber-necking (straining) to see what's happening at the far end of the churchyard.

Somebody gives the word. The crowd, armed only with a memorandum for the administrators of the area, finally sets off at about 9.00 a.m. in the direction of the old Bantu Affairs offices at Masenkeng [the local administration offices]. There they turn right in the direction of Zone 7, Sebokeng. Keeping to the tar road they will eventually arrive at Zones 11 and 12. They calculate the march will take half an hour. It will probably draw others to its ranks as it passes their area. The organisers hope so. They don't expect police to interfere, as it is a peaceful demonstration. Why, they even have some police in plain clothes walking with them.

Today the Vaal Triangle imploded. Father Lucas recalled being awakened in Sebokeng 5.00 a.m. to the sound of shouting outside at the busy Zone 12 T-junction. Bus commuters, attempting to go to work in defiance of the "declared" one-day anti-rent-rise stayaway, were being stoned. There was much shouting and some screaming. At 11.00 a.m., an enormous crowd appeared on the horizon, marching between Zones 11 and 12 in the direction of Nyolohelo Catholic Church, Zone 12, opposite the post office. In fact it was the march that I saw leaving from Small Farms earlier. Father Lucas opened the doors and gates of the church in anticipation of a mass meeting. The police practically surrounded it and noted the opening of the gates. They too seemed to be expecting a meeting. But the marchers passed and ten minutes later were still passing. Surely, Father Lucas recalls remarking, this is the biggest procession of people in Sebokeng's short history.

The police withdrew from the church to the lower part of the section that would later be known as "Beirut" in Moshoeshoe Street, obviously unprepared for such a massive throng of people. And then it happened. A camouflaged military helicopter, like a giant steel crab, roared up from behind the marchers at rooftop level, spraying tear gas into the crowd.

"O Nkosi yami! Safa saphela! Kwenzenjani kwelilizwe lethu?" (Oh my God! We're all going to be killed. What is going on in our land?), Lucas shouted. Panic, screaming, chaos, people trampled underfoot, running in all directions, anger ... Lucas will never forget this scene of human bedlam. He says he experienced a gut fear that stayed with him for weeks.

Our phones ring all day for more information on the breaking news. The Vaal Triangle is burning. Black smoke curling skywards dots the townships' landscape. Europeans glance uneasily at the townships from the Golden Highway as they drive past.

I spent last night in Vereeniging and found out as much news as I could over the phone. Since it is Monday I have no plans to go to Sharpeville today. I ring parishioners for an assessment of the situation in different areas of the township. My having been only seven months in the parish does not help as I have not completed home visitation and am still learning my way around.

Dr Kevin O'Hare of Vereeniging later told me: "The police had members of their staff at Sebokeng Hospital. The wounded and their families tried where possible to avoid going to hospital, but some, because of the severity of their wounds, had no choice. Other less severely wounded township residents, already fearful of arrest at Sebokeng Hospital, began to stream in to the consulting rooms in Vereeniging. Throughout the night traumatised victims of police shootings are attended to, early casualties of the Vaal uprising. That night every bandage, antibiotic and painkiller in the practice was used.

At 4 a.m. we cleared up and closed. The next morning no one would have known the activity of the previous night. It was the heaviest but most rewarding 24 hours that I have ever had."

The night sky shrouding the townships reddened from burning tyres of protest blocking all main streets. Young people crowded the streets fuelling the fires and built barricades to block further police and army incursions. Father Geoff Moselane, Sharpeville's Anglican priest, and his family were evacuated from their house after six tear gas canisters and nine rubber bullets crash through their windows from "unknown sources". That was a day to remember.

In the following days, five black town councillors were killed by angry residents.

Chapter 11

In the following weeks and months the townships boiled and
simmered and boiled over again as resistance deepened and spread,
even beyond the Vaal area. It was a time of terror, burning tyres,
mass arrests, arson, political funerals, the destruction of state property,
and of meetings. Emergency meetings, urgent meetings and *ad hoc*
meetings between the state, the people and churches.

Nothing illustrated how dramatically the churches were drawn
into the conflict more than the incident on Thursday, 6 September.
I had briefed Bishop Desmond Tutu, Reverend Allan Boesak and
Father Smangaliso Mkhatshwa (now mayor of Tshwane/Pretoria)
on our situation before their morning's press conference at 11 a.m. at
the South African Council of Churches. While I was in Johannesburg,
the clergy, Fathers Benen Fahy, Lucas Bambezela and Edward
Lennon, with Reverend Lord McCamel, had been meeting at
Father Ben Photolo's house at Evaton to hear his report on
(and dramatic intervention in) the extraordinary five-hour standoff
with the authorities on Sharpeville's main street the previous day.
(This was a report-back to the clergy by Father Photolo on how
he had, the previous day, mediated a near-violent confrontation
between Sharpeville residents and a large force of police in
which people presented placards reading "Rent R30" and
"Release the Priest".)

Meanwhile an anxious, angry crowd began to gather between
Zone 13 and Zone 14 in adjacent Sebokeng. The three clergy on the
way home from their meeting came upon the crowd and were quickly
co-opted to become members of an *ad hoc* delegation to negotiate
with the administration board on behalf of the residents. Later,
the Anglican priest Peter Lenkoe joined them. To use church jargon,
this was a ministry of presence by instant co-option!

Since the popular community leaders had by now been washed underground or into hiding by the intensity of the state's reaction to the upheaval, the next available level of local leadership was turning out to be the churches. Would they, could they, meet the challenge?

In crisis situations like this it became increasingly obvious that positions and decisions were often overtaken by events on the ground which called for new and more creative responses. Today, in this knife-edge atmosphere, there was no way back to the presbytery or friary except through the gauntlet of a people demanding your assistance.

This was not the time for ponderous theologies of accommodation, of non-intervention, of by-standing, of neutrality, much less of acquiescence. A theology suitable for the here and now was called for. And now. Right now.

The crowd had grown to about five thousand, and correspondingly a massive police presence was building up, with police nervously fingering their guns while observing the crowd from their vans. The assistant commissioner of police arrived from Pretoria (he had been assigned by a high-powered delegation of government ministers to accompany a tour of the riot areas). It was a high-powered group indeed: included were the Minister for Law and Order, Louis le Grange, the Minister of Home Affairs and National Education, FW de Klerk, the Minister of Co-operation, Development and Education, Dr Gerrit Viljoen, and the Minister of Defence, General Magnus Malan).

The assistant commissioner appealed to the delegation of clergy and residents to disperse the crowd. They replied that this would be impossible. The government ministers made a quick detour after their motorcade came upon the angry crowd of residents.

The co-opted delegation, after hurried consultations with the residents, moved off to the Orange Vaal Administration Board (OVAB) about three kilometres away, where they were informed that both the white town council clerk and the chief director were too busy to meet them. (The question of calling in the black town councillors wasn't considered by the authorities, which seems to suggest that they were not important for serious decision-making.)

The delegation returned to the township and carried this reply to the restless crowd. The delegation members were now impatient at the slow progress, and insisted that a senior police officer, Colonel Gerrit Viljoen – drafted in from Krugersdorp to contain the riots – radioed the administration board personnel to come immediately and start talking.

Nicholas Louw, town council clerk, finally arrived, and talks began over the bonnet of a car, supervised, on the one hand, by a large contingent of riot control police, and, on the other, by a great crowd of distraught residents.

A potentially explosive situation was averted when Louw promised that the rent rise would not be implemented, and that he would arrange a meeting as soon as possible between the residents' delegation, the black town council and the development board. This showed the power invested in his position. The car bonnet negotiations had been a success.

The promised meeting took place two days later. Louw, however, insisted when the delegation (see Appendix 1f for details) arrived that white priests could not be part of a delegation to discuss black problems. This caused a stir within delegation circles. Father Edward withdrew for the sake of the negotiations. This was all terribly embarrassing for Louw because now he was being forced to negotiate with natural community leaders and not with those forced on the community, that is, the Lekoa Town Council. Some town councillors were present, however, and countered everything the people's delegation stood for. The following points were put by the delegation to the authorities:

1. That the Lekoa councillors should resign. "This is not negotiable," replied the mayor.

2. That rent and services charges should be decreased. "No," replied the councillors after long discussion.

Owing to the length of the discussions, an independent inquiry into the allocation of business sites, the release of detainees, and a demand that police leave the townships were not discussed.

After the meeting, quite frustrated, the delegation went to the Anglican Church at Zone 13 for an immediate debriefing and to plan two community report-back meetings for Sharpeville and Sebokeng respectively. It was a short-term victory for the authorities.

I wondered whether the police, the Special Branch (an intimidating presence at the meeting, there to assess the new breed of leader the community had chosen) and administration officials realised that the clergy now felt obliged to inform the people of the townships as soon as possible about the outcome of this meeting. We knew the residents, especially the youth, could erupt in anger again when they heard about the intransigence of the civil authorities. We debated how violence could be avoided.

At stake here was the way to inform half a million people in five townships. It was Saturday evening at 5 p.m. The residents had to be told the next day. The community-based newspapers were well past their deadlines for Sunday's issue.

We decided that the pulpit was the only way. The next morning clergy in all the churches across the townships were to tell the people where to go for a special report-back in the afternoon. And while these discussions were proceeding, volunteer medical personnel were assisting the wounded in various churches throughout the region.

Chapter 12

Our Lady of Fatima Church, Sharpeville 8 a.m.

How do you address a grieving congregation after the horrific events of the previous week? Almost forty people had been killed during those five days, and mostly due to police shooting. How many had been wounded, were in hiding, afraid to go to hospital for fear of arrest?

What does a priest talk about in this kind of atmosphere? How receptive can a congregation be to the word of God under these circumstances? Indeed what word of hope is fitting on a day like this, a cool, sunny September morning? But grim too, as clusters of parishioners – the children more wide- and wild-eyed than usual – shuffled through the gate into Our Lady of Fatima church grounds, glad to be assured of the protective company of one another. What did they expect of religion that morning? What were they thinking as they blessed themselves with holy water at the entrance to the church?

Perhaps the church provided solidarity, a comfort, a familiarity, a folk venue, an ambience of peace for troubled minds where recent social disruption could be worked through and perhaps find meaning in a climate of near normality – and with the added dimension of faith, which united and strengthened troubled hearts. As a priest I was clearly obliged to speak – with sensitivity – about the evil of taking the life of another person and the angry destruction of another's property, about future reconciliation between present enemies. At the same time I had to retain the trust of the people.

With the other churches I too would appeal to the people to bring the names and addresses of all who had been killed. This was another decision taken at our meeting at the Anglican Church the day before. Vigilant monitoring of the changing situation was important because of constant government deceit.

Vesting for Mass in the sacristy, I silently prayed for myself, and for the people out there in the pews as the altar servers bustled about in last-minute preparations before proceeding to the altar.

A few minutes later the choir burst into song and the Mass was on. The liturgy that morning was full of suppressed communal energy finding an outlet in worship and fellowship. It was mixed with anxiety, confusion and anger. People searched for hope in the celebration. They shared their hearts publicly like never before at the prayers of the faithful which were extended to allow as many as possible to express their pent-up feelings. It was people's therapy. They listened to one another expectantly, revived their weary spirits, and found new solidarity in being together. Near the end, in a suddenly hushed church, it was announced that the report-back (of the meeting with the authorities) would be given at the Anglican Church at 2 p.m.

I felt very nervous as I prepared to go to Boipatong for the second Mass. It was a strange experience; to bear information that could trigger riots.

St Joseph's Church, Boipatong, 10 a.m., same day

As I arrived in the streets of Boipatong, I noticed the normal spirited activity of Sunday was absent. Opposite the church, at Tsirela (the town centre) the shops were closed and barred, adding to the deserted eeriness of the place – a ghost township. However I soon became aware of tension in the air conveyed by the hushed conversation of the people arriving for church. They were the only people in the streets that morning. And when the church bell rang to announce Mass, its sharp report seemed to pierce the stillness of the town. During the service, one of the altar servers limped, a victim of police shooting. Again the people were told where the report-back would be that afternoon.

When the Mass was over, worshippers gathered nervously at the church gate facing the deserted town square. I joined them and saw the reason. A solitary police Casspir was stationary at the taxi rank, while some riot police stuck a notice on a wall, banning today's two report-back meetings. The banning order was issued by the Vanderbijlpark magistrate, Ernest Marais Arndt, and banned all meetings, indoors and outdoors, "in terms of Section 46 (1) (B) of Internal Security Act No 74 of 1982 in the municipalities of Lekoa and Evaton as from 11.00, on 09.09.84 to 11.09.84."

As the police Casspir departed, parishioners rushed to read the notice. A hand tore it down. "For a souvenir, Father," explained Mrs Pinkie Tsotetsi.

Report-back meetings banned! The police had caught up on the clergy. But was it too late. It was now 1 p.m. and the two church-organised meetings were due to start at 2.30 p.m. Now what?

Sharpeville, same day, 1.30 p.m.

I returned to Sharpeville to St Cyprian's, the Anglican Church that was the venue of one of the meetings. A crowd was beginning to gather. A group of residents approached enquiring about the meeting, and I explained what I'd learnt at St Joseph's in Boipatong.

I visited AZAPO medical personnel treating people at the church who seemed unaware that an important meeting was scheduled there at 2.30 p.m. I learned that Father Moselane had gone to Nyolohelo Catholic Church, Zone 12. I returned to my parish at Sharpeville where some wounded were now arriving. I directed them to the doctors at the Anglican Church.

Nyolohelo Catholic Church, Zone 12, 1.30 p.m., same day.

Police arrived during Mass and demanded the keys of the church while Father Edward was distributing Holy Communion. "Do they want to lock the church themselves? I'm in the middle of Mass. If they want to see me, they can see me after Mass," whispered Edward to a messenger through thin tense lips. As with Boipatong, police stuck banning notices on the church door, which were unceremoniously ripped off and torn up by the altar servers. As people emerged from church they defiantly trampled the banning order underfoot. Some stayed back for the meeting. By this time residents were beginning to gather in the vicinity of the church. You could sense the tension. They stood around in small groups outside the Post Office opposite the church. They didn't know the meeting had been banned.

1.45 p.m. The crowd continued to grow outside the church. Some were already entering. Soon church ministers Lord McCamel, Peter Lenkoe, Geoff Moselane, Edward Lennon and finally Lucas Bambezela were ushered in. An emergency meeting was held to decide on strategy in the light of the banning order. By now the church had refilled. They decided to proceed as if it was a prayer meeting. Father Lucas, as the parish priest, spoke as if to open a prayer meeting, not an illegal public gathering. Could a prayer meeting also be illegal, wondered the clergy. The public waited expectantly for the news that was banned. Agitation rippled through the crowd outside and filtered into the church. The police arrived and ordered the crowd (approximately four thousand) to disperse.

The prayer meeting began to falter and die as the din from outside grew louder and pressed against the walls of the church. It had lasted three minutes. The commotion outside increased and exploded into pandemonium as the police opened fire on the dispersing crowd. A BBC man was inside the church, recording and interviewing as far as the highly charged situation, and his nerves, permitted. Major panic could have broken out at any moment in the church. The ministers appealed for calm. Lucas told the people through a loud-hailer to disperse quietly. They did so. Suddenly outside they heard the sharp crack of rubber bullets and the all too familiar whistle of tear gas canisters smoke-trailing through the air.

On the streets were screaming, panic-stricken people, fleeing fathers and mothers, youths shouting, tear gas, rubber bullets, beatings and lashings all round, as the police charged into the crowd. During the confusion Reverend Lord McCamel was arrested by the police and ten minutes later "released" by the surging crowd.

Inside the church a scene of another kind was being enacted. The ministers, priests and few remaining people were seen offering one another a sign of peace, strengthening one another's resolve to be strong in the present crisis. The dizzying stench of tear gas pervaded the church.

Outside stone-throwing spread as the angered crowd faded into the township. Shooting and shouting continued for some time. Finally the police departed. Calm gradually returned to the immediate area.

Edward tried to rest – he was drained. Community leaders departed discreetly through side exits. Lucas finally suggested that he and Edward make a dash for home in another part of the township.

They locked up. And since, in the heat of these very desperate moments, people could mistake Edward for a white policeman, they decided that he should lie down in the back of Lucas's car covered by his religious habit. After manoeuvring past streets of burning tyres, makeshift road blocks and blazing cars, they made it home, where they found parishioners preparing to go and "rescue" them from the scene of the day's battle. I rang from Sharpeville about coming over, but Lucas advised against it.

That evening the AZAPO medical team treated 149 wounded people.

Chapter 13

It was this and similar situations that led to the establishment of the Vaal Ministers Solidarity Group (VMSG) – see Appendix 1. It was nine days into the uprising and up to forty-two had been killed in police reaction when we called one of our many emergency meetings. The clergy met in Emmanuel Catholic Church in Sebokeng to prepare two public funerals. Canon Ben Photolo, an Anglican priest, was asked to take the chair. Technically, the meeting was banned. Thus if interrupted by the police, who were already cruising the dirt road outside the churchyard writing down car numbers, we would say we were arranging church functions.

Then an awkward moment occurred. There was a town councillor present – a Reverend Modise – representing his independent church. It was explained to him that if he had not resigned from the council he would be requested to withdraw from the meeting. He left.

Present were Lord McCamel (McCamel Church of God, Evaton), Isaac Tshabalala (Apostolic Church, Sebokeng), Johannes Mokoena (Apostolic Church, Sebokeng), Luther Mateza (Presbyterian Church, Sharpeville), Dan Marutle (Methodist Church, Sharpeville), P Mofokeng (lay church leader, Sharpeville), Peter Lenkoe (Anglican Church, Sebokeng), Geoff Moselane (Anglican Church, Sharpeville), Benen Fahy (Catholic Church, Evaton), Lucas Bambezela (Catholic Church, Sebokeng), Edward Lennon (Catholic Church, Sebokeng), and myself from the Catholic Church at Sharpeville. We made the following decisions concerning:

1. Funeral arrangements for those who had died during the riots. There would be two community funerals and the venues would be St Luke's Methodist Church for Sharpeville and Bophelong and Boipatong victims, and the McCamel Church of God for Evaton and Sebokeng victims. Times of services would be 10 a.m. to 1 p.m.

2. Aid to families of victims: We formed an executive committee to manage this. They were to make inquiries with local taxis and undertakers about co-ordinating and contributing towards the community funerals.

3. Legal aid: According to Ismail Ayob, attorney to Nelson Mandela, 120 had been detained. This Johannesburg law firm had been extremely helpful in the present crisis.

4. Racketeering: Common complaints brought to our attention at this meeting were: unfair pricing of food by some local shops, *tsotsis* (thugs) molesting residents, false and dishonest collections for police victims, hooligans looting, the burning of houses for arbitrary reasons, and using a climate of fear to exact personal revenge for perceived past injuries.

5. The VMSG was formed to fill the void created by the arrest of civic and political leaders.

All these matters were brought to the attention of our respective churches and congregations. We felt that the wide circulation of important information in the Vaal townships was necessary to counter official deceit or doctored news from the side of the government.

The VMSG enabled banned organisations to meet under the umbrella of clergy meetings. We knew too that the rent issue was not the real issue.

It was crucial that the ever-changing situation on the streets be analysed and discussed regularly at our meetings so that we would be in a position to understand and interpret events as they unfolded and perhaps, where necessary, to give them constructive focus and direction. Our collective wisdom honed by our Christian beliefs, I believe, served us well.

Meetings were conducted in an atmosphere of great gravity and urgency. They so often challenged our pulse rates and threatened our blood pressure! I often pondered the position of the clergy in this fragile situation. We all wondered about it. Certainly we begged God for guidance in the demands being made on us.

Like the distinguished anti-apartheid clerics such as Archbishop Tutu, Archbishop Hurley and Dr Beyers Naudé, Nobel peace prizewinner Chief Albert Luthuli was quite definite about his Christian obligations. "My own urge, because I am a Christian," he said, "is to get into the thick of the struggle with other Christians, taking my Christianity with me and praying that it may be used to influence for good the character of the resistance."

Yes, we did take sides, openly, as Christ did, thanks to the voices we were hearing from among ourselves. Following the Master we opted for the poor. We opted to see the world through their eyes and to listen to their throbbing heartbeat. We were led to hear the cry of a people in pain and tried to respond honestly.

It was not easy. Church ministers are not in the business of risk-taking. It is not what they're used to. Tradition governs much of their thinking – our thinking. Yet we knew we must try not to betray our Christian calling.

But knowing what that was in this developing situation was not easy. Those clergy whose sense of right and wrong, whose activist faith had been formed on a daily praying of the psalms, had no alternative but to enter even more profoundly into the lives of the people, without fear or favour, without hesitation or obfuscation.

I found myself thinking on the lesser-known side of my spiritual mentor, St Francis of Assisi, who didn't shy away from conflict resolution in his own day. I remembered especially his daring, his defiance of convention when in northern Egypt he walked through the packed Crusader battle lines to talk peace with the enemy, Sultan al-Kamil, the leader of the Arab world. Many at the time said his behaviour was scandalous, unheard of, totally out of place for a holy man. He had no place at the coalface of international politics and conflict, intoned Papal advisers. Francis, the most beloved saint in history, clearly thought otherwise.

Chapter 14

Funerals were frequent sites of political activity throughout the eighties, and one of the few places where people could gather, and even that was not guaranteed.

One funeral changed my life. I will always remember the date – Saturday, 15 September 1984. Together with the clergy, seven community-based organisations had organised two public funerals in the previous few days. Ordinary funerals for ordinary people require ordinary preparations the world over. Churchmen, imams and rabbis will tell you that. But here it was different. Nothing was ordinary those days. A funeral could be banned, suppressed or subjected to impossible conditions. As we prepared we had to take this into consideration. We hadn't wanted any police interference. They had interfered with funerals in other parts of the country. Given this, nothing had been left to chance. We had arranged that lawyers be present at both funerals in case the community needed a court interdict to contest police intervention. Students had been asked to respect the wishes of families for dignified funerals. Representatives of the SACC and the Catholic bishops had been invited. The Sharpeville mass funeral would be held at St Luke's Methodist Church and the master of ceremonies would be Reverend Luther Mateza of St Paul's Presbyterian Church. In the Sebokeng area the dead would be buried from the McCamel Church of God in Evaton. The master of ceremonies there would be the resident Minister, Reverend Lord McCamel assisted by members of the VMSG.

These were the most significant community funerals since the 1960 Sharpeville massacre. That morning I swallowed a Valium before leaving the house. My anxiety was at an all-time high.

Let my journal speak:

Sharpeville
All roads lead to St Luke's Methodist Church this morning.
Sister Bernard Ncube of the Companions of St Angela,
representing the Catholic bishops, arrives at 10.00 a.m.,
and, with a few others, we walk up to St Luke's Methodist
Church where today's funeral of Sharpeville and
Boipatong riot victims will be held. Silence pervades the
township. Grim faces follow our progress up the road
towards the church. Even before you reach the church you
can hear the fiery liberation songs of the comrades. People
swarm outside the church near the entrance. I spot
Motepe, a church lay leader, in his brown habit.
During the service, conducted by Reverend Luther Mateza,
all the pent-up feelings and emotions of the previous week
explode in a liturgy of song, dance and fierce protest
oratory. A litany where the 42 names (see Appendix 2) *of*
those killed so far by police is solemnly read to a deeply
hushed congregation by Reverend Dan Marutle of the
Methodist Church. An anguished, broken-hearted sigh
greets the name of Maud Nzunga, the seven-month-old
baby who died from the effects of tear gas after a shell was
shot into her room from the garden outside. While the
Reverend Cecil Begbie of the Witwatersrand Council of
Churches is delivering his address, a great commotion
accompanies the arrival of another victim from Boipatong
whose remains are marched into the church, shoulder-
high, and placed alongside the six other dead – or fallen
heroes. Speeches continue, interspersed with freedom
hymns and loud political acclamations. Pummelling the air
for emphasis, a local youth leader, referring to the police,
passionately declares, "We don't hate them, but we hate
what they are doing to us" – the sin, not the sinner – a
telling distinction.

The final prayers completed by the church ministers, the MC, amidst a growing din, describes the route of the funeral procession. The seven coffins are whipped up shoulder-high and rapidly borne through the crowded church by a COSAS guard of honour. I have never seen coffins leave a church in such haste. Then again I've never seen so many coffins in a church at any one time. But these times are different. By the time the clergy reach the exit, the procession is well under way and gathering momentum by the second. Rhythmic liberation chants set the pace. "Let's go over there," shouts a churchman to his colleagues, pointing, "and meet the procession as it rounds the corner and heads for the cemetery." We do just that, and draw a line of clergymen across Sharpeville's main road, hoping to provide the procession and motorcade with some semblance of order. But all is in vain. The pressure from over five thousand impassioned bodies is too great. We splinter, we're jogging; everybody is jogging. A priest appears and disappears. It's hot. Chanted political litanies fill the air. I'm jogging too under a hot sun. I'm wearing my brown Franciscan habit and carrying a small briefcase. Rather uncomfortable and perhaps a trifle indecorous. Religious habits are not meant for jogging in. But today … puff … this is … pant … irrelevant. After some time I realise I haven't spotted a minister or priest for some time. They are lost in the surging crowd. The students are forging ahead, thrusting fists into the air at regular intervals to emphasise a particular slogan. Feet thunder in unison. Dust rises.

By now we're passing Sharpeville Municipal Hall, still on the jog. I'm part of an immense human wave – and tiring rapidly. The younger lights have gone ahead. All this time I'm greeted or engaged in conversation by whoever is within range – and pant a response through bursting lungs.

I'm joined by two "minders" – students I don't know – who edge up to my elbows with reassuring glances, and with the intention of keeping my pathway clear and providing (first aid?) assistance if necessary. Though I am tiring I haven't collapsed. My "minders" keep encouraging me that we will soon be there. Faces glisten with sweat and political excitement. Seven coffins are somewhere behind us on the shoulders of 22 runners. The families bring up the rear in taxis and cars. Now we're passing the shops at Vuka section. People gesticulate at the lone white struggling to keep pace with the young turks.

We have long passed the older cemetery where the 1960 massacre victims were buried. The present cemetery has been re-opened for this public funeral.

At last it looms ahead.

And then I see them. And feel dread for the first time today. A large force of police, mostly mounted on their vehicles, is poised across the cemetery, parallel with the seven open graves. Poised as if for action. Ready and wanting to go into action. I remember what happened a few days earlier at Evaton cemetery. I want to scream out, "What the fuck do you want here? Can you not let a funeral be a funeral?" The atmosphere becomes supercharged as mourners absorb the shock of this terrible police violation of their mourning space. The police camouflage uniforms and conspicuous weaponry do nothing to calm the people. Indeed they have the appearance of men at war with the black community. In vain Father Moselane appeals to them to move away. It becomes clear now that the attention of the youthful mourners is divided between burying the dead and the naked show of strength (by the police) behind them. The slogans being chanted develop a strong anti-police, anti-Afrikaner, anti-town council flavour, and a new level of intensity is reached and breached. As we assemble at the gravesides, banners proclaiming various groups' political

affiliations suddenly appear over the heads of the crowd.
Church ministers sort out coffins as they arrive. The God
of the broken-hearted hears hurried prayers of
commendation, even if drowned in the passionate tumult of
political fervour. The mourners slowly begin to move in the
direction of the township, their chanting subdued and
scattered.

Suddenly there's a commotion in the departing crowd. A
glance in the direction of the police explains why. Two
police Casspirs disengage from the large police force and,
incredibly, push into the midst of the retreating crowd from
behind, remaining there to "oversee" the departure from
the cemetery.

Anger smoulders once again. This is planned provocation,
premeditated incitement! Or is it plain bad judgement on
the part of some police commander? Suddenly screams
pierce the air as shots ring out. A woman is struck on the
cheek by a rubber bullet. People scatter. Did someone
throw a stone? That's how the police will put it.

Meanwhile, we ministers are regrouping and gravitating to
an area between the crowd and the police lines to prevent
a possible clash. Already some of the youth are starting to
shout, and threatening to throw stones at the police who
are clearly on edge. For this reason, having encouraged the
people to keep moving in the direction of the township, we
approach the police and appeal to them to avoid
provocative manoeuvring. Deliberately we clergy decide to
remain in the cemetery to monitor any further aggressive
behaviour by the security forces.

Finally calm returns to our immediate vicinity, as the last
of the mourners disappear into the township followed
closely, of course, by the police. I'm walking back to the
church in the company of the African Methodist Episcopal,
Methodist and Presbyterian Church of Africa ministers,
relieved that so far there has been no serious violence.

At this moment I detect a car parked among the trees on the left side (between Vuka and the Stadium), and discern binoculars – "007" style – trained on us. It is the Security Branch men who earlier in the week had taken our names. Once again we seemed to be the object of their discreet presence.

A red car appears and we are offered a lift. This gesture proves significant. In the red car we decide to monitor the police. We notice clusters of police vehicles close to groups of people in the streets, and decide to tail these police vehicles, disembark when necessary and advise residents to refrain from regrouping or doing anything else that may provoke retaliatory gunfire on the part of police. In turn, we find ourselves followed by the Security Branch, who seem to be desperately trying to fathom what the clergy are up to. They ease up to about fifty metres behind us, stop and observe as we appeal to the residents for calm and restraint. Their presence, of course, inflames people anew, and makes our peace efforts doubly difficult. People from the streets keep pointing to them. We know, we gesture back. How else can you respond – give the Branch the "V" sign?

It is bizarre, a totally absurd spectacle – hundreds of mourners trudging home from an emotional community funeral, closely followed by large police-filled carriers. The police are followed by the reverends in the red car, which is monitored in turn by the Security Branch bringing up the rear. "What are those fucking predikants (preachers) up to?" one branch man kept murmuring, handling his rifle uneasily.

Meanwhile another community funeral was bringing Evaton to a near standstill.

Long before the funeral service began at the McCamel Church of God, Evaton, youth organisations had converged on the venue and commenced singing liberation hymns, chants and songs punctuated with passionate "Amandla!" closed-fist gestures. A profusion of banners proclaimed the bearers' aspirations. More priests and ministers arrived, including Fathers Benen Fahy, Lucas Bambezela and Edward Lennon, accompanied by their funeral leaders. The service began. The emotional temperature rose as freedom hymns ascended towards a listening God. Fierce oratory gripped the people who responded regularly and readily with gestures and chants of commitment. Different unofficial civic and political organisations (but, as according to plan, without declaring their name for fear of later arrest) took the stand and preached their message of hope. The brutality of the police was summarily judged, their deeds publicly condemned. "God," a street theologian declared, "is on the side of the oppressed."

Loved ones fainted, overcome by grief and the sudden shocking tragedy that has visited them. "I cursed and I wanted to know if there really was a God," a former member of the VCA, Teboho Maitse, recalled later.

After concluding church rites the funeral procession of perhaps six thousand set out for the cemetery. Approaching the Evaton graveyard, they were intimidated by two armoured carriers placed in the centre of the road. From the ground these war-brown, steel vehicles looked invulnerable, the armed police occupying them god-like. The mourners must, of necessity, have walked round them – literally rubbed shoulders with them. Anger rippled. The chant grew louder, lauding liberation heroes …"Tambo … Tambo …" or teasing the police, "Hippo … hippo." Fury reached new heights. At the cemetery (near the trees) the police were waiting in imposing force. Obviously it was the police strategy for the day. Various church leaders shared the graveside service. Afterwards the now-subdued mourners began to trudge home.

It wasn't to be a peaceful trudge, however. That night national TV did not show vicious police attacks on residents near the Evaton cemetery after the funeral – or the arrest of a bus.

A crowd of young people had hijacked a bus at Sebokeng to get to the funeral at Evaton cemetery. This happened regularly during this period. Deaths due to police shooting attracted thousands of young

80

people to both vigils and funerals. Police heard about it and stopped all buses coming from Mabitleng, the cemetery.

Probably thinking it was the hijacked bus, the police now "arrested" a bus hired by the Mabathoana family of Sharpeville to attend the funeral for a Mrs Skaledi, who was buried with other uprising victims on that violent day. The police brought the bus and its occupants to Sebokeng police station, detained them for the weekend and released them on Monday after charging them on some pretext. Later, on instructions from the Attorney General, the case was dismissed. I wondered, did Vaal Transport Corporation, the bus owners, compensate or apologise to their clients for the weekend they spent in jail?

Such was the intensity of police reaction to this funeral that at least three hundred were arrested afterwards. Father Edward spent the evening at the Sebokeng police station searching for his six altar servers who were among those arrested. In the process he collected the names and addresses of the detainees for the Johannesburg lawyers.

While these funerals were in progress the now underground VCA held a secret press conference at lawyer Ismail Ayob's offices in Johannesburg, outlining their present demands and future plans. That night, angry state agents allegedly burned the home of VCA vice-chairman, Esau Ralitsela in Sebokeng.

For whites ten minutes away, in the tranquil areas of Vanderbijlpark and Vereeniging, these two historic funerals had hardly happened at all. They were beyond the periphery of white consciousness. That very morning, at a church in Vereeniging, there was a well-attended lecture for ladies on "The Personal Appearance of the Christian Lady"!

Chapter 15

Families continued to arrive at our churches with the names and addresses of those who had been arrested, counting on the clergy to convey this information to lawyers. Media people were phoning regularly for an update on any developments. According to a newspaper report, 351 state and private buildings had been destroyed. Human Rights lawyers Ismail Ayob, Pricilla Jana, David Dison, advocate George Bizos and colleagues were daily attending three Vaal Triangle courts, attempting to bail people out and assist in any way possible. The courts were overcrowded. People were milling around outside. Priests were inside, gathering names and addresses from anxious families.

Some day, state prosecutors, judges, magistrates, police officials and court interpreters will tell their story of how these events impacted on them. Until then this story will remain incomplete.

In mid-September it appeared in *The Star* that the funeral of Joseph Sithole, a young activist allegedly killed by shop owners who blamed him and his colleagues for the uprising, would take place at the Nyolohelo Catholic Church, Zone 12 in Sebokeng. Lucas Bambezela visited the family to check this information. They knew nothing of this arrangement and in fact were not Catholics. They had expected the service to take place at the Baptist church of Reverend Lethale, where the Vaal ministers had allocated it. Meanwhile, the police took their cue from *The Star* report and drew up a police order, describing how the funeral would take place, which route would be used, the number of people permitted to attend, and so on. This order was addressed to Nyolohelo Catholic Church, Zone 12, and duly delivered at the priest's residence. It was pinned by the police on both church doors. Altar servers accustomed to working piously in the sanctuary, observing the police visits, immediately shredded the orders.

The huge number of mourners packing the small Baptist church and surroundings at Zone 13 on Saturday were oblivious of any police restrictions on the funeral. By the time the police discovered they had delivered the banning orders to the wrong church, it was too late.

But who was Joseph Sithole whose death caused such consternation in security circles and led to such police violence later in the day? He was a standard eight correspondence student, of impoverished parents on the run from the police at the time of his death. According to an eyewitness he was set upon and killed by local shop owners who accused him of starting the riots which led to their premises being looted and burnt down.

In 1998 Gcina Malindi recalled, "I am certain that Joseph, when confronted, tried to explain to his attackers what had happened and why. He was always ready to engage and debate rationally with people. It is a great pity that he was not given a chance to explain what the whole rising was about. His killers must be regretting what they did in view of what has happened in our country."

Strangely the security forces did not directly interfere with the church service that day. They accompanied the massive throng to the cemetery without incident and observed the burial from the far side of the cemetery. So far so very good, I thought optimistically. No violence! No overt police intimidation!

What happened next is legend in the story of the struggle. According to a participant witness, before the last prayers at the graveside were completed, the police began to encircle the large crowd and at the same time to advance menacingly towards the graveside. Rage, fear and terror took hold as people scattered in all directions, only to be driven back with tear gas (which was even shot into empty graves into which some had fallen), rubber bullets and *sjamboks*

Two years later, Brigadier Gerrit Viljoen told the court in Delmas at the trial of 16 activists on treason charges:

> *At the grave Mr Baleka, and groups of other blacks, were*
> *blatantly breaking all the restrictions imposed on the*
> *funeral. I decided this noisy and unruly crowd could not*
> *be let loose on the community. I ordered the police to*

surround the people and make arrests. Only the
necessary violence was used to quell the crowd.

Meanwhile, according to the eyewitness, the riot unit commander, Brigadier (then Colonel) Viljoen, *sjambok* quivering in his hand, was seen standing on his vehicle shouting, *"Slaan die kaffir!"* (Beat the kaffir), *"Donder die kaffir!"* (Lay into the kaffir).

Those who were rounded up were ordered to sit down in a certain area. Accused later of kicking Patric Baleka, who would later go on trial for treason, Brigadier Viljoen said he could not remember saying this (*The Star*, 22 April 1986).

After the wounded prisoner-mourners were marshalled together the Security Branch arrived and walked among them selecting those activists who appeared on their lists. They were taken away on a separate truck.

At the police station they were systematically beaten up again by about thirty police officers. Their injuries made them unrecognisable. "Simon Nkoli, a friend of mine of five years, could not recognise me. He actually asked me if I had seen Malindi, not aware that he was talking to me," recalls Gcina Malindi.

"Brigadier Viljoen's conduct on this day would normally have invited a criminal prosecution or civil proceedings against him. He and his riot unit's conduct constituted a gross violation of human rights. The police and army conduct at Joseph Sithole's funeral should have been an incident specifically put before the Truth and Reconciliation Commission," concludes Malindi, now an advocate in Johannesburg.

Among those arrested was Jacob Moleleki, aged 16, later shot dead by police while still in a police van and in the process of being released.

Chapter 16

*An invasion of armies can be resisted; but not an idea whose
time has come* – Victor Hugo

Seven thousand troops and police invaded Sebokeng in the course of
Operation Palmiet, the government's self-styled "peace offensive",
launched on Wednesday, 24 October 1984 "to restore law and order,
and get rid of criminal and revolutionary elements". Father Lucas
Bambezela, emerging from Emmanuel Church, Zone 14, first saw the
army as he travelled to his Zone 12 (Nyolohelo Catholic Church)
parish. It was raining and unusually dull, he remembers. He noted
that the roads appeared to be sealed off by soldiers in battle dress.

It was only on a second attempt that he was able to slip through
the roadblock. At the church he asked a soldier why he was there
and what was going on. The young white army recruit replied angrily,
"We don't know why we're here. We just woke up in Bloemfontein and
were told to come to Sebokeng."

During this military exercise, about four hundred people were arrested
for offences relating to influx control, possession of stolen goods, dagga
(marijuana), firearms and pornographic material. A pellet gun was
confiscated from the home of lay church leader Justinus Mohapi of
Sebokeng. For the army it was a show of strength.

The South African Defence Force (SADF) badly misread the mood
and intelligence of the population when they distributed hearts-and-
minds stickers stating, "Co-operation for peace and security" or, "Trust
me" or, "I'm your friend". It was as if the devil was asking Christ in the
mountainous wilderness to trust him. The people were neither cowed nor
fooled. Rather, residents going about their daily chores were thoroughly
amused at the extraordinary measures – this was the latest in a series –
that the white man was taking to restore apartheid's disintegrating
regime of law and order. There was a strong air of unreality about the

continuing social drama, and of course, like the state of emergency, it did not restore law and order. It did, however, serve to bolster and sharpen law and order within the ranks of resistance organisations.

~

The funeral of Lemmy Isolene at the St Peter's African Methodist Episcopal (AME) Church in Sharpeville was held the day after the army invasion. Lemmy, a 16-year-old bus-stop hawker, was known in Sharpeville while guiding his blind father around town. Police shot him on his way from an earlier funeral (Mma Ndambambi). It was a sadly typical vicious circle: I dreaded the aftermath of each mass funeral. It was shooting time for the police – most likely after someone threw stones at them.

Reverend Luther Mateza (Presbyterian), Reverend Washington Malumbazo (Presbyterian Church of Africa), Reverend Dabula (AME), Reverend Phillip Molefe (International Assemblies Centre), and I conducted the funeral service.

Like other funerals, it was supercharged with the youth dominating the proceedings but at the same time, respecting the wishes of the presiding ministers and priests. In speech after speech they vented their anger and frustration. Anti-government rhetoric was interspersed with freedom songs and declarations of "Amandla!" accompanied by clenched fists punctuating the air. Later, Reverend Lord McCamel, chairperson of the area church ministers, addressed the congregation. Halfway through the service there was a commotion near the doors, usually a sign that police were in the vicinity. Quickly, to forestall panic in an enclosed area, the ministers moved from the sanctuary to the side entrance of the church, there to be confronted by the man in charge of riot control for the area, Colonel G Viljoen, and a subordinate officer.

The colonel demanded that the speakers stop talking politics or he would arrest "these people", that is, all 400 people in the church. My flesh crawled in the presence of this man. His assistant threatened to arrest me and the three other ministers if we didn't "control" the people in the church. As this church-door standoff was going on, the emotional temperature inside recorded an all-time high, and one continuous chorus of protest rage rang out.

We had little to say to the colonel and we returned to our places at the front of the church. Reverend McCamel appealed for silence, and explained the situation. He exhorted the mourners to sing "orthodox" church hymns appropriate to the occasion. He then asked me to address the congregation.

Still simmering from the altercation with the police, I hesitated, wondering if it was appropriate for a relatively unknown Celtic priest to speak at this moment. It was a risky move for a white person to address the crowd after the standoff with the white colonel at the church door. I felt small and vulnerable. I moved towards the raised pulpit with pounding heart, not knowing how I would be received or what I would say. Silence descended.

That day, I spoke in Sesotho, the predominant language in the area. I hoped I was coherent. The crowd was astonishingly receptive. A white addressing them in these "anti-white" circumstances was mind-boggling. Law had prevented them from living or working in close enough proximity to whites ever to relate to them. Happily this white was speaking a language they could relate to. Hundreds of young eager faces strained to see the speaker and hear the message. I think I spoke about Christ's friends and relatives who were caught up in the political turmoil of his last days, his deep depression at Gethsemane, followed by his detention and ruthless execution on Good Friday. I compared it somehow with the present critical times, but with the assurance and certainty that the equivalent of the Easter Resurrection, the liberation of South Africa, which would follow.

That evening, senior security police listened to a recording of my sermon but my white nasal rendering of Sesotho and Biblical imagery confused the black translators and it came to nothing. I returned to my place and was thanked by my colleagues. This was a high point in my relations with the people of Sharpeville, and indeed with the Vaal Triangle.

It was a full three hours later that the service finally drew to a close. Cars and taxis filled up quickly. My *bakkie* was overloaded even before I arrived. It wasn't hijacked, only commandeered for the funeral. Things were like that those days.

Soon we were on our way to the cemetery. Once again, as in all similar situations, the large youth presence led and controlled the funeral procession. Teenage girls and young women, with high-pitched voices in new rhythmic chants, encouraged their menfolk forward, not only towards the cemetery but also in the struggle for the liberation of every last brother and sister. Most countries have hallowed stories of their women's contribution to national emancipation.

Every time we passed contingents of heavily armed police in their armoured vehicles the tempo of verbal defiance rose. The *Maburu* (Boer) police, the Lekoa Town Council, the despised mayor, the Casspirs – they all featured prominently in the repertoire of yet another advancing wave of humanity.

The enormous procession was attracting new mourners as we snaked our way through the unpaved streets of Sharpeville. Finally we reached the cemetery, where the chanting and slogans, undiminished, were now interspersed with the final commendation prayers. The rites concluded, the now more muted crowd began to leave the cemetery for home.

Chapter 17

But all was not over. What happened next is described in an affidavit I made at the time in late October 1984 (for the Catholic bishops who had decided to investigate police brutality):

A 16-year-old youth, Lemmy Isolene, who the previous week was shot by police at Sharpeville, was buried at the local cemetery on 25-10-1984. After the funeral services had been completed at the graveside and as the last of the mourners were returning to the township and had drawn parallel to the houses, police Land Rovers (mostly yellow) in a clearly premeditated, precisely executed exercise, crept up swiftly behind them. Doors flashed open, out poured white and (one) black policemen, camouflaged, wielding yellow sjamboks (whips). All hell broke loose. Like animals of prey, they set upon the people with such sadistic abandon as to defy description. Girls, women, children and men were sjamboked mercilessly and without the least provocation. People screamed for mercy, scattered over fences into private property, hotly pursued by the police, raining blow after blow on the defenceless mourners. In five minutes the area was deathly quiet again except for the police regrouping, returning to their vehicles and moving off. A small group of people (about eight or ten) attached themselves defensively to me and another church minister, hoping that the police would not attack clergy, and therefore not them either.

I was about 20m away when I witnessed this. The police hadn't noticed me. I counted about five pairs of shoes, mostly women's, abandoned in the street by fleeing mourners after it was all over. Time: 12.30 p.m.

Later that morning I was unceremoniously stopped by Colonel Viljoen in his blue police car. He wanted to know where I was going with so many passengers – really mourners fleeing police assault. I replied that I was returning to the home of the deceased to wash hands according to African custom. Reluctantly he said, "Go on," after looking at me, eye to eye, with total distrust – our second unpleasant meeting that day.

Clashes between police and people electrified the townships. Often on those occasions I saw police vehicles careering in all directions in search of action. The result was deserted streets, garden gates closed, anxious peeping curtains waiting until the danger was past before venturing out again. I returned to the church exhausted.

But the security forces were already hatching a new plan.

~

It was raining heavily on a Wednesday evening when through the office curtain I saw seven army trucks trundling past the church and deploying troops in full battle gear in the area of the dump at "Seepoint" section. Here we go again, I thought. Reports had been coming in that all entrances to Sharpeville had been blocked, and people entering had been fingerprinted with the usual indelible red ink. Residents, returning from work, were mystified, angered and a little suspicious of this ink.

The army left later that night. It had been a trial run for the big one. Low-intensity rebellion continued to define life in the townships.

Three weeks later, on Saturday, 24 November, the community of Sharpeville embarked on operation clean-up day. As punishment for the residents' refusal to pay rent, the municipality had suspended rubbish collections in Sharpeville and Boipatong. Since there had been a schools boycott in all the townships since 3 September, many hands made light work when it came to cleaning up the weeks of accumulated rubbish in open spaces throughout the township. So, since morning, hundreds of children, armed with shovels, pick-axes and enthusiasm, were to be seen in large animated groups loading *bakkies* and lorries at refuse points around the town. Cars passing clean-up points were requested to contribute R2,00 towards the costs of the operation. Local businessmen and van owners provided transport to take away the refuse. Church leaders were exempted but donated anyway. Petrol could be contributed too. This community effort went on for much of the day. But then something happened.

At 2.30 p.m. the South African army, in an awesome show of military strength, rolled up Sharpeville's wide main thoroughfare past the decoratively walled picnic area, which had been built by the army in recent years in an attempt to placate the angry residents. They cordoned off sections of the town for house-to-house "pass and permit" raids. It was almost reminiscent of a World War Two clean-up operation in a rural French village.

A long row of brown military machines the height of the surrounding houses peeped out on the main road from side streets, conveying the impression of invincibility. Along the main street, mighty steel-plated military ambulances stood ready in the centre, with Land Rovers parked before and after. In this "Operational Area" of the Putsoa Stene district of Sharpeville, young white boy-soldiers lined the centre of the narrow township side streets, rifles at the ready, not knowing what to expect on this their first visit to a black residential area in their own country. They were evidently astonished by what was happening to them. Their superiors had committed them to strict secrecy for this exercise.

For more than two hours these young, confused teenagers stood on patrol, trying to deal with culture shock while their colleagues went from house to house discovering urban Africa for the first time in their privileged young lives. They were in search of pass offenders, hooligans and revolutionaries. I wondered if they noticed the buckets of water in front of many houses at the ready so that residents could wash their faces to fight the effects of tear gas. A pall of eerie silence tinged with tension pervaded the normally cheerful bustling Saturday afternoon atmosphere of Sharpeville.

The military cordon extended up past Moedi School, and I was blocked from getting to the church. They were not allowed to let anyone through, an officer told me, awkwardly. I returned down the long grey line and got through the blockade at another point, thanks to the good offices of a more understanding soldier.

The patrons of the corner shebeen near the church, having observed my first unsuccessful effort at getting through, greeted my arrival at the church with cheers – a small victory.

The army went from house to house, and the people of Sharpeville will tell the story to their children's children – the story of the day the army came "to catch a thief". The sight of the military carriers lumbering through their home town like a herd of thirsty elephants searching for a waterhole was etched in their memory.

Throughout the whole operation the population displayed enormous resilience born of a lifetime of endurance lived under the brutality of apartheid and all its ramifications. They remembered 1960. They remembered 1976. 1984 was merely another chapter – but the beginning of the final chorus.

Chapter 18

Next day, Sunday, public relations officer Sarah Crowe, legal adviser Nicholas Fink Haysom and Victor Gillinge (all from SACBC secretariat) managed to get through the official police/army roadblock but were stopped at four unofficial youth roadblocks. It was only when they indicated that they were heading for the church that they were allowed through. Thankfully they were not searched, as the purpose of their visit was to finalise affidavits about criminal police activities for future publication. Clerics, including myself, had secretly collected affidavits and witnesses and were due to meet them.

Driving to Boipatong from Sharpeville and back again for Sunday services, I was allowed through all unofficial youth roadblocks but was waved down at seven police and army checkpoints. I was laden with affidavits against these very people. I was not confrontational. it is not a good idea to be confrontational when you're carrying damning evidence against the security forces buried under Bibles in your briefcase on the front seat. So I chatted up the police as they eyed my grubby carrier bag, and asked the soldiers for their trust-building sticker handouts which said "Trust me". Maybe my presence confused the soldiers who were new to the area. They were eager to give me stickers. It put them off the scent. I was sweating and not just because it was 30 degrees outside. I was dehydrating after five hours of church services in cramped dilapidated buildings with no ventilation. Each time I pulled away with a deep sigh of subsiding relief, a visceral expression escaped my lips into the empty steamy interior of the van – "*masepa*", or was it "*kak*" or "shit"?

The nights in Sharpeville and Boipatong were dark. The electricity had been turned off by the administration because of the rent strike but the residents had adapted to the new situation. The green transformer boxes dotting the streets were summarily hacked open and manipulated by amateur electricians, so that some residential blocks again quietly "recovered" electricity. In solidarity with those who were still in the dark – and in order to ensure that the authorities remained unaware of the continued flow of electricity – it became an unwritten law that power would be used only for heating or cooking, but not for lighting. Candles were to be used. Television sets were to be turned on only when the white flicker of light was not visible from outside. Much damage was done to Eskom and Orange-Vaal Development Board electrical property – a factor which may have led to the blanket resumption of electricity for all, both in Boipatong and Sharpeville, some time later.

~

Meanwhile in the leafy, white, conservative sanctuary of Vanderbijlpark, another private war was being played out. Although white schools had not been part of the developing schools boycott in the townships, two days after the army invasions of the townships, Sancta Maria reported a drop in the attendance of white children. In fact, many white children did not attend school that day in the PWV area because of the rumoured possibility of kidnapping by black groups. Such was the influence of right-wing agitators working on white fears.

But the problems for this school went back to January 1978, when the Dominican sisters in Vanderbijlpark had admitted three black children to Sancta Maria School, pioneering open education in the Vaal Triangle and beyond.

A war of words ensued between the nuns and the Transvaal Education Department (TED). The school was ostracised by neighbouring white schools. Even Sancta Maria parents became worried about these new developments. Some removed their children from the school. Other parents, much later, went into serious shock when one of their children told them that a priest at assembly had prayed for the downfall of the government. For some parents this was bordering on treason.

At the same time the Department of Education and Training (DET), not to be outdone by the TED, insisted that the flourishing night school for black adults (525 were on the rolls in 1978, including 72 teachers) must be relocated to one of the townships. The Dominican sisters, in the spirit of their founder St Dominic, persisted in both projects, and eventually won through.

The woes of Sancta Maria were different to those of Assumpta Primary School in the heart of Sharpeville. Here the dangers were not of the rumour variety. At any moment a violent skirmish between police and residents, mostly youth, could spill over into the school, causing panic and putting the lives of the children in danger.

Although the sites of struggle were secondary schools, sometimes primary schools were invaded by older students who were determined to bring all on board in the name of that struggle. Parents had to decide daily whether it was safe to go to work and whether it was safe for their children to go to school. For principals like Sister Eilish Higgins or Cecilia Mogopodi, guiding a school in those circumstances was an acquired skill. They developed a strategy of survival. The main school gate would be kept closed during learning hours. This was to keep at bay periodic surges of street activists engaging the security forces on the run.

The streets surrounding Assumpta were regularly scanned by the staff for approaching unrest, and information was passed to the principals of adjacent primary schools. When danger was forecast children would be released in small groups and told to walk and not run, home directly. This was to contain panic. Their teachers would hold their collective breaths as the little ones bravely left the school grounds holding hands in shared solidarity.

Chapter 19

By the end of October 1984, seven weeks into the uprising, the VMSG (see Appendix 1) had met with the Evaton Chamber of Commerce, the Orange-Vaal African Chamber of Commerce, various taxi associations, social workers (some feared for their lives as they worked on the government's development board), the Red Cross (they asked to use the churches instead of state-run clinics for the distribution of food relief), and schoolteachers – though not yet school principals and certainly not inspectors. The church ministers always took the opportunity to explain the bigger social picture unfolding in the area. As a consequence it was generally agreed that town councillors should resign, that rents be decreased, and that students be released from detention.

Business and professional people do not normally lead the charge for political change. Others do that. But the business community was now rethinking its position and its understanding of the direction political developments were taking in the townships. These meetings helped businessmen evaluate and adjust their positions accordingly.

The caring professions too were re-appraising their own positions. Nurses, in particular, found themselves at the cutting edge of the upheaval, having to care for the wounded and dying in hospitals. The police too wanted to know who were the wounded and dying. This put the nurses in a difficult position. They had to establish their loyalties early on. They came to understand the point of view of the clergy.

We were shepherding in social and political change. Thinking globally and acting locally underpinned our actions. We sensed that the Vaal Triangle was emerging, albeit ponderously, as the core area from which new impulses for change were being tried, tested and advanced. It was, for those civil groups that came to us, a speeded-up, fast-forward conversion encounter which they carried back to their constituencies near and far.

There were indications that teachers and social workers were beginning to re-examine their loyalties too, a necessary rite of passage in any national struggle for democracy. It was fascinating to see township teachers who traditionally were noted for their dogged adherence to official policy begin imperceptibly to change direction. I saw this first-hand when the principals and teachers of the Vereeniging circuit wanted to give a donation to the churches' victims' relief fund (Appendix 1g). The rendezvous was set up furtively for a day and time to be disclosed only hours in advance. A teacher, Julia Matsoso, organised the hand-over by eight school principals – cloak and dagger style – at the church in Sharpeville.

It was a Wednesday morning at 8.55 a.m. when two cars swept into the churchyard in quick, quiet succession. Eight doors flashed open. The occupants poured out and into the church office. Brief introductions, embarrassed smiles, passing over of bulging envelope and they were gone.

The churches had negotiated an end to the three-month school boycott. But youth at Boipatong were slow to get the return-to-school message. The township had no electricity. Communications were weak. And anger still smouldered. Periodic stone-throwing still continued.

One December afternoon I drove to Boipatong for parish consultations connected with marriage preparations. Weddings had been suspended during the heat of the insurrection. Now they were doubling up; there was to be a rush of weddings during the uneasy lull. The situation was still far from normal. I drove from Sharpeville across the open veld and entered Boipatong at Lebohang Secondary School on my way to conduct Mass at St Joseph's Church, my eyes trawling the likely flashpoint spots whence a brick or two might arc in the direction of my lone vehicle, my body hunched over the wheel in tension, to the hostel where youths stared at the white driver and recognised the *bakkie*. I turned the corner, and drove past the makeshift football field called the "stadium", and finally to Tsirela section and into the churchyard where someone had opened the gate. I sighed with relief!

Altar servers arrived for the service, prepared the altar and disappeared home in fear of later police assaults. Very few came for

Mass for obvious reasons. The streets are dangerous after dark. I concluded church business quickly.

In fading light I left for Sharpeville with parish teenagers Tsietsi and Mkhulu thoughtfully joining me as minders along the road. It was raining heavily. My *bakkie* lurched through great potholes hidden under rushing floodwaters.

It was dark when I arrived at the church at Sharpeville. The rain had stopped and the churchyard was flooded. At the office I found a note under the door reminding me about the sacrament of reconciliation, confession, for the religious education children at four the next day. I left it on the table as a reminder, then went through the dank dingy sacristy into the darkened church. I felt a need to pull back into my own private space.

The red familiar flicker of the sanctuary lamp was the only thing that broke the blackness – a calming presence, a focal point. I knew I was not alone.

Nevertheless I felt a profound weariness, a heaviness coming over me. I was stumbling into my own interior world. Impulsively I prostrated myself on the sanctuary floor, which smelled of candle wax.

My diary read:

> *I find myself praying without words – fighting within myself. Self-pity wells up. Takes over. Will this uprising never end, Lord? Is there no relief? Why is it so sustained, so intense, so repetitive, so pervasive?*
> *And then I think of those young people out there. Those who were so passionately involved in seeking change, so committed, so determined, always against such great odds. How dare I complain?*
> *Still, Lord, I want to tell you that this is getting to me, getting too much.*
> *Silence. Deafening sound of silence. The God of Silence. Your pregnant silence, Lord, doesn't impress me one bit! Let it be. What's the use? I am too tired and confused to argue with Him.*

It reminded me of other times in different but similar circumstances when I engaged God in noisy, angry exchanges as I paced up and down a deserted church. People would have thought I was crazy, needing help from the men in starched white coats with grave countenances and hidden syringes. But then the spiritual sages tell us that God (the Force or whatever the reader believes in) can take tough prayer, angry prayer, noisy prayer. He had to take it from His prophets and psalm writers. Jeremiah, they say, got furious with God in his little hut. (But then they bundled him off to Africa.)

I eased myself up after about twenty minutes, careful of my football-damaged knee. I probed with my hand and found the spot where I sit each morning for meditation.

It is a time of listening to voices from the heart and beyond. I'm jaded. Sitting still in a typical ghetto warehouse-like church, looking nowhere, for in the uncompromising darkness there is nowhere to look. I close my eyes and enter even deeper into myself. Sensing all round me the lingering human energy of recent community-driven meetings and services. A car drives into the churchyard, pauses; there are no lights, and it leaves. I jump as a stone clatters on to the still cooling tin roof of the old building. Catapult kids chasing birds on their way home from play.

My churning internal world slowly subsides. Familiar and unmistakable sounds of township nightlife recede gradually to the outer limits of consciousness. Daydreaming at night-time! The solitude of it all.

Is there a certain loneliness hovering around me? A subtle, pervasive alienation seeking to express itself, to be named and identified? A sort of coming together, in and around me, of a combination of strange and unlikely elements converging to make things fall apart?

Formerly accepted cultures, ways of doing things, ways of thinking, are taking a pounding these days. Things and familiar situations are beginning to break up, to melt down.

*I'm still trying to make sense of the ever-changing signals,
symbols, and signs of the unforeseen, the unexpected crisis
in the daily life of Vaal townships. What new critical
demands will these times make on us in the coming days?
Or even tomorrow? Perhaps even tonight.*

*The loneliness is heightened when you know your fellow
clergy friends (if they are married and in a loving
relationship) will return home this evening to an
understanding family there to unload their burden,
to find a listening ear and perhaps a soothing caress.
Deep dark silence.*

*But I'm calmer now. My wilderness within is becoming
friendlier. I lift myself up, switch on a light and reflect for a
while on some hopeful, life-giving guidelines from the Bible.
Evening prayer it is called. Satisfying.*

*Time to go. I make my way through the sacristy and out.
I lock up. The streets have become noticeably quiet.
I cross the muddy yard (stepping over the extended stoep
or patio, which a parishioner had graciously installed,
and which had become the first-ever illegal memorial to the
memory of the Sharpeville dead of 1960 and the Vaal dead
of 1984) and in the matchbox flat kitchen find a plate of
fish and chips heating in the stove. That was the car that
drove in and out. Steve Lehobo, a Sharpeville store owner,
leaving a treat for the evening. In fact, come what may, the
Lehobo family always left something hot on Wednesday
evenings. As did the Lebajoa family on other days. And not
only them. Others too. Bless them all. They are so loving.
I boil water for tea feeling almost upbeat. The ringing phone
breaks the silence – a call from Sister Angela Murphy. To let
me know that her churches-supported domestic skills project
has relocated to Vereeniging due to the widespread
disruptions at Evaton.*

*I switch on my little short-wave radio to catch the BBC
news about these townships. Usually more accurate and
independent than our own mostly manipulated news.*

*Ironically our censored version of the radio news is brought
to us sponsored by paragons of truth and correctness such
as insurance or banking concerns. I scan the local
newspapers, especially the black community-based ones.
I wonder what they are saying about us today! The black
view and the white view as always. And locally distilled by
many censorship laws. At least they are reference points,
but often not much more.*

*The foreign media normally get it right. They come and ask
the right questions. Like Mallory Saleson from the Voice of
America who never misses 21 March, Sharpeville massacre
day. The townships are the news these days. Living close to
breaking world news is frightening and adrenaline pumping.
But you feel good that the news is getting out, that the
world is listening. I tremble with hope.*

*I became aware that my incoming mail – apart from
accounts – had slowed to a trickle. People asked if I had
received their letters. No, I had to reply. Thus I had to make
use of neighbouring church box numbers in white areas to
improve the situation. Years ago, a friend working at
Vereeniging post office assured me that some white
colleagues used to travel to Johannesburg for weekend
"piece jobs" in which they were apparently employed at
intercepting anti-apartheid mail. Be that as it may, it
wasn't until June 1995 that a Michael Leach confessed in a
Sunday Times "kiss and tell" article that as chief
administrator in the Department of Posts and
Telecommunications security department he had helped to
set up a giant national surveillance network, a vital function
of which was to copy, open or pass on anti-apartheid
sounding letters to the police strategic communications
section for security processing.*

*Tonight I'll sleep better. The only sound is the rushing
storm-water drains outside. The thunderstorm this evening
put an early end to the normally vibrant street life of the
township.*

Not so last night. Uprising or no uprising, I fell asleep to the sound of cowhide drums celebrating the homecoming of a newly graduated traditional healer. Competing for attention on the full-mooned, warm summer's night had been the loud hypnotic strains of Peter Tosh and Bob Marley, mesmerising their local followers into bopping the night away under my window. The air was pungent with dagga.
I read myself to sleep.

Chapter 20

If the people were suffering, the black councillors – whose decision to increase rent and service charges had sparked off the uprising – weren't having an easy time of it. A bizarre side saga was playing itself out across town, at the Sebokeng administration buildings at Houtkop, where the Lekoa town councillors, who had fled their homes, were in protective hiding.

The following is an extract from the diary of one of the councillors:

The Councillors were housed at Houtheuwel, in JC Knoetze Hall. During the day they held meetings to solve the problems that were increasing by the day in the Vaal Triangle.

It was pleasant during the day when other employees of the Council and Development Board were around. From 16h00 they knocked off and went to their houses. Those without houses remained behind to look longingly at those who had homes. Telephones were left for the use of the councillors to contact their friends and next of kin. That was the only consolation when everybody else had gone home. This connection did not make them feel "alone in the world". The bill must have swollen out of all proportion by the end of September 1984. We knew from the reaction of the officials.

It would be wrong not to say something about the team that prepared meals for us and kept checking on us time and again: Mrs SM Steenkamp, 55 years old, and her helpers, among others Miss Martha Ratona and Mr BJ Scott. These ladies and a gentleman woke up early every morning and went to their homes very late. Theirs was to see that catering was done and all their wonderful work can be summarised in two words: dedicated and indefatigable. Every morning while we were asleep they were around preparing the breakfast for the day. At 16h00 all other employees of the Development Board went home, but not Mrs SM Steenkamp and her crew. They were busy preparing our supper. Their work never ceased for there were the police and soldiers who also had to get grub from the kitchen.

Mr BJ Scott was the Town Secretary of Lekoa Town Council. When there was any problem the Councillors had, they communicated with him and he would handle the situation to the best of his ability. At some stages he sacrificed his personal belongings to the advantage of the stranded. May his tribe increase! At his humble abode, which was not far from the Administration Offices, he kept some cattle that were milked by his employees. A can of milk was delivered to the Administration building every day to be consumed by whoever liked milk. This was a gift from the bottom of his heart.

Colonel Kruger was the man in charge of the Defence Force in the Vaal Triangle. He was a very energetic and able man. At about this time he had received information that "the tunnel to the Councillors is nearly complete". Whatever that meant was for them to consider. It could have had a literal meaning or a proverbial one, but they meant that the way to get to the Councillors was nearly completed. The only pity about the tunnel was why get to them (councillors) through a tunnel? It could have been less costly to ask them for an interview and talk to them. Surely they were not going to refuse to speak to the people when they were chosen by the same people to represent them?

Part Three
The A B C of an uprising

Chapter 21

"Four versions ... four ... exist of the life of Christ. Which one would you have liked to chuck out?" – Truth Commission Chair Desmond Tutu after the first round of submissions by political parties produced four different versions of history, *Mail & Guardian,* 24 December 1997

My Dad was great at telling us about the weather. His forecast was really important when we were going to the Phoenix Park in Dublin for a few hours in the outdoors. We trusted his opinion more than the wireless forecasts. He would go outside the shop on the Dublin Quays, and with hands deep in pockets and shoulders thrown back, study the sky for some time (pedestrians sometimes stopped to see what he was staring at but he never noticed), observing the movement and shape of the clouds and come back with a definitive explanation of the weather conditions for the next few hours – or even for the next day. He was always right.

But what about trying to forecast future social and political events at a given place and time? For instance, the Vaal Triangle in South Africa during the 1980s? Sometimes I ask myself: Did the Vaal Triangle really fall apart after the events of 3 September 1984? Or will historians see this time as a great milestone for change whose time had come? Was the Vaal Triangle the final catalyst ushering in another South Africa? An October 1984 survey in *The Star* found that most white people in the Johannesburg area thought political agitators were responsible for the ongoing violence and that the rent increase was "not the real reason". This was the general feeling in government circles too. "Bus loads of agitators came from outside," claimed EC Mahlatsi, mayor of Lekoa. Nicholas Louw, his town clerk, concurred when he told an USCO (formerly the Union Steel Corporation) meeting on 6 December that it was " youths from outside [who] instigated the riots".

In a meeting earlier with social workers, Louw blamed the new Tricameral Parliament, which excluded blacks. An anonymous pamphlet blamed the VCA, as did Mahlatsi in an interview with *City Press* in November.

Surprisingly, Lekoa town councillor Jonas Tsoai broke ranks in an interview with the *Sowetan Sunday Mirror* in December 1984 and blamed his own council. As did fellow councillor, Arthur Zulu Jokozela, when he told the Delmas Treason Trial: "The rent increase which was to be implemented in the Vaal Triangle in September 1984 was a material cause of the unrest which swept the area that month." (*The Star*, 19 March 1986). Others blamed the UDF and the churches.

Would Christ, if he had walked the angry streets of the townships in 1984, have listened to these commentators? For he once said: "You superficial people! You understand the appearances of the earth and the sky, but you don't understand the present times" (Luke 12:56).

But what was the official version?

The Van der Walt commission of enquiry was set up by the government to investigate the causes of the education crisis in the Vaal Triangle. This one-man commission of inquiry, given two weeks to complete its work, took submissions from "132 people and organisations". In March 1985, it handed the DET an edited version of the original 970-page report. The report was finally tabled in Parliament in April 1986. One wonders why it was withheld from the public for so long, in spite of the verbal promises of publication given to the VMSG by the Deputy Minister for Education and Training, Sam de Beer.

Among Professor van der Walt's findings were:
(a) Police tactics were at fault.
(b) Education authorities ignored warnings by teachers of an "explosive situation" building up.
(c) There was a feeling that the black education system was inferior and offensive to one's dignity.
(d) The success achieved by the school youth in 1976 had encouraged children to try again.

(e) A sense of disadvantage compared to white students was evident.
(f) The rent increase could not be regarded as the primary cause of the riots though it was the last straw.
(g) Pupils saw rent increases as eating up money put aside for their schooling.
(h) The real problems were found in local conditions and local government.
(i) The tricameral system of parliament was a spark to the unrest.

Undertaken by the Potchefstroom University for Christian Higher Education at the time, the exercise was nonetheless flawed from the beginning for at least three reasons. The time frame was too brief. The report was coloured by the limitations of a white person who, although sincere, could never really comprehend the vast sea of underlying emotions, perceptions and experiences that made up the social framework of black urban township life, seriously wounded by the ideology of separateness. And finally, only "132 people and organisations" came forward for interviews or made submissions, and these were mostly professional people. Yet despite these shortcomings, the report's recommendations were valid, and self-evident to blacks. *The Annual Report of the Institute of Race Relations*, 1984, summed up the underlying causes of the upheaval:

(a) Dissatisfaction with the system of African education. School disturbances in different parts of the country began in January 1984. Later in the year – around July – these school protests merged with community organisations that were protesting against the increases from seven to ten percent in general sales tax (GST).
(b) Economic causes. Gordon Hood, managing director of the OK Bazaars, said in late 1984, "In my years in retailing I have never encountered what appears to have become accepted practice in 1984 – the phenomenon of raising the price of basic foodstuff several times a year". The Institute of Planning Research (IPR) of the University of Port Elizabeth found that in September 1984, the Vaal Triangle was the most expensive place in the country for Africans. The IPR also found that the average rent in the Vaal Triangle townships was higher than the average paid by Africans

elsewhere in the country. It was precisely this flashpoint that sparked the violence during the 3 September 1984 stayaway. It was protest against the proposed rent and service charges increases of R5,90 for state-owned units and R5,50 on privately owned houses. At the same time, the Evaton Town Council announced similar increases in residential permit fees. Furthermore, the household subsistence level (HSL) of an African family in the Vaal area was R330,25 a month, as against R327,11 for Johannesburg, the next most expensive area. The Bureau for Economic Research (BER) of the University of Stellenbosch supported this finding.

(c) Opposition to the new constitution and the exclusion of Africans from the Tricameral Parliament. PW Botha was elected the country's first Executive State President on 5 September 1984, two days after the uprising began.

(d) Appalling, blatant corruption in local government circles. During the 1985/87 Delmas Treason Trial, the following details came to light:

"Mr Piet Mokoena said that, of 12 liquor licences and premises awarded in the Lekoa (Vaal) area shortly after his election in 1983 – worth a total of R10 000,00 – nine were awarded to councillors. He himself had received a licence, premises and goodwill worth R1,1 million after becoming a councillor and had not paid anything to date (13/03/86) except monthly rent. He conceded that the Orange Vaal Administration Board, shortly after the elections, awarded 12 liquor licences to the extended family of Esau Mahlatsi, the mayor of Lekoa." (*The Star*, 13/03/1986).

Advocate Bizos for the accused said in addition to the 12 liquor outlets that the Mahlatsi family controlled, they had interests in eight more, acquired through the Lenthana Company. This brought to 20 out of 25 licences in which the Mahlatsi family was involved. It would take another 15 years before council disclosure of business interests or transparency became accepted public topics of discussion.

Mahlatsi was still mayor of Lekoa in 1986. Nicholas Louw, town clerk of Lekoa Town Council, denied a monopoly existed among the members for Lekoa Town Council (*The Citizen*, 8 April 08/04/1985). Result: an uprising.

Chapter 22

The first recorded (in South Africa) rent boycott was undertaken by residents of the Vaal Triangle and Evaton in September 1984 – Truth and Reconciliation Commission of South Africa Report, 1998

The rent and services boycott that started in September 1984 continued until the 1990s. The churches too were participants. It was highly successful as a peaceful means of protest, so much so that even the following government efforts failed to break it:

1. To undermine the collective decision not to pay, residents were asked, during house-to-house raids by the security forces, to sign agreements to pay.
2. By December 1984, Proclamation 186 of 1967 had been resurrected whereby employers were empowered to withdraw money from employees' pay packets and forward this "rent" money to the administration board. This failed, as employers did not want to bring civil unrest onto the factory floor.
3. Youth camps were set up in various parts of the country to win the "hearts and minds" of youth so that they would prevail upon their parents to break the rent boycott.
4. An invitation to State President PW Botha to visit the Vaal townships and a request to him to re-introduce a compulsory stop-order system to force rent defaulters to pay their tariffs.
5. Cutting off electricity of defaulters.
6. Evictions.
7. Appeals on TV by local councillors (which angered residents) and street leaflet campaigns (using the wrong African languages, for example, Setswana instead of Sesotho).

After 75 violent deaths the communities of the Vaal had stopped listening. More than a decade later, the new democratic government had great trouble bringing the boycott to an end. It had developed into a culture of non-payment.

And irony of ironies, in spite of the public's refusal to pay rent and service charges – "Asinamali" (we have no money) was the call, monthly dues at my parish were raised by 100% in December 1984, with the positive approval of the congregation. Clearly a different culture of giving existed within the Christian community. People were being necessarily selective. It was another small breakthrough on my learning curve.

But there was a deeper issue at stake: the survival of the community. Its gut defences were invisible but in place. Hence the failure to kill the boycott.

Robert James Scally in his book *The End of Hidden Ireland* [7] tells of the Irish peasants of the 19th century and how they resisted the British Empire. "Their means of resistance – conspiracy, pretence, foot-dragging and obfuscation – were the only ones ordinarily available to them, the 'weapons of the weak', like those employed by the defeated and the colonised people elsewhere."

These not easily discernible but well-tested dynamics of resistance, survival and self-preservation came into powerful play as the state turned up the pressure on residents to abandon the rent boycott.

All this clever reasoning will be of interest to historians and politicians. Young Johannes Rantete, however, probably summed up the feelings of the township people late in 1984 in his praise poem called *Sebokeng You Are Great:*

> In that unmeted anger you broke out into
> Violence to overcome the forces of oppression
> Imposed on you by your fellow brothermen.
> That wrath you showed was more than
> That of a tempted black mamba
> When you demolished everything to ashes.
>
> You made a history that none of your residents will ever forget.
> Your reaction so shocked the government
> That it could not believe the damage done
> Were only a protest against the rent hikes.

[7] Oxford University Press, 1996

Wrath of the mamba, zeal of the united,
Courage of the history makers –
I bow down to your everlasting greatness.

Chapter 23

The strength of inter-religious solidarity in action against apartheid, rather than mere harmony or coexistence, was critical in bringing that evil system to an end – Nelson R Mandela

When the Catholic bishops published their now famous report – "Police conduct during townships protest: August to November 1984" – it was generally greeted with incredulity on the part of whites and astonished acceptance by township people.

The controversial booklet was for the most part based on affidavits secretly collected, often late at night and often in the most bizarre situations, by the VMSG late in 1984. It was the first time any church or institution had publicly confronted the apartheid police force with evidence of its own lawlessness – an encounter between the men of the mitre and the men in camouflage. Herbert Koaho (NGK), Edward Lennon (Catholic), Peter Lenkoe (Anglican) Lucas Bambezela (Catholic) and myself represented the VMSG at the launch of the booklet, and the Secretary General of the SACBC Father Smangaliso Mkhatshwa (now mayor of Tshwane), and Archbishops Butelezi, Daniel, Hurley and Orsmond, presented it to the international media. Among the activists present was the former UDF leader and current Minister of Finance, Trevor Manuel.

In former years every South African Minister of Police knew in his heart the necessity of having a ruthless police force to implement the grand design of his government. Opposition to police brutality was taken personally by the minister and by means of heavy bluster, appropriate whingeing, smear campaigns, even lambasting of church delegations, critics were crushed, discredited, neutralised or simply ignored. It was in the light of this and more especially the deplorable police behaviour in the Vaal townships during September, October and November 1984 that the bishops decided to act in a decisive manner.

The report provoked an intense public debate in the national Afrikaans and English press on the methods, outlook, perceptions, activities and equipment used by police in the black ghettos.

Later government reports (Kennemeyer[8], Van der Walt) on police behaviour in black areas quoted from the church document. In fact the report was a not-so-veiled condemnation of the policing of Brigadier Gerrit Viljoen, who was in charge of riot control in the Vaal Triangle. And it was understandable if he took it personally.

Among the Brigadier's arsenal of riot control methods documented in the report was the Trojan horse ambush of people in Evaton, by his men from a bus hired from Vaal Transport Corporation (VTC) on 15 October 1985. VTC never denied it. And scorn upon scorn – a VTC bus (showing contented township life scenes) was depicted on thousands of leaflets distributed by the police in the Vaal townships advising people to reject the troublemakers and return to the "peaceful" days of the past. This irony was compounded by the fact that at another time in the 1980s, perhaps in an effort to undo the damage, the VTC had issued commuters with thousands of community-friendly leaflets extolling "the bus to trust" (Bese yeo o ka e tshepang).

In 1998, the TRC concluded that "security forces also used 'ambush' tactics against civilian protesters".

The SACBC report went on to describe the indiscriminate firing of bullets and tear gas at private homes where at least two residents were shot through the eyes. Nicholas Ngudlwa, 10, was shot dead in September 1984 by a Sergeant Pereira who was later found guilty of homicide and fined R600 or 12 months in prison suspended for three years (*The Star*, 16 September 1989).

The Sharpeville parents of young Maud Nzunga, the seven-month-old child who died after tear gas was shot into the room where she was lying, or the children and grandchildren of Martha Ndabambi, who was carried home delirious, having inhaled tear gas shot from a helicopter, will never be convinced that their loved ones died of anything but tear gas – at least indirectly. The report documented these deaths, and others – as well as the police rape of two underage Sharpeville girls in November 1984. The report

[8] In June 1985, Mr Justice Donald Kennemeyer issued his report on the police killings at Uitenhage.

even collected the variety of abusive terms used by the police in the heat of the moment and sometimes in a state of intoxication.

Police reaction was swift and predictable. The bishops had "ulterior purposes" in publishing this book, said a spokesman; indeed it revealed "untruths as regards detail, chronology and events" (*City Press*, 9 December 1984).

The police also had their media defenders. Emelia Jaroschek, writing in the *Sunday Times*, said that Brigadier (then Colonel) Viljoen was a "remarkable peace-maker" and a "police colonel who brought remarkable calm to the Vaal Triangle's riot-torn townships".

Reports like this continued to misinform the non-black public about the emerging bigger picture. Indeed, in September 1984, South African television had falsely reported that rioters were burning the churches in the Vaal Triangle. Yet the only damage to churches was done by security agents who in late 1984 firebombed the Catholic churches at Sebokeng and Evaton, and savagely tear-gassed the home of Anglican Father Geoff Moselane.

The police were clearly stung by the audacity of the church. Their bad name had become international news. They needed to save face. Damage limitation was called for. Through the SACBC, after a meeting between Sarah Crowe, Archbishop Denis Hurley, SACBC president, Father Smangaliso Mkhatshwa, the SACBC Secretary General, Edward Lennon and myself at Krugersdorp with divisional commander Colonel Steyn, they asked to meet those who had made affidavits criticising them. The church later abandoned this procedure when it was found that that the police only intimidated those who bravely agreed to meet their aggressors. Finally the police withdrew, even when it was agreed that they could continue their questioning, but only on church property and in the presence of a priest or lawyer.

The bishops' report was confirmed by the findings of the TRC in 1998: "Police accused of using excessive force could rely on the full support of their superiors, the silence of their peers and the full indulgence of security-conscious judicial officers."

The facts had been established. For once the police didn't like the facts before them. The churches had taken them unawares. They had

115

stood up to the government in exposing its security forces. And got away with it.

In 1997, the now retired Hurley made a telling remark: "The apartheid government was more scared of us than we of them – we should have realised it earlier."

Police morale began to slide. They now intensified their surveillance inside church congregations.

Chapter 24

Clergymen who openly involve themselves in politics should remove their robes, resign and enter politics – Kerkbode, official newspaper of the NGK

Encountering the state inside the church was uncomfortable for church ministers and priests. "The spies are restless," wrote the poet Mongane Serote in his book *Third World Express*. They were indeed. Every parish had its suspect informers. People still hesitate to talk about it. Informers – *dimpimpi* – were voluntary and involuntary. Some offered information about "Father" for money. Others were beaten into offering information. Usually the Security Branch tried to elicit information from those closest to the priest or minister.

Good-natured parishioners, well-meaning members of church committees or councils, sometimes advised me about the wisdom of saying certain things publicly which might upset the mind of the state. One had of course to weigh this wisdom with the demands of the Gospel or one's obligation to preach the truth and thus form a community with a conscience.

It was too easy to succumb to the floating temptation of the time to keep "on the right side of the law" or not "to talk politics" or to do or say nothing in the name of "prudence".

This very dilemma grew in intensity with the successive States of Emergency, from mid-1985 to the end of the decade. The state clamped down on people's annual commemorations of past violent clashes with the state such as the 16 June 1976 Soweto uprising, the 21 March 1960 Sharpeville massacre or the 3 September 1984 Vaal Triangle uprising. These memorials were banned outright. But that did not prevent an emotional build-up in the townships as the date of the commemoration approached. Police and army were always out in force and the Security Branch was on overtime as they roped in willing and unwilling collaborators and positioned them for all eventualities. This included slipping them into the back of churches with the last rush of Mass-goers just as the Sunday service was about to begin. Unsurprisingly, our phone lines seemed to fall dead before these commemorations.

They did not always stay at the back of the church. Cecil Pienaar was a loyal Security Branch officer who had been accused of torturing some young people from the coloured township of Rust-Ter-Vaal, outside Vereeniging, in the mid-1970s. He often sat in the front pew, prepared to report every holy word uttered by a seething Father Dominic Hession standing one metre away. Picture the scene. Picture the angry feelings of the congregation. Picture the spy's own emotions of betrayal. And multiply that thousands of times throughout the country.

My own home-grown way of facing such a situation was to allow myself to be carried, in an apparently detached mode, by whatever way the people wished to highlight the occasion, for example, at services by spontaneous public prayer for specific social needs, "political" sketches by the youth, the singing of *Nkosi Sikelel' iAfrika* during services. The police used to ask detainees, during interrogations, who was promoting the singing of this hymn at the end of Mass at the church in Sharpeville. I wonder whether Libidi Korotsoane, our choirmaster, knew this at the time. I always appreciated his initiative.

I remember our youth in Boipatong commemorating the Soweto 1976 uprising with a quite dramatic sketch during Mass. At one point in the drama the "police" ran up the church aisles and "shot" a group of 15 "protesters". There were "dead" bodies all over the sanctuary. Richard "Bricks" Mokolo (a church lay leader and political activist who on 11 June 1985 was beaten up by the auxiliary police called "Kitkonstabels" and tortured by the Security Branch, for "inciting people to burn houses and encouraging residents not to pay their rent") emerged solemnly from the sacristy dressed as a priest to perform the last rites. It was difficult to keep a deadpan, fatherly face in the midst of all this "bloodshed" and blessings.

Yes, humour intruded too. Sometimes introducing the sign of peace during the Mass I would deliberately encourage the congregation, especially those at the back, to greet lovingly those strange faces beside them – the possible informers – assuring them that as shy "newcomers" to the parish they would be accompanied to the church office for registration afterwards. I could not resist the bit of liturgical fun. God smiled too, I know. And it developed healthy vigilance in the congregation.

I didn't take an active part in these anniversary Masses. My contribution came the following Sunday when people were more relaxed and the social tension had subsided.

My sermon on such a day, delivered in a light-hearted vein, informed the public (with my tongue firmly in my cheek) that under the Emergency regulations I was not allowed to recall or even mention, for example, the anniversary of the Vaal uprising in which 75 had been killed in 1984, that the Sharpeville Six or the Delmas treason trialists appreciated their continued support, that there had been 67 deaths in detention up to then or that there were presently 300 political trials under way. These would have the appearance of side remarks, oblique references in the context of the larger sermon or homily on the Gospel of the day. A message of hope was conveyed to those for whom it was intended.

Later in the Mass a parishioner, while explaining some church business, shared other consciousness-raising news items such as the fact that posters reminding us to pray for detainees who – "Remember those who are in prison as if you were in prison with them" [Heb. 13:3] – had vanished from the church during the night. Informers, when they were there, would hardly have noticed, as our Sunday celebrations at Sharpeville were quite spiritually distracting to your average Gerry Mpimpi (Gerry the Informer). By Monday he was somewhat confused about what he had heard or seen, so much so that his handlers at times thought he was holding back.

Working hard behind the scenes, as always, were our regional and local justice and peace people.

It is quite probable that the Vaal Triangle clergy were targeted by the State Security Council's Project Epic, set up to counter the

119

revolutionary and political theology of the Roman Catholic Church and "Project Frog" was designed to target the SACC and other "enemy organisations" (*Southern Cross*, 27 July 1997).

The state was indeed relentless in its pursuit of intelligence gathering, managed by the government's "Sanhedrin" or council of senior security generals with heads of subsidiary state groupings. Tshepo Koebe, a former altar server (at least fifteen of our altar servers were detained during this period), was questioned about the parish structures while in detention – who was heading these structures? And what were their functions? They wanted to know who handled the parish monies, and whether non-parish funds were channelled through the parish by Father Benen, Father Geoff or myself. They probably knew that the Church had been a secret channel for funds from the European Community for would-be political exiles all along.

According to Shaka Radebe, a COSAS leader, most of those arrested in the Vaal Triangle were questioned about the church ministers, and specifically about the role of some white priests and their relations with local black clergy, and those connected with the SACC.

A favourite question of Security Branch officer Captain Steenkamp was whether I attended meetings on church property. It was crucial for the Branch to know if priests were in any way stimulating opposition to the government. For that very reason I normally didn't attend meetings but formally and informally met community leaders in other circumstances on a regular basis. Thus there would be less pressure on detainees on my account.

Some church youth even found it in themselves to protect priests. When asked whether priests knew that the Sharpeville Youth Congress was meeting in a church room, they replied that the priests didn't know; that they thought it was a choir gathering! Telling lies to heretics (if you believed apartheid to be a heresy) or to sinners (if you believed apartheid to be a sin) in order to protect a priest. What a moral quandary to be in!

Church youth detainees were informed by their interrogators that their church was divided. The Pope, they were told, didn't agree with violence. The state media quoted the Pope out of context and clearly wanted to create the impression that local bishops and the Pope were at odds about the South African situation. In fact, as far back as 1981, Police Minister Louis le Grange was trying to drive a wedge between Bishop Desmond Tutu and the member-churches of the SACC: "Member churches must now seriously ask themselves how long they are prepared to entertain the fact that the SACC support subversive elements." Did Le Grange believe his own lies and deceptions at the time? Many of his followers did. I wonder how did they feel when 16 years later General George Meiring in *Days of the Generals*[9] admitted that the police were "inherent liars".

Even the anti-church leaflets found regularly on the morning streets or church yards failed to have the desired effect of neutralising the faith communities Of course, the churches countered in different ways – the pulpit, the press, and at meetings.

The state tried and failed to smash the VMSG by the detention of two of its members, Father Moselane and Reverend Lord McCamel. But the state underestimated the influence of the churches among the people. And profoundly so.

[9] Hilton Hamann. *Days of the Generals.* (Zebra, 2001)

Chapter 25

While he was in detention, Reverend Lord McCamel's mother died. I called for Sister Theresa Seeta, his cousin, at her family home at 11.20 p.m. on a typical cold winter's night. We slipped out of a slumbering Sharpeville, bound for the McCamel Church of God. Eve, the mother of the detained VMSG chairman, was to be buried that night according to the last wishes of her deceased founder-husband, between the hours of 12 midnight and 3.00 a.m.

Reverend Lord McCamel, after six months of detention, was released to conduct the funeral of his mother, a compassionate move on the part of his apartheid captors. His wife had expressed the wish that the Vaal ministers be present when her husband appeared, as a silent gesture of solidarity with a colleague living under severe pressure.

At about 1.00 a.m. (now Sunday morning), three brown-robed Franciscans pitched up along with other church ministers to do what was required of them in this most bizarre of situations. There was no public lighting in this area of the shanty ghetto.

But the practised eye discerned figures lurking behind trees or sitting in stationary official-looking cars parked in the outer, unlit areas of the imposing church building. The vigil ceremonies had been under way since midnight in the church.

In the family residence adjoining the church, there was a hushed air in anticipation of the "homecoming" of Reverend McCamel, mixed with the sadness of the loss of a loved mother and sickeningly compounded by the presence of so many plain-clothes police and soldiers.

The subdued atmosphere was broken at 1.20 a.m. when two of the younger children rushed into the house to announce that Papa had arrived. Three minutes later, the bearded, imposing figure of Reverend McCamel entered, accompanied by four seemingly embarrassed black heavies who never left his side for the next two hours.

Tearful embraces, lumps in throats, sad brave smiles, kisses from the children and midnight handshakes. He greeted us, the clergy, personally and warmly, and asked me to lead the assembled group in prayer. I can't remember what the Holy Spirit inspired me to pray about – I felt much emotion at the time – but I knew that some sort of co-existence if not accommodation between South Africans, sometime in the future, was part of it. Spontaneous prayer under these grotesque circumstances was a disturbing experience. To be real, it had to touch the core beliefs of the black police guards standing by, for they were uneasy and most likely plagued by repressed guilt. They kept their eyes self-consciously lowered.

Also, it had to have a message of consolation for the bereaved, and of hope for the Reverend McCamel, who was not allowed to speak to us in private. I stumbled my way through it. It was heavy going. We talked guardedly for some time. Everything was recorded. Cups of tea were passed, even to the guards. Clink of china, subdued conversation, and then to the church. It's not often you see a congregation breaking down in mid-song when their minister makes his entrance. But it happened that night. Many wept.

How often do you see a minister laying his mother to rest, surrounded by six heavily-armed soldiers and security personnel at 3 a.m.? It conjured up a host of disturbing emotions, which took days to subside.

It was a one-off experience and indelible. Only apartheid could produce it. Reverend McCamel was whisked back to jail moments after the last prayers at the cemetery, his church congregation still singing the final hymn at the graveside. In agitated silence they filtered back to the buses. Soon dark stillness returned to this, the "silent town" of the living-dead, but this time with the smell of fresh soil and the damp of new dew, a hint of dawn on the far horizon.

Part Four
Return to the epicentre

Chapter 26

Will no one rid me of this turbulent priest? – Henry II

The surveillance of the clergy was to be expected. Already they were being blamed by visible and invisible voices for the violence.

An unlikely source of information in this respect came from the right-wing Christian newsletter *Signposts* (Vol. 3 No. 5 1984). At the time it was secretly funded by the government. *Signposts* told its readers that according to DC Ganz, Chief Director of the Orange-Vaal Administration Board, "Most meetings where this fiasco was planned took place in houses and churches in the Vaal Triangle with the whole-hearted co-operation and direction of the ministers involved. In these meetings in churches the burning of shops and the driving out of community council members was planned. United Democratic Front speakers were presented to promote the matter." He said the issue of increased rent was "used just for appearance as a kind of smoke screen by the agitators".

In fact, up to December 1984, among the reasons advanced for the violence or uprising were:

- "I have reason to believe that priests are behind the unrest in the Vaal Triangle" observed a Vereeniging magistrate – off the record.
- "Father Moselane, an Anglican priest of Sharpeville, and churches, were involved," Mr Steve Nkatlo, a Dobsonville town councillor, alleged while attending the funeral of the murdered deputy mayor of Evaton.
- "A priest and churches" said leaflets that were planted on township streets.
- Church ministers at a meeting on 25 January 1987 were told by former Lekoa mayor, Sam Kodisang, that "church ministers triggered the unrest in 1984".

The Minister for Justice, Louis le Grange, at least was more discreet when after a tour of the area on 6 September 1984 he declared gravely: "There are individuals and other forces and organisations behind what is happening in the Vaal Triangle." Later he spoiled what insight he may have had, however, by adding "certain adults have again used children and youngsters to do their dirty work for them".

In reality the antipathy between church and state had a long history. In the 1970s, meetings related to culture and the arts were usually held at church venues. The police, for fear that these events would become tinged with politics, always monitored them one way or another. Plays for example had to be approved by the censor board before public performances. Nevertheless cultural activities tended to be a home for veiled anti-government sentiment – a spark in the darkness that was gathering momentum, spurred on by the uprising of Soweto in 1976.

By September 1983 the spread of opposition fever was gaining momentum on all fronts in the Vaal Triangle. The urgency of regular community meetings was becoming ever more apparent. Churches were fast becoming sites where people's grievances could be aired and debated. The UDF was clearly energising and inspiring these gatherings with fresh hope. New local leaders were surfacing. Thunder rumbled ominously on the horizon.

All this was of concern to the local authorities, who threatened to cancel churches' deeds of lease if meetings "other than church meetings" were held there. On Tuesday morning, 13 September 1983, an official acting on behalf of the director of the Orange-Vaal Administration Board, DC Ganz, delivered a terse letter, addressed to "Stand 4896 Zone 12, Sebokeng", which was in fact Nyolohelo Catholic Church, Zone 12, advising that the stand may be used only for *bona fide* church purposes. They added "if this condition is not being complied with, the Orange-Vaal Administration Board may be compelled to cancel the deed of lease". (At this moment in another part of the world, Soviet Premier Yuri Andropov was ordering Polish Premier Jaruzelski to restrict the activity of the Polish church). Anglican and Methodist churches received the same threat.

As local pastors, we ignored these instructions, indicating to the board that they should bring their concerns to the attention of our bishop in Johannesburg. A polite though earnest letter debate ensued between the bishop and the board, on the meaning and interpretation of expressions such as "non-church meetings", "meetings of a political nature" and meetings for "non-church purposes" – the theology of administrators versus Christian social teaching.

An inter-church meeting convened at St Michael's Anglican Church, Zone 13 Sebokeng, with Anglican and Catholic bishops in attendance, concluded unsurprisingly that religion and life were an integrated whole and did not fall into two categories. If people, denied the use of school or municipal halls, wished to air their grievances on church property, in church halls or even in churches, then that was all right. This was not groundbreaking theology for most churches. The matter was closed.

Meanwhile meetings of residents multiplied in churches. Alas, more threatening letters arrived from the board, including one on 5 January 1984, requiring the signature of the recipient, Father Lucas Bambezela (copies were required to be sent to the bishop and to the regional superior of the Franciscan Order). On 13 February 1984, a letter from the board to the Catholic Diocese of Johannesburg complained about gatherings which "tend to encourage deterioration in the relationship between blacks and government-instituted organisations", for example, administration boards and local black authorities. The threat of withdrawal of leasehold was no longer mentioned.

For years some churches had been seen as natural if not traditional local points of enlightened Christian social thinking. Thus they were able to accommodate within their teaching the voices of growing social dissent. Priests at local and regional level were often long-time friends of key movers for political change. This facilitated smooth relations between churches and society in those changing times.

Furthermore, church venues, strategically situated, as they were throughout the townships, especially the Sebokeng-Evaton-Sharpeville grid (and the country at large), enabled genuine community leaders to reach a wide audience. Later the state in the celebrated Delmas Treason Trial would endeavour to prove that violence had been fomented at these meetings.

All this time some of my Franciscan brothers who were expatriates were acutely aware that the Security Branch paid great attention to their every intimate action and public utterance, especially since the 1970 deportation of our colleague Father Peter Shanahan.

It was in this social context that priests and pastoral sisters (like popular Holy Rosary Sister "Maletsatsi" Day) were challenged to proclaim the Good News of liberating salvation, often in locally rooted stories or parables as Jesus had done. These stories raised spiritual awareness and challenged listeners to think new thoughts and ask new questions about the social, spiritual and political circumstances governing their daily lives. For their part, some church-going faithful in the townships might have wondered at the "political" role their local church seemed to be assuming. Socialised into a false conscience by apartheid, they were a little weary, a little uncomprehending of all these impatient meetings at their local church. At times they let their anger be known in their church councils. In fact this was an interesting phenomenon thrown up by the insecurity of political change, which sometimes threatened to split congregations among themselves or from their pastors or bishops. It was a time when many ministers suffered divided Christian communities.

For other churchgoers, however, there was a deeper awakening of long-repressed yearnings for emancipation.

Local authorities noted these new developments with unease, nay alarm. "The churches can no longer be trusted," they murmured darkly.

~

We deemed it important to have access to channels of communication to community-based newspapers and to leaders elected by the people but now in hiding. The clergy was therefore in constant contact with the VCA (then in hiding) through Reverend Lord McCamel, who normally attended their secret press conferences at the offices at Ismail Ayob's legal firm in Johannesburg. The Anglican Reverend Peter Lenkoe was our very effective link with the community-based newspapers, especially *The Sowetan*, the *Sowetan Sunday Mirror* and the *City Press*, for our press statements. Typical of our news releases was a regularly updated list of the dead, which normally differed from that of the police. At one stage this led to a public challenge by Sheena Duncan of the Black Sash to Education and Training Minister Dr Gerrit Viljoen (*Rand Daily Mail*, 25 September 1984), who used our latest list of recently killed residents to argue the minister's view that most of the Vaal dead were "external elements".

Dr Viljoen, confronted with this disparity, could not be contacted for comment. The minister's views reflected those of the Lekoa Town Council at that time. The VMSG regularly issued statements relating to numerous meetings where community affairs were discussed, for example, the January 1985 school boycotts. We also used the foreign media extensively when necessary, such as the day a band of colourful bishops adorned in tribal dress descended on the Vaal townships.

~

They came in solidarity "with all who have suffered in the recent unrest in the Vaal Triangle and in other towns in South Africa". On Sunday, 27 January 1985, 28 bishops poured into Sebokeng and celebrated Mass at Emmanuel Church, Zone 14.

It was dubbed, predictably, by the *Sunday Times* (27 January 1985), as the "Mass of the rubber bullet" because a rubber bullet was brought up to the altar in a solemn procession during the highly emotional service. In fact other symbols of people's anguish and grief were also brought up to the altar, such as a rent invoice symbolising the rent and services strike, the bishops' booklet on police brutality, school books symbolising problems in the education system, a tear gas canister, a list of those killed mostly by the police (but also including the names of murdered councillors), and a plastic bag containing a change of clothes for a detainee.

The widespread international exposure this event was given was crucial to its success. It had been planned with particular care with this in mind. Much later Father Edward Lennon and I smiled at the memory of "inciting" the community, including the bishops of South Africa, Botswana, Namibia, Lesotho and Swaziland, to ignore the Emergency regulations by arranging an entrance procession through a section of the township to the church at a time when such acts were strictly forbidden by law. It was the longest church entrance procession in South African history.

We had deliberately given the visit a low regional profile so as not to provoke the police to overreact. After the lengthy supercharged Mass we arranged for the bishops to spend the day in small groups visiting places of past conflict and the homes of the victims of police shooting. The Security Branch was intensely angered when next day they discovered what had happened.

The fearless *Rand Daily Mail* gave the procession – of hundreds of township people, visitors and bishops – full-colour treatment on its front page. Press photographers couldn't resist columns of bishops in full regalia walking the ghettos. There was a hint of the opera *Aïda* about it, but a serious purpose, too, appropriate to the times. Another point had been made. The churches would not be cowed. The police agents monitoring the township's political pulse had been taken by surprise. One policeman parishioner with a developed conscience questioned by Security Police later about what Archbishop Denis Hurley had said at the service, replied with feigned innocence that the Archbishop spoke about love. And of course he did, adding, "There must be change, for without it there can be no peace, and without change my greeting to you is a complete and utter mockery." An executive member of the right-wing Christian Resistance Group and Johannesburg regional chairperson of the Conservative Party, Clive Derby-Lewis, condemned the event as "heresy" and "open rebellion against the admonitions of the Pope" (*The Citizen* 28 January 1985). Derby-Lewis has since left the Catholic Church in a huff. Later he was jailed for the murder of ANC leader Chris Hani.

Police anger intensified against the Vaal churches. It was turning to rage. Informers were failing to provide accurate information to their handlers and were increasingly nervous. Police field men were stretched to the limit and many were showing visible signs of severe stress. At that moment, senior officers in the Security Police were examining more creative approaches to curb the influence of the clergy.

Chapter 27

The local management centre (headed by the local SAP station commander and the SADF company commander) liaised with churches, youth groups, vigilantes, traders, sports clubs, journalists, opinion makers, shebeen owners, cultural groups, moderate political organisations, teachers etc. – Max Coleman in *A Crime Against Humanity* [10]

In the middle 1980s, the Lekoa (Vaal) Town Council produced a master plan to break the rent boycott. Part of this strategy was to try to harness the township youth, training them at special weekend camps so that they would persuade their parents to abandon the rent boycott. Conservation, Christianity, communism, history and culture were part of what was discussed at these weekends. Principals at Vaal Triangle schools, and other parts of the country, were asked to make available their brightest pupils for "holidays" at, for instance, Riverside Lodge near Ladybrand or Golden Gate Highlands National Park near Phuthaditjhaba. Some teachers were also recruited and trained secretly by the South African army outside Cape Town.

The managing director of this national scheme for youth re-education was a political scientist, Dr David Marx of Bloemfontein, ably assisted by a former senior clerk of the Development Board, Lexon December. They would establish Eagles clubs in pursuit of their special vision for the youth of South Africa.

At the time, Lexon December explained innocently how they got their funding: "Every year we'd go overseas with Dr Marx and there we would get to talk to various firms about funding." Elize van Vuuren, public relations officer for the Eagles clubs, with all the honesty she could muster, said, "I believe that big business gives us money because we are against communism and for democracy." In late July 1991 it was finally revealed that the Eagles clubs, operating mostly in the Free State and the southern Transvaal (with a staff of

[10] Coleman, M. (ed.) *A Crime Against Humanity: Analysing the Repression of the Apartheid State.* David Philip, 2002.

80), had indeed been funded under "Strategy 44" of Military Intelligence, working through the Local Management Centre headed by the police and army.

The Vaal Triangle arm of the organisation – *Vaaldriehoekse Swartjeug Projek* (Vaal Triangle Black Youth Project), later called Eagle Giant Research – was located in a second-floor apartment in the Allied Building in Vanderbijlpark. The regional manager was Piet du Plessis, a former sports organiser in the Sebokeng Development Board. Du Plessis enlisted the help of Zacharia Tlali of Sharpeville, Joseph Kheswa of Zone 13, Sebokeng, and Johanny Manoto, originally of Parys but then living in Sharpeville, to do his fieldwork.

Isa van Rensburg and Petro Pepper were also on his staff. They were a good team and worked zealously to capture the "hearts and minds" of young people. It's hard to know how many parents, teachers and teenagers the Eagles seduced, but Gerry Mokethe, their Sharpeville leader, at one time calculated at least twenty people in the township had joined it. Certainly it had the support of the old DET. Apart from schools, choirs, youth clubs, women's organisations and other community groups were natural recruiting grounds. It was mostly a case of involuntary collusion by many of these groups. They simply did not know they had been infiltrated.

The planning document, which was drawn up by Du Plessis, stated, unashamedly, that "standards such as Christianity, moral standards, honesty and many others, enjoy a low priority among most blacks – particularly the youth. Since a greater part of the black population no longer have positive standards the social order has decayed" (*The Star*, 19 December 1985).

To advance the cause of freeing African society from decay, numerous catchy slogans were used: "We stand for God and country"; "We work for peace, justice and unity"; "Christianity, education and non-violence"; "Let the Eagle fly high". Some peripheral church ministers, both black and white, were roped in to give the scheme legitimacy. Strangely, churches associated with the Vaal Council of Churches were never invited to participate.

The regional treasurer, according to a member of Eagles, was John Gogotya. Gogotya, a one-time Soweto businessman, one-time church minister, one-time door-to-door salesman in Sharpeville and self-made politician, knew and ignored the fact that people called him a sell-out. He was known in Soweto for distributing anti-boycott pamphlets in an operation called Operation Advance and Upgrade. In 1987 in a loud splash of television publicity he established a sort of political movement called the Federal Independent Democratic Alliance (FIDA) which, according to its mouthpiece *The Democrat*, was to take "moderates" to the negotiating table in 1990. He opposed "one person, one vote" and was happy that "the state of emergency has allowed many blacks to sleep peacefully at night. Many of the detained children found life more bearable in prison away from intimidation or being used as cannon fodder" (*The Star*, 11 June 1999). Like Marx of Bloemfontein, Gogotya travelled overseas where he campaigned against disinvestment, sanctions, and so on. He was the chief township organiser of the youth camps and was often seen hiring classy tourist buses and distributing largesse such as sports gear to township children on weekend junkets to national parks, organised by Eagle Giant Research of Vanderbijlpark.

Again like Marx, he denied any link to the South African government – until Thursday, 30 August 1991, when the bubble burst in the pages of *The Star*, on 1 August 1991. The government had been supporting FIDA all the time under the code name Capital, a project of Military Intelligence.

Always on the move, just before the 1998 national elections John Gogotya left the National Party to join the ANC.

~

As a pastor in Sharpeville in the mid-1980s I found it imperative to make inquiries about the "snake in the grass" activities of Eagle Giant Research in the townships and to alert other church ministers and priests, especially as it impinged on the life of the churches. I was not in favour of our youth being subverted by vaguely visible lackeys of the state. I spoke about the phenomenon in church, warning the youth to beware. I needn't have worried. The young people had already visited the local headquarters of Eagle Giant Research to see for themselves. A sharp disagreement had ensued when a spokesperson for the organisation refused to name – when pressed by the youngsters – the "communist" priests working in the townships. Benjamin Mofokeng takes up the story:

> In March 1987 we, the members of the St Mary's Catholic Youth Club, were invited to a meeting in a building at Vanderbijlpark. This, we assumed, was an authentic meeting aimed at advancing the youth activities in the Vaal area. This meeting was arranged by a white group referred to as "The Eagles". The meeting started very interestingly, but I happened to notice that it was a meeting aimed at securing and grooming future informers. They were to see to it that all formations which rightfully resisted injustice would be crushed from the root. I together with my colleagues in the youth club started to peacefully protest against this cruel form of indoctrination. The response we got from the convenors was to say, "I seem to know too much" and that I will pay dearly for [my cheek]. The meaning of that comment is not yet clear to me, but the interpretation was that my days would be cut. The meeting did not come to a harmonious end, due to the fact that we were literally expelled from the building at gunpoint.

The battle to win the souls of the youth did not end there. One Saturday morning while the youth were cleaning the church premises, former youth detainee Nathanael "Slow" Lenka rushed into the office to say that Security Branch policemen were walking through the church inspecting the posters on the walls. Moments later in walked four strapping plain-clothes men. I thought perhaps they wanted to discuss the next day's inter-church prayer meeting for emergency detainees, to be held at the church. But no, they did not mention it, though one of them popped outside to enquire of Nathanael why the youth were cleaning the church. For Sunday's Mass, replied Nathanael innocently. Back in the office the visitors seemed interested in the books, papers and notice board as the conversation continued.

No, they wanted to talk about the youth, they assured me while taking in the contents of the room. How could they work with the church to help the youth avoid being influenced by radicals? – a test question to elicit my thinking on the subject. No, not to elicit my thinking but rather to read my reaction because this was a learning mission they were on. On Monday they would report to their superiors.

I went into mild shock at hearing this question, bells ringing all over my head. Clammy palms. A cold sweat. For I am not by any means a brave person. My face expressionless at first, and I contrived enthusiasm for their sudden, unheralded and curious interest in youth affairs. I ask for their suggestions, of which there were none. Some small talk followed and cute name-dropping. Did I know Marilyn Cooper, one of the founders of St Peter's Advice Centre at Vereeniging church (and later the church at Sebokeng)? Yes, I replied. I also knew Marilyn was under investigation at the time. Momentarily they had digressed from youth affairs. They had made their point. Then they got back to the youth.

Again I feigned enthusiasm for their interest in our youth and agreed that they deserved to be assisted in every way possible. In case I should need help from my four stalwart visitors I asked them to write down their names on a piece of paper, which they did after only the slightest hesitation: Peter Cronje, Peter Swart, Shawn de Villiers and Johan van Rensburg.

Then, warming to the situation, I asked them for their phone numbers. With beguiling eagerness I grabbed my pen intending to write beside their autographs. One by one, starting with Shawn, they said they had no phones. In fact I could have given them the number of their Security Branch superiors. It was laughable. I wasn't angry but challenged. The air was thick with deception – *their* trade. I suggested that we meet again to pursue their idea of forming a Vaal Youth Organisation. All agreed readily. I knew they wouldn't turn up on the appointed day. And they did not. They did, however, turn up the next day to observe at a distance from darkened car windows those attending the prayer meeting. One was wearing a grey suit and tie because it was Sunday and he had come direct from his church to the observation street corner.

Chapter 28

*"While I was a student at Southern Illinois University in 1985, the
International Freedom Foundation with right-wing Christian leaders
Jerry Falwell, Pat Robertson and selected South Africans in tow took
every TV opportunity to besmirch the South African Council of
Churches and the Catholic Church in South Africa. They accused
these institutions of promoting violence and necklacing in the country."*
Khekhethi D Makhudu

The pamphlet war for the souls of township people got into full
swing after September 1984. It raged between the security services
and all who opposed the government. Some pamphlets were
distributed openly by security forces; others were placed by stealth
after dark in key areas. These pamphlets were designed to sow
confusion in opposition circles. It was in this area that the churches
came under censure or even attack: On necklacing: "Are our religious
leaders speaking out against these monstrous deeds?" asked Youth for
Peace – sponsored by Concerned Businessmen. "Priests go to the
pulpits and preach the Gospel and not death and destruction," read
another leaflet from Concerned Residents in Sharpeville. The trade
unions were also attacked in this way for "deceiving" the people about
work stayaways.

The attack on the churches now went international. Russell Crystal,
a man of many parts and many pasts, spent a record nine years
honing his political skills at the University of the Witwatersrand
during which he set up the conservative Students Moderate Alliance
and, later, the umbrella organisation, National Students Federation; all
with taxpayers' money. The purpose of these "set-ups", we were told,
was to counter the nefarious activities of the university's democratic
movements. Later, broadening his vision, Russell went abroad. His
country, he believed, called him to counter the bad press South Africa

was getting overseas during the 1980s. Meanwhile he had done his national service in military intelligence and was well positioned for his next career move. "Operation Babushka" was the code name for the IFF, which, according to apartheid spy Craig Williamson, was funded by the former government until 1992 to the tune of $1,5 million a year.

"Gypsy" was the *nom de guerre* for the then sleek, fair-headed National Party member who headed the IFF offices in Braamfontein, Johannesburg. Gypsy's job as executive director of the IFF (established in 1985 by Jack Abrammoff, an American conservative who once represented the late Zairean dictator Mobutu Sese Seko) was to persuade a hostile world that South Africa was okay. According to former Security Branch member Paul Erasmus, the South African Military Intelligence was the channel for funding IFF projects around the world in such countries as Belgium, the United Kingdom, Israel and especially the USA.

~

Now it came to pass that in the mid-1980s the local branch of the IFF flew an alleged self-confessed participant in four unknown necklace murders, and two Kwa-Zulu traditionalist ministers, to the United States to try to deflect a renewed sanctions campaign against South Africa. According to *The Star* (5 July 1987), the "Gypsy" Crystal said, "He had been instructed by his head office in Washington to arrange for an alleged former ANC activist, Ms Salaminah Borephe and two ministers, the Reverend Phangumza Mtungwa and the Reverend Chanyise Mabaso, to travel to Washington where they were to appear at a Congressional hearing sponsored by the Republican Party Study Committee. "We decided to provide a balanced view," said Mr Crystal with appropriate gravitas.

A balanced view indeed! Ms Borephe – the alleged necklacer and alleged, but unknown, pupil of Jordan High School, Evaton – was prevailed upon to disseminate the outrageous contents of a five-page document manufactured by the IFF in Johannesburg (see Appendix 3). The "Gypsy" and his researcher, Wim Booyse, collaborated in the project as did ultimately the facilitator and controller of the International Freedom Foundation (IFF),

Brigadier Ferdie van Wyk of army intelligence (*Sunday Independent*, 6 July 1995). The report, written with the help of the former Security Branch of the Vaal, demonised the clergy of the area.

It was written to deceive foreign and indeed South African white readers. It cleverly gave the impression that English was the second language of the speaker or writer. For the most part, names were avoided to prevent suing for defamation.

The content was something else. It was riddled with mention of UDF's affiliate COSAS, or that the Students Christian Movement (SCM) was a front for communism, when everyone knew that they were a born-again Christian youth movement with Pentecostal leanings. Again, that the South African Students' Organisation, (SASO), a black consciousness youth movement, had been ordered by whites to have schools burnt in 1976 or 1977. Everyone knows that white people didn't order black consciousness people around, much less order them to burn their own schools.

But let's look at what Russell Crystal and Wim Booyse were saying about the clergy. A few imaginative quotes will be enough.

"We were told by church Ministers how good was communism. The Anglican Ministers taught us in the Catholic churches how to make petrol bombs."

"The church Ministers told us that the Russians had sent the weapons [which he was distributing] and that the children from 16 to 18 must take a gun (AK-47) to kill white people."

"Then the other Reverend of Anglicans in Sharpeville together with Lord McCamel and the others from Sebokeng Anglicans … told us that the community councillors must be killed on the 3rd September."

"On Sunday 2nd September, there was a meeting of the residents at the Roman Catholic churches of Zone 12 (Sebokeng) Evaton and Sharpeville where the Ministers told the people to kill the community councillors the following day."

Chapter 29

Not they who can inflict the most, but they who can endure the most will emerge the victors – Terence MacSwiney, Irish patriot, 20th Century

Most people had left the church precincts in Evaton except Lefa Motsamai, who was still tinkering with his amplifiers after a dance session in the old hall. It had been a hectic September Saturday in 1981 with meetings, an extended funeral and consultations going on for most of the day. I was tired. It was nearing dusk and in case darkness descended too quickly, I was looking for candles and matches and checking over things for tomorrow's parish services.

Suddenly there was the stamp and tramp of running footsteps on gravel. Through the lace-curtained window in the office I saw teenagers taking a short cut, running madly through the churchyard. I wasn't sure whether they were being chased or were *tsotsis* chasing some unfortunate, with their knives drawn for blood.

As I drew away from the window a shadow abruptly blocked the entrance to the office. COSAS activist, Gcina Malindi, perspiring and panting, collapsed on the office floor. Hyperventilating, gasping for breath and clutching his chest, he murmured, "I've heart pain." Thinking that I had a heart attack in front of me I flew into a panic and offered to get him to Sebokeng hospital immediately. "No," he said, "I just need to rest and to hide from the police." I helped him into the already darkened side sacristy. Thankfully the police hadn't seen him rush into the office.

Five years later, Malindi appeared as accused No. 5 (H.V. 5/85) in the infamous Delmas Treason Trial, accused of every anti-apartheid "crime" the state could think of. It happened like this.

Tuesday 11 June 1985 marked the first appearance in the Pretoria Magistrate's Court, amid unusually tight security, of 22 prominent

South Africans (*baferekanyi* or terrorists, according to state radio) accused of high treason, alternatively of terrorism, subversion, five counts of murder (of black town councillors) and of furthering the aims of the banned African National Congress.

The accused were among the top echelons of black anti-apartheid leadership in South Africa. No trial was to attract as much interest since the historic Rivonia trial that saw Nelson Mandela and other nationalist leaders sent to prison for life in the 1960s. Indeed both sentences, that of Mandela and the present accused, were handed down in the same Court C in Pretoria's Palace of Justice, and the common link between the two trials was Advocate George Bizos who was junior council at the original trial. In the present trial he was ably assisted by advocates Arthur Chaskalson, Karel Tip, Gilbert Marcus and Zac Jacoob and by instructing attorneys Caroline Nichols, David Dison, Ismail Ayob and Pricilla Jana. The trial, however, for the most part was held at Delmas. It lasted for more than three years of long and dreary argument.

Sometimes what was happening behind the scenes was more interesting than what was happening in court. For example, the state needed many witnesses. For this they offered enticements. I heard about some of them. State witnesses were given R7 daily, making the silent journey from Section 29 to Section 28 detention, which carried more privileges – for example, a radio. Some co-operated only reluctantly with the police, and not all did it to the state's satisfaction. During the trial the husband of a female Section 28 detainee was promised, by a prominent black Vaal Security Branch officer, that his wife would "come out of prison a rich woman".

Early in the hearing the judge, Mr Justice Kies van Dijkhorst, made a bet with one of his assessors, Professor Willem Joubert of Pretoria University, of a bottle of whisky that the accused would not dare go into the witness box to testify and face cross-examination. He paid up when they did.

Later when Joubert disclosed that he had signed the UDF's Million Signatures petition, the judge dismissed him as his assessor, saying he could not judge the case impartially. Joubert issued a sworn statement accusing the judge of being politically biased against the accused, to which the judge responded by accusing Joubert of incompetence and bias in favour of the accused.

Van Dijkhorst continued the trial with a single assessor, Willem Krugel, who, the defence said was a known member of the Afrikaner Broederbond (*The Star*, 28 November 1996).

~

One pleasant sunny Friday in June 1986 the trial, which had long ago been moved to the remote Transvaal farming town of Delmas, an hour away from Johannesburg, had been going on for a year. A police sergeant from Somerset East had been explaining how he and colleagues had been monitoring anti-government meetings in the local community hall. Under cross-examination by George *"Matla a Tlou"* – Strength of an Elephant Bizos, he described in detail how the tense gathering of local black town councillors had simulated resignation before an angry crowd. He was asked to explain in detail. It went on and on. At 1.10 p.m. the court adjourned until Monday.

In the happy confusion that followed, the clergy, including Father Edward Lennon and I, were invited to come forward and sit with the accused, in the area normally reserved for the defence team – amidst bulging briefcases, volumes of court material, videos and televisions. After the discreet exit of judge and assessors, the bench had become an altar – for a wedding was about to happen. Anglican Bishop Nkoane was there to do the honours, assisted by fellow Anglican priest, Geoff Moselane (accused on five counts of murder and terrorism and refused bail). The groom, Lazarus More, was also a "terrorist" and "mass murderer", as were the two witnesses, Mosiuoa Lekota (now Minister for Defence) and Aupa Hlomuka. All present were defendants in the trial, except of course for the bride, Golda Magauta Maphisa.

I thought to myself, never have so many terrorists and revolutionaries celebrated so movingly a marriage ceremony on the precise spot where, at some future date, they could be condemned to death by hanging.

Lekota, married and living in Durban before his arrest, was the natural choice to say a few words. In his address, which could not be quoted at the time, he portrayed the family as a symbol of unity necessary in the struggle for liberation in South Africa. He emphasised the ultimate reconciliation of all the peoples of the country, though this task would not be easy. "The most extraordinary scene I've ever seen," remarked Church of England envoy, Terry Waite, who was later taken hostage by Islamic extremists in Lebanon.

Chapter 30

Twice weekly I was awakened at 6.30 a.m. by the warm-up roar of the special trial bus departing from the church at Sharpeville *en route* to Delmas, picking up families, friends and supporters in the neighbouring townships of Boipatong, Evaton and Sebokeng. At one stage during this trial, according to a later *Weekly Mail and Guardian* report (August 1995), Sergeant Gary Pollock, while a member of the Security Branch, ambushed and shot the tyres of this Delmas-bound bus. His handlers at Strategic Communications (Stratcom), the dirty tricks arm of the former State Security Council, fired him up into believing it was a busload of revolutionary ANC nasties.

Much later, when the trial finally moved back to Pretoria, dependants and friends of the Sharpeville Six availed themselves of this transport to visit the condemned in Pretoria Maximum Prison.

Since the trial deeply impinged on our parishes, Edward Lennon and I attended the proceedings as often as possible. Indeed on one occasion Edward was asked to leave the courtroom during a cross-examination of the widely discredited government-backed township mayor with whom he had had words at a public meeting leading up to the September 1984 rising. Regularly we met our colleagues from other churches there.

Encouraged by the dedicated work of Petrus Thapedi, a Sharpeville Justice and Peace Committee member, I often found myself involved in the task of facilitating the search for defence witnesses during this long, drawn-out trial. A feature of this ministry was to create a social climate among potential defence witnesses whereby, often cowed and fearful of the vast threatening security apparatus, they could be induced to come forward and offer their services to the defence's legal team. Churches were meeting points for such work.

During the trial it also became extremely important to facilitate the release of a sort of "people's pressure" on the trial judge and assessors by regularly, publicly and discreetly signalling at every opportunity that it was good to attend the Delmas trial, that it was the serious duty of each resident, nay, that to do so was a Christian response in faith to a serious community need. Simultaneously, it was of crucial importance to promote the opinion that the trialists were not simply youthful political firebrands, but mature reflective Christians who were suffering because of their enlightened understanding of the sayings of Jesus Christ. This pastoral policy often flooded the Delmas courtroom with hymn-singing – uniformed church grannies who found strength in their common cause and at the same time inspired hope in the trialists that the broad community was squarely behind them. The people responded gallantly – and after the new South Africa was born the trialists came back to thank the people of the Vaal for their loyal support in those bad old days.

Meanwhile the local Detainees' Parents Support Committee (DPSC) had set up a very effective organisation based at the church in Sharpeville, which co-ordinated transport to the two major trials (Sharpeville Six and Delmas) and regularly workshopped the families, dependants and friends (especially those of the Sharpeville Six) on their legal rights, visiting procedures and a host of related problems. For the bewildered, often alienated, families of the detainees, the DPSC was a source of strength and a sign that someone cared.

In fact this venture went back a few years. In 1983 Bishop Tutu, as general secretary of the SACC, sent the fieldworker Tom Manthata to the Vaal to gather information on the general state of repression in the area. It was decided to set up a Vaal Information Centre (VIC) in Sharpeville. In time, this became a cover for a local DPSC branch.

The main drivers in this valuable work were Shele Papane, Gift Moerane, Mpolokeng and Steve Jona, Grant Taaso, Abe Welcome, Thami Zondo (later to startle the government as a hunger-striking detainee), Jerry Makhale, Vusi Tshabalala and Peter Skosana (years later to become executive mayor of Sedibeng). The same is true of their colleagues at Sebokeng – Aupa Mareletse, Mmamokete Lentsoe,

Sakie Thagudi, Sy Molotsi and Thomas Maleka – operating out of the ever-jocular Reverend Herbert Koaho's NGK Church at Zone 13.

The state set up its own Security Forces Support Committee (SFSC) to counter the DPSC. The arrest of leading Sharpeville DPSC members Papane and Zondo was certainly the work of the SFSC. Key support came from Valli Moosa (now Minister of the Environment), David Webster (assassinated in 1989) and attorney David Dison. Dison linked the Centre to Amnesty International, whose members secretly visited the area and became a channel through which information was sent to the outside world.

At Sharpeville I sometimes strayed into meetings to signal solidarity for the work in progress. Thirty or forty representatives of detainees were usually to be found there in deep discussion about practical day-to-day matters. Sometimes members of the short-lived Sharpeville Civic Association (SCA) were there listening to the problems of the community, with Phillip "Chippa" Molefe (years later an executive with the South African Broadcasting Corporation) in the chair, such as the still-aproned, just-out-of-the-kitchen wife complaining about her wayward husband who she was sure didn't come home the night before because he was with a former girlfriend at Vuka section, near the Presbyterian Church. Or complaints about the comrades, who, sensing that crime had to give way to the more immediate aspirations of the populace, tended to over-police the townships, sometimes to the point of harassing people. Community discipline had to be maintained during a time when normal policing had fallen away, particularly when community leaders such as the trialists at Delmas were in prison.

At Modderbee Prison east of Johannesburg, the morale of the 22 trialists was always quite high. For reasons of strategy the language of communication with white warders was Afrikaans. The spokespersons were normally "Terror" Lekota, Tom Manthata, who worked at keeping a political balance in the group, and Father Geoff Moselane. Every evening, between 5 and 6 p.m., there were political discussions and a shared analysis of the daily news as gleaned from the newspapers. They also discussed the progress of their case and the skills involved in answering questions during court procedures. Reading time was between 9 and 10 a.m.

Lekota was the link between the group and Nelson Mandela on Robben Island. He got to know Mandela while completing a previous five-year sentence there. Now Lekota regularly received mail (through the good offices of lawyer Ismail Ayob) from the Island, informing the 22 that "the old man" was fit and well. The Island prisoner encouraged them to be strong, and wondered whether he would be welcoming them to Robben Island one day soon.

For recreation, indoor games included snooker (Lekota was the best), draughts, *marabaraba* (favourite of Mphuthi), snakes and ladders, ludo, monopoly (loved by Molefe – later premier of North-West province – and Ramakgula), chess (the favourite of Hlomuka) and scrabble (Chikane). Outdoor exercise included running and soccer (favoured by Lekota, Ratsomo and Molefe, though Molefe was inclined to be a little laid-back). By far the best player was Thabiso Ratsomo. Manthata and Hlanyane were the keenest joggers while the others played soccer. Nobody will forget the day Manthata was hit by a stray ball, or the day Moselane was tripped by a fellow player and from the floor charged the aggressor. "Wait, wait, Moruti," they cried, calming the aggrieved priest, or the day Simon Nkoli was downed by a pile-driver from "Competer" (short for Comrade Peter) Mokoena.

Hlabeng Matlole's good-natured complaints, Gcina Malindi's gift as a reconciler and Gerry Tlhopane's stoic acceptance of his situation were important gifts to the group. Tradition wasn't forgotten either. When Lekgwakgwa Ramakgula's mother died, "Competer" (also known as "Smash" to his soccer friends) stepped in to perform the traditional rites of *ho hlatswa* – cutting his hair and washing it in aloes, which had been brought by the family.

And tradition was spiced with humour. On the day before a state witness was due to give evidence against him, Lekota, whose clan name is Basia, informed his astonished colleagues: "While you were asleep I slipped out of the prison to consult with my ancestors who told me there will be no evidence against me tomorrow." And indeed the next day the state witness completely changed her evidence against him. In fact, she told the court that she had been tortured and told to tell lies about Lekota, "the one without the front tooth".

David "Bra Day" Mphuthi occupied a special place in the life of the of Delmas treason trialists. Sometimes called "Mr Clean", Mphuthi was distinguished for the lengthy quality time he preened himself each day, paying meticulous attention to showering, laundry, polishing shoes, grooming hair, moustache, dressing and, a trifle incongruously, eating the meagre meals provided by the prison. His studied, serene approach to even the simple things of life gave his comrades a much-needed lift, and bonded them the more. Indeed his ability to abstract himself from reality by these ministrations was in itself his strategy for survival.

There were even times during the trial that called for a celebration or two at Modderbee – celebrations of small but deadly serious victories such as could only happen in a court case that carried the death penalty. When the judge and assessors fell out with one another, that was good. When a state witness was exposed as a liar that was good. When one of the accused was allowed to marry in court – that too was good. When some of the accused were released on bail that was great. They were significant victories for life and a wee celebration was called for.

A prison "bash" (a township public party) was out of the question. The prison authorities wouldn't understand. They wouldn't even try to understand. A *braaivleis* (barbecue) was also considered out for obvious reasons. No, a celebration would have to be discreet, clandestine. Which in itself was a small thrill!

How do you make a party in a prison and a private party at that? What are the ingredients of such a get-together? No invitation cards to be sent out for sure. The usual edibles sent in by friends outside or through the prison tuck shop would constitute the main course. But, wondered someone at a preparatory meeting, there was still something missing. What about some "forbidden fruits" to enhance the occasion? Something crucial to any celebration. A new thrill element now entered the discussion. Heads turned slowly in recognition.

It was then that the word "sebata" was born into the vocabulary of the *baferekanyi* of Delmas. It meant a wild animal that devoured a person's insides – alcohol. And so the idea of tactfully challenging the prison security system by smuggling in alcohol was born. "No," says

Manthata, a teetotaller, "we did not drink out of depression. We were too committed and concerned about the state of our country and its people. We knew what a shame it would be, to us, to our families and to the cause of the anti-apartheid struggle, should we ever be found drunk. All of us felt bound to preserve and guard the reputation, long established by the founders of the liberation movement, regardless of ideological persuasion or party affiliation."

In fact often during court appearances at the trial at Delmas, certain people were known to slip a few rand into the waiting hands of a particular policeman. He would drop in to the local bottle store, buy a good brand bottle of something, and slip it into the briefcase of one of the trialists in the holding cell below the courtroom. This was happening downstairs while upstairs an unflappable George Bizos (head of the defence's legal team) slowly rotated his bulky figure, peering over half-moon frames as he trawled the faces of the silent, mostly supportive presence of that day's visitors in the public gallery – this practised motion while he nonchalantly hammered home a point, a point which Judge van Dijkhorst, most likely, disregarded.

Just as a certain stout in Ireland is said to have medicinal qualities, and a common soft drink is sometimes recommended for stomach conditions in South Africa, whisky, declared Mokoena, was his and should be everyone's magic elixir for almost all conditions. Not all were convinced, like the strict non-drinking evangelical pastor Hlabeng Matlole or the no-nonsense Thabiso Ratsomo who raised the issue in the first place. It just wasn't right, they felt, and besides, the matter had been cleared up at the Friday "housekeeping" meeting by a majority vote against the introduction of "forbidden fruits". Matlole said he afterwards took Lekota aside and chided him for abstaining during the vote, saying that a leader should lead by good example.

Notwithstanding, on many a summer's evening after the accused had returned to Modderbee from Delmas, the prison toilet or certain cells took on the trappings of a *spot* or *shebeen* (without, however, the homely presence of a *magrizza* or shebeen queen) where the "water of life" was shared and great healing of hearts and spirits took place. A sort of born-again experience! At least for some.

But one day, things really got stuck. The prison authorities, suspecting something, instituted a search of the dependants when they returned from the court hearings at Delmas. Oh dear – consternation!

It was no one's fault really that a bottle of whisky (*umuthi* or *sebata*) was found in Father Moselane's briefcase nestling against his prayer book. You see, the policeman at the court must have mixed up the briefcases – a case of mistaken identity. A deceptively shy Father Geoff was adamant that this was the case.

And when the trial began to falter in the courtroom, prison warders never noticed the sudden, unusual interest in five-litre cartons of "fruit juice" sent in by their recently released comrades. It was always a happy occasion when these cartons arrived. Their contents had an unadvertised flavour!

Long after their release the Delmas 22 still remember and retell these funny life-giving incidents when they meet.

Chapter 31

When the long-awaited emotion-charged day of judgement arrived, the historic Pretoria courtroom was jam-packed with families and friends of the accused, ambassadors, ordinary people and anti-apartheid activists. Practically speaking it was the end of an era when family ties had endured great emotional strains, jobs had been abandoned, and many of the accused's children had grown up separated from their fathers.

The judgement handed down by the judge and surviving Broederbond assessor was a litany of disapproval of the accused, their views and the style and nature of their politics. It was a judgement fraught with inferences and vague circumstantial evidence gleaned from 31 unrest areas of South Africa. The judge, in compliance with the wishes of the state, found them guilty on 8 December 1988.

These were their sentences:

Patrick "Terror" Mosiuoa Lekota, 40, married, UDF publicity secretary who had spent six years on Robben Island for work he had done in the Black Consciousness Movement: 12 years.

Popo Molefe, 36, married, UDF general secretary who had been detained in 1976, ten years.

Moss Chikane, 40, married, UDF leader: ten years

Tom Manthata, 40, married, SACC fieldworker, detained on three previous occasions, student of black consciousness, i.e. psychological liberation of blacks: six years.

The following VCA members were sentenced to five years imprisonment: David T Mphuthi, 48; Hlabeng S Matlole, 64; Sekoati Mokoena, 34; Lekgwakgwa Ramakgula, 35; Gcina P Malindi, 20; Naphtali Nkopane and Jacob Serame Hlanyane. All these sentences were suspended for three years except that of Gcina Malindi, whose full sentence would have to be served.

"We view the present trial as an interim affair. Somewhere in the future lies a date when black and white South Africans will take a second look at these moments in history. They will vindicate us," said the accused, after sentencing, before being led down to their cells. Prophetic words.

This was the last great apartheid show trial. Time was running out for the regime. And they knew it. There was mounting apprehension in government circles. The pressure from below was pushing up alarmingly against the steel mantle of the South African security forces. Never before was the world so united against South Africa. And the country was feeling it. This was clearly evident in the statements of distinguished national and international observers after the trial:

Archbishop Desmond Tutu: "If these ... men have committed treason, then I have committed treason and should face charges too." He said the court findings were an "extravagantly painted portrayal of what would be a normal process in a democratic society."

Former United States State Department spokesman, Charles Redman: "It's inconceivable that their political activities would have qualified as treason or terrorism in this country or in any democracy. The clear intent of the government during this trial has been to neutralise prominent black opponents through protracted judicial proceedings and imprisonment. This misuse of the South African judicial system for political purposes is deplorable." The German Embassy issued a statement saying the judgement "criminalises peaceful opposition against the apartheid regime." Reverend Frank Chikane, President of the South African Council of Churches said: "Almost anybody, provided they are in the black leadership, could qualify for treason."

Visiting United States Senators, Sam Nunn (Georgia, member of the Senate Armed Services Committee) and David Boran (Oklahoma, Chairman of the Senate Select Committee on Intelligence): "We believe that the policy direction reflected by the Delmas Trial, unless reversed, will lead to a serious deterioration of United States-South African relations."

International Commission of Jurists envoy, Patrick Macentee (Chairman of the General Council of the Bar of Ireland): "The Delmas

Trial was an opportunistic device to use the killings of 3 September 1984 for the purpose of discrediting and criminalising as many individuals and organisations opposed to the government as possible. It was profoundly offensive to the concept of impartial justice under the rule of law and to democracy and freedom."

Mosiuoa "Terror" Lekota explained his attitude: "If you give up and try to come to terms with everyday oppression, it's like choosing death. Catholics say despair is mortal sin and they're right. It is wrong to give up hope. Being alive means keeping fighting."

On 29 January 1989, Mr Justice van Dijkhorst gave leave to appeal to all five convicted and for a "special entry" to be made concerning alleged irregularities in court proceedings, in other words his controversial dismissal of one of his assessors. The Delmas treason trialists were finally acquitted on a technicality.

While the Nuremberg trials after World War Two lasted a mere ten months with an indictment of 200 pages, this trial, called the Delmas Trial, in which none of the accused was convicted of violence of any sort, had endured for nearly four years with an indictment of 565 pages.

The story of the trial may be told in simple figures:

No. of accused:	22
Co-conspirators:	911 individuals (including Archbishop Tutu and 50 organisations and church groups)
Acquittals:	three discharged in 1986, eight in 1988
Convictions:	11
Court days:	442 (longest in South African legal history)
Pages of Indictment:	565
Pages of Evidence:	27 194
Exhibits:	14 425 pages, 42 videos and radio tapes, five rolls of film and numerous photographs and maps showing various churches and environs
No. of State Witnesses:	152

No. of Defence Witnesses:	126, of which 120 were disbelieved by the judge, according to Advocate Bizos for the defence
Pages of Judgement:	1 521
Bail applications:	Bail given to six (Patric Baleka, David Mphuthi, Lekgwakgwa Ramakgula, Petrus Mokoena, Jacob Serame Hlanyane and Thabiso Ratsomo) in November 1986 after the release of three accused (Mkambi Malindi, Lazarus More and Simon Vilakazi) due to insufficient evidence. Of the remaining 13, nine were given bail in 1987.
No. of times accused no. 22 (Ratsomo) reported to a police station as part of his bail conditions:	840 (twice a day whenever there was no court appearance)
Estimated cost:	More than five million rand (how many houses would this have built?)
Duration of Trial:	Three and a half years

"He is well-spoken, articulate, intelligent, tending to be verbose, will tell lies unashamedly," remarked Mr Justice van Dijkhorst about Lekota in summing up before sentencing during the Delmas Treason Trial. Considering Lekota's sense of discipline (schooled by German priests at Mariannhill) and, much later, his proven anti-corruption stand as premier of the Free State this, to say the least, is a little ironic. By 1996, however, it appeared that Van Dijkhorst had undergone a change of heart.

Allister Sparks, who had been there later, wrote: "An amazing act of reconciliation took place in Mmabatho last Saturday, November 25, 1996, when the Premier of North-West Province, Popo Molefe, organised a reunion of the 1985-1988 Delmas trialists – and extended a hand of absolution to the controversial judge who sent them to jail." (*The Star*, 30 November 1996)

I had also attended the event with colleague Edward Lennon. It was a thanksgiving function in honour of the churches for, as Molefe had said that the accused did not bear any grudge against the judge or their prosecutors. "They were just doing their job. This is the healing time and it's important to have people from different backgrounds celebrate together."

~

And celebrate we did. Even before I entered the stadium that November morning there was a sense of expectation in the air that was very tangible. There was excitement too as I met and recognised faces and personalities from the dark past, now radiant in triumph after a job well done. (No, not a job well done but rather a single-minded response to rid South Africa and the world of apartheid in the face of enormous, institutional and social pressures to desist, conform and accept the status quo.)

This was an *imbizo* (traditional meeting) of former "rebels". As such, wide-eyed (sometimes wet-eyed) bonhomie and bear hugs characterised knots of arriving guests as they closed in on the main entrance to Mmabatho stadium, a Star Wars-type of sports arena built by apartheid in a former homeland.

Ushered into the marquee in the centre of the stadium, sitting at a central table, was the judge himself, Justice Kies van Dijkhorst. I was flabbergasted. I had looked at him so often in such critical awe at Delmas on his high bench like some kind of all-knowing, all-wise but fatally flawed Buddha. This morning with his wife (she once sent a cake to the trialists) he appeared uncomfortable and even vulnerable. He appreciated my greeting and looked at me quizzically when I alluded to the time he ordered me out of the courtroom because my arms were uncovered. An accused had quickly passed me his jacket and saved the day. Today, however, the judge, who could have condemned him to death, sat next to his former accused no. 19 – now premier of North-West Province and host of this public gesture of reconciliation.

In the next half-hour I watched in amazement as former Delmas treason trialists made their way, as they arrived, to the judge's table to greet him and his wife. A truly astonishing sight! Tentative smile of recognition as the judge tries to place the face before him.

Sparks continued: "Molefe made a speech unstinting in his exoneration of the judge: 'The laws of evidence that governed the type of trial such as Delmas,' he said, 'left little if any room in which judges and magistrates could exercise a discretion. We therefore never blamed the judges as such for applying the letter of the law. The blame fell squarely on the shoulders of the politicians who designed those laws.'"

"The judge in turn spoke of his thoughts during the trial. He came to realise that neither side of the racial divide understood the other. 'The Afrikaans press did not even carry the Delmas trial. You need a black paper to get the proper picture. The contents of UDF documents showed me how others thought. It was an eye-opener. At the time a wall of glass separated us. We saw each other but we did not hear each other. And because we did not hear, we became indifferent and that was tragic. Today Premier Molefe has offered me his hand and I take it with both of mine,' the judge concluded in his speech."

The 1902 Treaty of Vereeniging (between the British and the Boers, and excluding Africans) firmly divided the peoples of South Africa for decades to come. William Plomer in *The Boer War* has written: "Out of that bungled, unwise war, an Alp of unforgiveness grew". Today that "Alp of unforgiveness" from a past white-on-white "unwise war" was giving way to an Alp of forgiveness from yesteryear's excluded South Africans.

Part Five
Stoking the fire nicely

Chapter 32

"They don't want to deal with the truth" – Jacques Pauw, author of *Prime Evil*, the documentary on Eugene de Kock, on why few whites make up the one million viewers who watch the weekly TRC Special Report on television, *Mail & Guardian*, 24 December 1997 to 4 January 1998

On a bright summer's day in August 1983 I visited the famous Ann Frank Huis Museum in Amsterdam, Holland. It is the attic home where the young Jewish girl, Ann Frank, and her family hid from the Nazi police during World War Two. Tragically, the family was discovered, arrested and deported to concentration camps, and all but her father died in the gas chambers.

It was a moving experience. As in all memorials of social nightmares you slip into an unconscious silence – you almost feel clammy, as you wander from room to room, the horrors of the past political depravities reproaching you from the photo displays. You want to be alone with your thoughts and emotions. Conversation is out of place, you feel. Like at the Holocaust memorial (Yad Vashem) in Jerusalem – or future memorials in our country.

As I prepared to sign the visitors' book, I was alerted to something familiar. My eyes caught the words "South African" just above where I was writing. Somebody from South Africa had been there very recently. He wrote under "remarks" an astonishing public admission: "I am a South African and I still would like to kill blacks in a gas chamber." Signed – a white South African (I have withheld his name). Then, below that followed a response from another visitor to the museum-attic: "I am a white Australian and I hope the above 'person' gets to push the button to turn on the gas chamber, it fails and he electrocutes himself."

I was still coping with this disturbing experience as I crossed the city to the Franciscan sisters' hostel where I was staying. In the entrance my eye caught the black cover of their visitors' book. I'm glad I opened it. It made that day for me. It was a sign of hope. It said: "Thank you for upholding the traditions of St Francis" – Charles Yeats, Durban, August 22,1983. (Yeats is a South African who had been imprisoned as a conscientious objector.)

There you have it. Two white South Africans giving public witness to their beliefs in a foreign city in the eighties; one sad and hurting – profoundly so, the other happy and thankful – profoundly so.

Most people of European stock in South Africa during apartheid probably found themselves somewhere in between. Their world view was conditioned and managed carefully by the government. For the most part they had to depend on second-hand accounts of what was happening in the neighbouring black townships. The system of government many of them voted in would continue to deny them the right ("unauthorised entry prohibited") to know how blacks lived, how they got to work, how their children got to school, how their parents socialised, how they managed to make ends meet. They would come to know generally unlettered African domestics who had skilfully honed their behaviour and outlook to accommodate the likes and dislikes of their employers. The aspirations of especially articulate and educated blacks would have remained largely unknown to them.

Archbishop Denis Hurley said at the time, "most whites in Johannesburg probably have a better idea of living conditions in England and Holland and Portugal than they have of living conditions in their nearest township." With exceptions, they never noticed "the daily trooping of people into jails and farm prisons, lock-ups and police cells". Many accepted *mapantiti* (prison labour) without question.

They – again with exceptions – accepted as normal the conveyer-belt justice over *dompas* (pass book) infringements handed down in township magistrate's courts throughout the land. They were spectators when from 1957, at least a hundred clergy were victimised in some way: their passports were confiscated, visas refused, temporary residence permits withdrawn, banning orders issued, orders of house arrest issued, and so on.

Decades later white South Africans were still struggling to normalise relations with black South Africans. "It is a sad reality that many white

South Africans still do not comprehend the depth of pain visited by apartheid's war on the dreams of young black people," Professor Mampela Ramphele, then vice-chancellor of the University of Cape Town, remarked in 1996. South African cabinet minister Kader Asmal in his book *Reconciliation Through Truth* puts it forcefully: "There is a risk that privileged South Africans, if they forgo the opportunity to reconcile themselves with uncomfortable historical facts, will find themselves in a kind of psychological exile, or an escapist historical dungeon." While it is true that some white South Africans have recognised their bystander complicity, those fellow countrymen who found the TRC hard to digest perhaps even as a form of doing penance (only five percent of white people viewed the TRC hearings on television) would do well to ponder the words of Bishop Comiskey of Ireland who himself has been visited with deep personal suffering:

> *To seek forgiveness is to attempt to effect a healing, to bring a closure. So long as this remains undone, there will continue to be fertile breeding grounds for resentment. "Resentment" literally means "to feel again" in the sense of revisiting old wounds, going back over old injuries, rekindling old rages, constantly reinventing oneself as victim. There are those who will say of attempts to seek forgiveness and bring closure to wounds: "Why rake up the past, why stir up old hatreds and resentments?" To these I would say: "Resentments never die, they just fester away." They simmer beneath the surface of life, ready ammunition for the fearful and embittered ... Forgiveness and seeking forgiveness, like charity, must begin at home.*

The UN Conference on Racism in Durban in 2001, in its statement on historic slavery, confirmed this. It finally declared that the Arab and trans-Atlantic slave trade (an earlier form of globalisation gone badly wrong) was a crime against humanity. This declaration came in the wake of a growing sense of indignation by the countries of the world for past deeds now seen as repulsive and inhuman.

Chapter 33

*The Vaal was particularly badly affected by the destabilisation
tactics of the late 1980s and early 1990s. The government sponsored
dissident groups in places like Sebokeng, Boipatong and Sharpeville –*
Truth and Reconciliation Commission of South Africa Report, 1998

In February 1990 President FW de Klerk announced the release of
political prisoners and the unbanning of liberation movements. However,
the end of apartheid did not mean the end of strife. Fires continued to
burn.

Gertrude Motapanyana was returning home after a casual visit to her
friend, Mercy Maphotoma at 7.20 on the night of 12 July 1993. They
had been discussing church matters. As she was approaching Molantoa
BP garage at Zone 12 extension, Sebokeng, shots rang out from a
passing white Cressida. She was knocked forward – almost lifted off her
feet – as two bullets slammed into her back. Gasping for breath,
writhing in agony, Motapanyana passed out as blood covered her brown
Seshoeshoe dress. The car jolted away at high speed, leaving dust and
darkness in its wake. Initial silence on the street, then shocked screams
as the awful truth swept through the neighbourhood – another wild
senseless shooting. Soon afterwards I met her at the hospital.

~

It was 7 p.m. The evening was quiet. Dusk was falling over the
township outside my office in Zone 14. The street was still busy with
people filtering home from work. I was deep in discussion with a
senior police officer who was a parish Bible teacher. Down the road at
a place called Korporasie Gobizitwana beerhall, a massacre was under
way. We didn't hear the gunfire. The policeman was not called to the
scene. I visited the site later.

Congealed tufts of bloody human flesh marked places where drinkers had been coldly cut down. Eight AK-47 bullets had shattered the white tiles in the toilet as clients rushed for shelter. They did not make it. Heaps of decaying, crimson human gut covered the toilet floors. When the shooting began it must have been a scene of dazed panic and blind consternation. Over a hundred patrons (mostly from the former Transkei) were in various degrees of intoxication. A heavy pungent smell of decaying flesh and stale, spilled beer (Special Leopard) pervaded the hall. Walls and even the high tin roof were punctured with bullet holes.

Stepping over puddles of drying blood, I was shown around by the owner. We moved in silence between upturned chairs and tables where the wounded had fallen the night before. I felt helplessly vengeful as my eyes wandered around the shattered warehouse-like hall of death. Finally I felt my way to the exit, glad to be out in the crisp sunny morning air. Knots of neighbours were talking in hushed voices. A greeting passed.

Living in a climate of officially contrived and secretly condoned violence by other means, I studiously ignored the presence of white high-ranking police and army officers.

I saw them eyeing the lone white clergyman as he emerged from the beer hall. Their conversation faltered, a little taken aback. It picked up again, questioning the presence of a priest in these places. Even then I knew they had had a secret manipulating hand in it. I wondered how much they trusted one another. What did they tell their wives on restless nights? I drove off. No, I was not nauseated except by their presence. I did not feel like vomiting. But there was a certain familiar numbness and rage and my insides were churning for the rest of that May day in 1991. Terrified citizens wondered who was sending killers into the township nights.

Chapter 34

Billy Mokoteli was a popular man about town with many community interests. People found him easily approachable and often came to him with their concerns. He had a nice way with them. They trusted him implicitly. His pick-up van was a familiar sight around the township.

One warm night in April 1992 after clocking in for work at the well-known Cape Gate factory, adjacent to Boipatong, he was found murdered 13 km away at Zone 6 Extension, Sebokeng. He had not clocked out or reported that he would be absent. According to security guards someone had come looking for him in a kombi, which in the case of Billy was normal enough.

Within hours, rumours of the how and why of his violent death were racing from kitchen to kitchen in the small ANC-leaning community of Boipatong. Natural death or mere murder were rare in the early 1990s in the Vaal Triangle. Something sinister was afoot, many thought, but no one said so openly.

Two days later strange white men came in a police lorry, and without greeting the bereaved Mokoteli family or identifying themselves as the police went to the back yard of the house as if searching for something. They came twice, once under cover of darkness, and departed empty-handed each time. These visits, observed nervously from the squinting windows of the neighbourhood, only served to add to the huge social pressure that was mounting daily on the family of the deceased.

A tangible fear shrouded the service and indeed the whole township on the morning of Billy Mokoteli's funeral – a fear, they said, that "drugged thugs with Inkatha links" might attack the mourners, seeing his death as an assassination. Terrified family, friends and sympathisers were ready to fade into nearby houses at the first sound

of an approaching *impi* band. Indeed so transfixed with fear were they
that some wet themselves. "You could smell the urine. You could see it
on the ground," one recalls. Their fear squashed all embarrassment.

Now nine years old, Billy Mokoteli's daughter, Diaketseng, suffers
from clinical depression. Some say the trauma of those dreadful days
leading up to the funeral was off-loaded from mother to daughter
during breast-feeding. The Billy Mokoteli mystery deepened
afterwards. Somehow it became received opinion that he had been an
Inkatha Freedom Party (IFP) operative. Not even his wife, Mando,
had known about it. Six weeks later the hostel dwellers of Kwa
Madala, nearby, attacked the township in what became known as the
Boipatong massacre.   ~

The Boipatong massacre came two years after an earlier
conflagration on 22 July 1990 in Sebokeng, which followed the launch
of the IFP in the district.

> *It has been established that the first massacre, on 22 July
> 1990 in Sebokeng, following the launch of the IFP in the
> district, opened the floodgates of violence in the PWV,
> leading to 38 massacres and costing the lives of
> over 1 000 people.* [11]

Thereafter the IFP were no longer allowed to live at the Sebokeng
hostels. They went to Iscor's Kwa Madala hostel out of which they
operated in the coming years.

I would guess that the men of Kwa Madala hostel, including the
gangsters taking refuge there, were feeling the strain of being
ostracised and expelled by the Vaal community. ANC supporters had
often attacked some of their members and their property, usually after
an Inkatha raid. It was believed that Inkatha attacks were planned at
this hostel near Boipatong. Emotional ethnic speeches emanating from
KwaZulu-Natal and visits from fiery IFP politicians (some from
Driefontein near Ladysmith) to the hostel soon created a tinderbox.

A particular pattern developed in which attacks occurred over the
weekends, took place at night, and involved unknown gunmen driving
in unidentified vehicles. The security forces were unable to apprehend

[11] Coleman, M. (ed.) *A Crime Against Humanity: Analysing the Repression of the Apartheid State.* David Philip, 2002 p.180

the perpetrators. The subjects of the attacks were the people of the Vaal and especially those living in the Sebokeng hostels from which they had been expelled. Sites of organised attacks were taxis, funeral vigils, bus stops, stations, beer halls, nightclubs, hostels and especially trains. In fact urban commuters went into a sort of communal freeze, eyeing trains as ogres of evil and death.

It is common knowledge that the security forces and Iscor (Vanderbijlpark, owners of Kwa Madala hostel) were inexplicably unable to contain, much less prevent, the carnage, this in spite of numerous approaches from the churches, trade unions and other organisations. (Official dry responses were commonplace, even humorous: "Yes, we're working hard to bring peace and stability to the area but there is one we want to arrest called Gift Moerane" said Col. Steyn to a church delegation comprising Naphtali Nkopane, Isaac Kolokoto and Gift Moerane). This is a matter of record and perhaps it is here that any future inquiry into the Boipatong massacre should begin.

In fact, community leaders were convinced that there was a strategy behind the "go slow", "softly softly", and even "nudge nudge" attitude of the police and Iscor management in the area. And the suspicions of the community leaders were correct. There was indeed, as a Soweto woman remarked, a fox behind the wolves that are killing us.

Later it emerged that Vlakplaas Commander Eugene de Kock had been there, stoking the fires. Supplied with illegal weapons, *skelm wapens* – by, among others, Security Policeman Paul Erasmus, De Kock had operated in Vereeniging and had supplied guns and hand grenades to Themba Khoza (then a Transvaal IFP Youth Brigade leader) who was arrested red-handed at the Sebokeng hostel with guns in his vehicle. The Khoza charge sheet later went missing in the Sebokeng police station. It appeared that Vereeniging and Vanderbijlpark were staging areas to destabilise the Vaal Triangle townships.

According to TRC investigator Piers Pigou (*Mail & Guardian*, 9 October 2000) although the Vaal Triangle had been an epicentre of repression and death during the mid-1980s and early 1990s, only three policemen from the area had applied for amnesty – and they had

164

been implicated by De Kock himself in connection with falsifying evidence about Themba Khoza. Years later apartheid assassin Ferdi Barnard told the TRC amnesty committee that hit men provided guns to Zulu hostel dwellers to carry out a series of massacres across the Reef, including the Boipatong massacre. The covert police structure called Crime Intelligence Services (CIS) with a safe house in the Vanderbijlpark area – plot 177 Reitstraat, Rosahof) was supposed to be dealing with so-called gun running. In fact, according to a recruit, the CIS, headed by Captain AG du Plessis, was targeting political activists in the area such as SACC fieldworker Saul Tsotetsi. The churches, secretly informed by a potential but horrified recruit, Daniel Kodisang, brought the matter to the attention of the *Weekly Mail & Guardian*, which exposed it in May 1992.

Indeed, according to a report in the church-owned *New Nation* newspaper (July 1993), the police had a "Yankee Squad" whose task was to recover illegal firearms and which had on its payroll notorious gang leader Victor "Khetisi" Kheswa who lived in Kwa Madala. Kheswa, who was arrested for mass murder, died in police custody in that month after he threatened to reveal his secret co-operation with the security forces. The state pathologist's post mortem claimed he had died of natural causes – a virus that had induced heart failure. A separate examination on behalf of the IFP and the Kheswa family found he had died of "conditions including acute suffocation, electrocution, hypothermia and occult toxic substances"[12].

These killings were directly responsible for the establishment of informal "defence units" throughout the affected areas. I knew the unit commanders at Zone 14 Sebokeng. They emerged from the community and were passionately concerned with defending that community, of which I was a member. I believe there was a genuine need to protect neighbourhoods. When they were formed and active in the area people slept better at night. I did. Yes, there were terrible abuses at times. Very often they were dealt with. But all things considered, they certainly met a felt community need in our district at this particular time. They were reminiscent of defence committees set up in Northern Ireland in the late 1960s to defend the Republican minority from Loyalist attacks.

[12] Marinovich, G. & Silva, J. *The Bang-Bang Club: Snapshots from a Hidden War.* Heinemann (2000); p. 79

It was, after all a township solution to a township problem.

Not all would agree, especially outsiders. *The New York Times* (31 July 1992) reported in an article alarmingly entitled "Bullied by its Children, a Township is Festering" that the residents of Sebokeng refer to their self-appointed defenders as "com-tsotsis" (a combination of "comrade", the township badge of militancy, and "tsotsi", the township slang for thug). Yes, the "com-tsotsi" phenomenon did arise but later, once abuses had set in. Certainly, Gertrude Motapanyana and many others in 1992 felt safer when the youth patrolled the streets at night.

One of the effects of this turmoil in the district was to provoke otherwise traditional conservative Christians to come onto the streets in protest. In late 1992, Benedict Mofokeng, Bridget Lefhiedi and Laurence Lehloka of the regional Sacred Heart Sodalities organised Masses (con-celebrated by South African and Japanese friars Rogers Sihlobo and Nicholas Nemoto) for the victims and solidarity prayer-walks to the Joe Slovo informal settlement which bore the brunt of the Boipatong massacre both in Boipatong and Vereeniging.

Meanwhile a struggle to the death – up to now a side event – was unfolding on the streets of Sebokeng between a defence unit and a ruthless gang of criminals who terrorised the area. And activist Saul Tsotetsi was about to go public with compelling evidence of third force involvement in township slaughters.

Chapter 35

Elimineer vyandelike leiers (Eliminate enemy leaders) – TRC, 1998

Saul Tsotetsi, 37, was employed full-time in justice and social ministries work at the SACC's Vaal branch, based in Vereeniging. He began his service with the SACC in 1984, following his release after serving a seven-year sentence on Robben Island. His work centred on peace-making and reconciliation, and he was frequently called to mediate in conflicts between police and community members and between administrators and students.

On 22 March 1992 he was killed by a hand grenade during an attack by unknown people . He had been scheduled to meet two days later with a representative of the Goldstone Commission on public violence, to turn in evidence concerning the causes and motives for local violence. At the time of his death he had just completed a detailed investigation into the massacre of 39 mourners attending a night vigil before the funeral of defence unit member Christopher Nangalembe, murdered when he was seen to be exposing the allegedly Inkatha-inspired activity of the Kheswa gang.

In his ten-page affidavit he showed how he had penetrated the underbelly of Vaal townships' gangland and found there a maze of interconnected political and criminal activity. Kheswa stood out prominently as the instigator of the kidnappings, rapes and killings at Sebokeng.

Tsotetsi claimed that it was this group that massacred mourners at the subsequent vigil for the funeral of Christopher Nangalembe. In his report he described the failure of the police to protect the mourners even though they had been warned of the serious possibility of an attack.

A few days before he died Tsotetsi told an audience: "The reason for me to sacrifice my personal ambition to the extent of risking imprisonment was because I believed, as I do now, that taking a stand against apartheid injustice was and is an obligation on my part as a Christian. In other words, even if the future government can inflict injustice of whatever kind I will stand up against it. This is an obligation that I am prepared to stand and die for." In 1998 the Saul Tsotetsi Recreational Centre was opened in Sebokeng in his memory.

Chapter 36

Traditional rituals were performed, muti was sprinkled on us,
and we attacked at night – TRC hearing on Boipatong massacre,
Sowetan, 7 July 1998

He (Mthembu) and others had killed both adults and their children
because "… a snake gives birth to a snake" (*The Star,* 14 July 1998).

It all began to get to me at Mathope's tin shack. I was directed to a
group of women sitting together in front of their frail tin dwellings.
Then I noticed the little body of Aaron Mathope, nine months old,
lying head up as if asleep, but blood-soaked (they had removed the
cloth cover for me), skull crushed and lifeless.

As usual a few quiet introductory questions set the scene between
the dazed families and myself. After a prayer they directed me around
the side of the box shack. Somebody out of the crowd stretched out a
hand in greeting to me. Local church leader Wilson Baloyi, a member
of the Secular Franciscans, who had been accompanying me for some
hours on this death walk through the dusty streets of Boipatong,
tugged at my sleeve. "That's Aaron's mother," he whispered, pointing
to the prone, blanket-covered shape of the child's mother, sprawled
where she too had been cut down hours earlier. Blood still seeped
through the cheap grey blanket, darkening as the hours passed. Large
numbers of traumatised locals were shuffling in and out among the
shacks of the encampment, nodding silently and talking in low,
shocked tones. No cars or taxis challenged the brooding silence.

A lump began to form in my throat. My breath seemed to shorten.
Tears formed in my eyes. I just gazed at the blanket, numbed and
wordless. As I worked through my emotions in silence, others joined us
and we were just together, wordless, in our common loss.

Baloyi drew my attention to more blanketed heaps, just beyond a
makeshift wire fence. Mother Mokoena and her neighbour had also

died that night in a deadly hail of bullets. The two women had died slumped over as if they had been chatting to each another across the garden fence.

Someone came through the crowd, greeted me and shoved a piece of paper into my hand. It showed he had counted 21 dead so far. I prayed, haltingly again. (It would have been inconceivable for a church minister not to pray. It was expected in all circumstances, but especially in such as this.) But what do you pray about when a tragedy of these proportions engulfs a normally God-fearing community? How do you relate religion to life in these numbing circumstances? How did God reach out to the hearts of these stricken families there and then? Where was God's face this morning? "Modimo o teng" (God is among us), whispered Baloyi, noticing my hesitancy. Others seemed to concur as they sought to make sense of the nightmare, some eight hours after the killers had completed their murderous work.

This community had just been ravaged by a two-hour, well-planned slaughter. They were waiting for me to pray words of hope and consolation. True, as the winter dawn broke over Boipatong and the adjacent informal settlement, eyes had dried from exhaustion, the crying had ceased, screams of terror had died away and the wailing had become muted. But this was clearly only a shocked lull; a communal intake of breath as the enormity of the horror became known throughout the townships. Only hours earlier defenceless families had been trapped in their own homes as crazed night marauders exploded into their living rooms with blood-stained hatchets, pangas, knobkerries and home-made spears held aloft to destroy whatever stood in their way. "Usuthu" was their blood-curdling cry as they literally attacked whatever moved. What do you pray about in a situation like this?

As I said, "Let us pray," heads bowed, eyes closed in devotion and I began to address God in a stumbling, incoherent way, punctuated by silences, as my emotions brimmed over. Anger ... confusion ... shock ... and shame. Soft sobs among the crowd. It was the 19th time in four hours I had prayed over grotesquely contorted corpses. It was the sixth such massacre whose results I had witnessed in the past two years. Christian memories tumbled into focus; the madness, the consternation, the shocking speed and turn of events that marked the final dark days of the life of Christ. "Crucify Him!" raved the hysterical mob. Mary and some friends saw her Son executed in the cold clinical way of all executions. And He wanted to forgive the executioners who were paid to do a job. The serial killer Herod had launched an official massacre of babies in the local townships of his time. The massacre of the "Holy Innocents" they called it. (See Appendix 5.) I mumbled something about this for a few moments.

On entering another cluster of shacks I saw police mortuary workers discreetly filling in their forms, before removing the remains of a man who still lay in his bed of blood; of a woman who was struck down while hiding in a shed, and of a teenage girl who was clubbed to death while trying to escape her drugged killers. She had been a visitor to the area. Praying and blessing of victims continued.

I then moved on up the street into the township proper. White and black riot police, clad in their camouflage fatigues with N4 guns at the ready, stood around nervously, close to their Casspir and Hippo transport vehicles. I was scrutinised as I passed, avoiding eye contact. Mother Namane distracted me with a smile and a greeting. Her husband, Zek, a church reader, would act as interpreter the next day for Nelson Mandela's visit.

Finally I arrived at Wilson Baloyi's house. Some years beforehand, due to his participation in the Vaal rent and services boycott, Baloyi's furniture and TV had been confiscated by the state. Now the alleged "state-aided" killers, using guns and all sorts of weapons, had bludgeoned their way through his heavy, meranti hall door, burst into his sitting room, and deposited a large suitcase with stolen wineglasses and old shoes – loot from a previously ransacked house – on his sofa. Seeing Wilson himself retreating to the back room where the family had fled, one of them went for him with a hatchet. As the attackers tried to break into the room, pounding and pushing the door (it was covered with hatchet cuts) with all their crazed strength, he gave one last superhuman heave, sending one of them off balance. Just then a shout went up outside, "Let's go," and the attackers made for the door – but not before they grabbed his radio, carried it outside and smashed it against the ground as they vanished into the winter night in the direction of another defenceless home.

~

Many more things could be said, have been said and will be said about the plunder of Boipatong on the night of Wednesday, 17 June 1992. The media were late on the scene that morning. They couldn't find Boipatong, which is what the name Boipatong means – "hiding place". I gave a few interviews and returned to Sebokeng. Parishioners were already cleaning around the house and church. I opened a beer, plopped onto a sofa with two broken springs, and looked at the wall, trying to sort out this morning's horrifying images.

Later that evening, between incoming calls, my mind, a little more settled, went back to an incident the night before in the Vanderbijlpark township of Bophelong. My diary ran as follows:

> *I'm discussing parish renewal with lay leader, Mrs Daisy Oliphant, mother of SAFA president Molefe Oliphant, when an urgent phone call comes through from Mrs Beauty Selela, a church leader from Boipatong. I take the phone and chat briefly with Beauty Selela before handing the receiver to Daisy. Mrs Oliphant was to immediately contact Peace Action (a grouping of 24 non-denominational organisations, including church groups, available to react quickly to possible situations of violence) about a strange rumour making the township rounds. The rumour was that something terrible was to happen on that night, possibly at Sebokeng or in some other township. Black ambulance drivers based at Houtkop (the seat of administration) had been told by white senior officers not to use the ambulances on that night – a strange instruction. Needless to say the drivers were mystified and given the engineered mood swings of the townships in those days, discussed these matters among themselves and with others. Among those others was Mrs Maria Mojapelo of Sebokeng who rang to inform*

Selela, a retired clinic matron at Boipatong. She, Selela,
was now telling Oliphant.
After eating that night, I had left for home at Sebokeng.
I wasn't sure what to think. I had hoped it was only a
rumour and dismissed it from my mind. Besides, the
parish elections were coming up and occupied my mind
as I had driven back to the township. One hour later the
slaughter had begun. Very early next morning Father
Mawethu Potolwana took a call from Mrs Beauty Selela
that something terrible had happened in Boipatong.
Bleary-eyed I set out for the township.

Days later, President de Klerk, on an official visit to Madrid, Spain, attacked the ANC, saying, "I find it a pity that the ANC is politicising this event in our country … I regret any inference that the government is involved in this act."

The months following the Boipatong massacre were probably the most crucial months in modern South African history. While the townships seethed and raged with anger, while unions promised mass action countrywide, while Mandela (who blamed De Klerk and the IFP for the massacre) and De Klerk traded insults, and while the economy began to grind to a halt, transition negotiators Cyril Ramaphosa (ANC) and Roelf Meyer (NP) were secretly meeting on a regular basis to try to find common ground in order to return eventually to the negotiating table.

And the violence was not all one-sided.

Chapter 37

There was a loud cheer as he was set aflame –
a newspaper report of the lynching Sam Hose
after a church service, Georgia, 1899

It was 10.15 a.m., 16 June 1992 – Soweto/Youth Day – but not yet recognised officially as a national holiday. It was a bright, sunny, township morning. A small crowd was coming from the direction of Zone 11, Sebokeng. Perhaps it was an initiation school, a *maqai*, returning home from their camp just outside Evaton near the Golden Highway. But no, it wasn't, the time of year was wrong. Usually these traditional schools operated during the summer holidays in December.

At the sound of agitated voices, Disebo and Tshidi turned towards the oncoming crowd. They suspected that something might be very wrong. For, out in front of the swarm, was a girl probably in her early twenties who appeared distraught She was being taunted and pushed ahead of the group. She was wearing a floral nightdress wrapped at the waist by a towel.

Tshidi and Disebo decided to follow the group, asking the stragglers to explain the purpose of the angry crowd. They were told that the victim – for she was clearly a victim – was an active member of the IFP, had recently been seen carrying a gun, and was allegedly involved in killing people.

The mob was now swearing at her and a shout went up, "Ha a bolawe (Kill her) because," they roared, "she is a killer herself." "Where are the Inkatha guns?" they screamed at her. Strangely, there was no response from her. It was eerie, the two girls told me later. She didn't even react when someone struck her with a sjambok.

Now the crowd was asking for a tyre at houses along the street. Fearing the worst, the residents pretended they had none. Again the girl did not react as the crowd shuffled on, howling for blood.

By now they had reached the outskirts of Zone 12 near a public dumping area. "Rea mo chesa, Ntja" (We are going to burn the dog), they screamed. "Ncheseng" (Burn me), the girls heard her say, and the pack set on her, knocking her senseless with rocks. Meanwhile someone ran up with a tyre hastily removed from a flowerbed in a private garden.

Tshidi and Disebo deliberately fell behind. Disebo instinctively, with her hand shielding her mouth, gasped to Tshidi to stop. This was becoming horrific. Intervention was out of the question, as the mob had taken on an ugly personality of its own.

The young woman still showed no signs that she understood that death might be imminent. Frenzied, the mob went to work. The old car tyre was shoved under her, stuffed with papers and plastic bags. A wide-eyed youth hurriedly splashed petrol over the tyre and the human form. A match was thrown onto the pyre and flames exploded upwards – still no movement or protest. She died in silent agony.

Disebo and Tshidi had heard that the IFP sometimes provided its members with certain medicines or drugs in order to "kill others without remorse or to be killed themselves painlessly". The rumour had come from the Inkatha stronghold at Kwa Madala hostel near Boipatong. They were aware too that this killing was not seen in isolation. It had happened in the wake of numerous drive-by murders that had plagued the Vaal townships since 1990. Anger, rage, fear and helpless frustration during the early 1990s lurked below the surface of the township psyche.

The result was summary justice of a chilling kind. And it was fed and nourished by a decade of overt bloodshed, to say nothing of the pummelling the already battered African family was taking. The perpetrators of this vicious act were themselves victims of their own, often brutalised, neighbourhoods.

Through killing this young woman these children believed they were doing the community a service, ridding it of an obscenity. And true to gut human instincts, when similar acts of social revenge happened in other countries and other continents, no residents interfered for fear of being branded friends of the enemy themselves. Later, the TRC explained further:

*From evidence before the commission, it appears that the
burning of a body was a sign of contempt for the victim
and his or her deeds. No act could convey a deeper sense
of hatred and disrespect. The practice was also used to
make an example of the victim so that others would be
inhibited from behaving like the deceased.*

When Tshidi finally slept from exhaustion in the early hours of the
next morning she had nightmares. Disebo tells me she cannot ever
again pass the site of this grisly execution. She's afraid of "seeing
something".

Part Six
Apocalypse

Chapter 38

It is often victims who are cursed by memory, while perpetrators are blessed by forgetting – The File, Timothy Garton Ash,

It's true the newspapers seldom spoke of the activities of the Security Branch in the townships. Their instinct was to be invisible at all times. They aspired to be grey colourless people who slid in and out of places where people stopped to chat or do business or have a drink. This practice, however, did not make them anonymous. In fact, people could always identify them by name, rank, car, and mode of activity, and a few were legendary in the community for the way they went about their work. Some black Security Branch personnel even believed deeply in what they were doing. For them it was right and just to defend the country against communism. Others were in it only for the job. In the end, when apartheid began to cave in, many black Branch members felt badly betrayed by their white superiors.

While the apartheid government was in power, detainees got to know the Security Branch personally. They had profiles on them and readily compared notes.

Indeed their victims sometimes gave them unwanted exposure afterwards. It is important that victims talk about their nightmarish memories. It is part of their healing. It enables them and their violators, in different ways, to come to terms with their past. It helps the nation to lay the ground for recovery, forgiveness, reparation and moving on.

But there is also another point to remember. After the youth uprising of 1976 the state was determined to suppress all youth formations with a social, political or even social-religious agenda. Thousands left the country to join liberation movements. Let us remember those who stayed and faced the consequences. They were largely unknown since most of the leadership had left. They kept the torch of hope burning. In the following stories, violators and victims from that time come together in the worst of circumstances.

Cosmas "Sampie" Thokoa was one such victim, a survivor. He was arrested at 1.00 a.m. on 12 June 1978 with many other Young Christian Workers (YCW) throughout South Africa. A resident of Sebokeng, he was interrogated on the third storey of Vereeniging Police Station by a phalanx of senior police[13], including a superintendent known locally as "The Monster".

The following are extracts from my parish notes on this case:

"You'll die like Biko, you can't stand my interrogations. Sobukwe fell, Mandela fell and Biko fell. And you will fall too," warned Steyn as he worked on his victim.

(At this time I had a nasty encounter with Steyn concerning Security Branch smearing of priests working in the townships. Our informants detected plain-clothes men spreading rumours that we priests were engaged in unholy alliances with the beauties of the location. A charming thought – coloured by the Immorality Act – but not too inventive. The old sex card used by all security services throughout the world to compromise the opposition. Clearly it was meant to neutralise our pastoral work with the people. During the tense meeting, monitored by a second silent deadpan officer, Steyn contrived to appear indignant that his men would behave so unprofessionally, and with some bluster all but called me a liar. As I was leaving the meeting I enquired about the condition of Cosmas Sampie Thokoa in detention. It was to let the Colonel know that any torture of Thokoa would be noted and publicised. Steyn assured me that everything was fine. Which, of course, I did not believe. Remarkably the smear campaign ended just then.

During most of the interrogation, which was done in three shifts, Cosmas was handcuffed to a chair. Sometimes they wrapped him in an electric blanket after which Colonel Conradie plugged it into an electrical terminal. The shock was excruciating, Cosmas told me afterwards.

---

[13] The victim named these men as Colonel "Panyapanya" Steyn, Colonel Conradie, Superintendent de Beer, Superintendent Macholo (called "The Monster") and Superintendent van Heerden.

179

Was it sick humour or a form of sick arrogance? Anyway, one memorable day, policemen, including De Beer, stood four matches on his head, supported by his hair, and proceeded to light each of them. Then they sang, "Happy Birthday to you", as the flames burnt lower and lower. As Cosmas's hair began to singe they blew out the matches.

A black constable called Ali had to be withdrawn from the interrogation programmes, seemingly because he was too violent and indeed later was retired as medically unfit. Sometimes Cosmas wasn't allowed to sleep for three days and had to eat standing. After he entered into an exhausted sleep they would wake him within 15 minutes. Exposing Thokoa to cold conditions was also a strategy to "soften" him.

During this time, the victim chose to say nothing of his torture to a visiting magistrate, fearing it would be used against him during the interrogation. Most days he was beaten on the head.

After six weeks of interrogation at Vereeniging he was sent for trial at Kroonstad in December 1978. Accused of subversion and sedition as a member of the non-denominational YCW , he was later acquitted and became Transvaal secretary of the Black Allied Workers Union and a secret member of the Pan-Africanist Congress.

By 1981 he still did not know why he had been arrested. The psychological after-effects were still with Cosmas – lack of concentration, irrational fear, worrying about simple things, lack of responsibility. It is possible that today thousands of South Africans while they go about their daily work in politics, municipalities, NGOs, trade unions, and the arts are still damaged from their experiences of police brutality. Many are not even aware of the damage that was done to them. After his release I ministered to him in the area of the healing of nightmarish memories.

Chapter 39

Among those of our local youth arrested for YCW activities in 1978 was an Evaton altar server, Danial Mokobane. I asked the altar servers to bring his arrest to the attention of the congregation themselves as a way of rallying our youth and raising awareness among adults and parents. On the Sunday following his arrest the servers remembered him in the intercessions with the following request for prayer. It's a poignant reminder of the past: "In humility, I stand before you this morning. One of our altar servers has been arrested and is in detention as I speak to you. We don't know why. His parents are in deep distress. They went to the police station but the police did not want to talk to them. We ask you, our congregation and all the altar servers, to please keep him in your prayers."

A few days later I found an urgent note under my office door from a distraught Mrs Lydia Makume from Sharpeville, informing me that Lucia Masooa had been taken away and that the police were searching for her own daughter, Mamoroesi (18). The police (Malakia, Beukes, Rafube, Tshabalala, Steyn, Moagi and others) had called, she said, and were aware that Mamoroesi had gone to a YCW meeting at Pietersburg in the Northern Transvaal. Mrs Makume wanted me to ring Pietersburg immediately and warn Mamoroesi that she was "highly wanted by the Special Branch". Actually at that moment – 15 June 1978 – they were already in the process of being rounded up. They were detained and gave false names having deliberately carried no means of identification. After three days they were brought to Pretoria where they were released. Fearing to return home, the 11 YCW activists who had been arrested were offered accommodation by the distinguished theologian, Father Albert Nolan, at the Dominican house in Johannesburg. They stayed there for a month before returning to the Vaal and Cape Town.

Facilitating communications between the YCW "hunted" (throughout South Africa 30 were detained between May and July 1978), their parish bases and their Johannesburg headquarters, became of crucial importance at the time. These young resisters were motivated by Bible discussion that preceded all their activities. Their ecumenical example inspired others of their peer groups at the time and prepared the groundwork for more overt anti-apartheid action in the early eighties.

Show trials followed with the state determined to destroy the movement. The widespread persecution of the YCW in the late 1970s by the South African state was headline news (Pope Paul VI expressed concern about it) which even involved public recriminations between Cardinal McCann, the head of the Catholic Church in South Africa, and the notorious bespectacled Minister of Justice, Jimmy ("Biko's death leaves me cold") Kruger. (That same year the same Jimmy Kruger declared triumphantly before the Natal Congress of the National Party that the three enemies of the state were the YCW, the Christian Institute and theologians!) The inspiration behind the YCW in the Johannesburg diocese were the indefatigable Dominican friars Benedict Mulder and Joe Falkiner, who encountered much police aggression at this time. With Father de Fleuriot, they helped to keep the movement intact during its darkest, most glorious hours. Police packs continued to stalk the young activists. One of those activists was Simon Nkoli.

Simon Nkoli, another member of the YCW movement, was arrested in August 1978. At the time in an urgent note he had told me they were closing in on him. I was to contact him immediately at Santa Maria Convent, Vanderbijlpark. Later they arrested him and in clinical Security Branch terminology opened with:

"We're friends of yours," and continued, "What organisation were you a member of?"

"YCW."

"You should leave it, man. It will get you thrown into jail."

Then the heat was turned up.

"Don't pretend to be surprised because we know what you have done wrong. And I know what you have done too."

"What have I done?" asks Nkoli.

"*U jala mafere-fere bathong hohle moo u yang teng.*" (You create confusion, fire up people, wherever you are). Another favourite security line to create distrust within anti-government activist ranks was, "We were told this by someone."

"How long have you been in the YCW? What office do you hold? Who contacted you first? Do you accept our advice or not? Where do you attend church? Who is the priest?"

And again, another classical question designed to sow confusion in opposition ranks: "Do you know Joyce Mokhesi? Do you know where she is?" And then the most sinister question of all:

"Do you think Joyce told us about you?"

In the middle 1980s Nkoli was one of the accused in the famous Delmas Treason Trial. Acquitted, he went on to achieve national and international recognition as a gay and AIDS activist leader before his untimely death in 1998.

~

Samuel Ntoane was 20 and living in Orlando West, Soweto, when some time in February 1978 he heard about yet another midnight raid on his home. Certainly he knew that they were searching for him. He felt for the family every time it happened. The frequent disruption of his family also angered him because he was helpless to do anything about it. It was the lot of politically aware blacks during the years of oppression. It made life very insecure and unpredictable. Young families were badly disrupted by it.

"*Maak oop, maak oop!*" shouted moving figures (the police) in the dark outside. Someone was banging on the front door. It had to be whites as they only use front doors. The family was inside. While they were familiar with night raids, the fear and terror of the event never leaves you. Samuel was not present that night – which angered the police. Somebody had got their lines crossed in the intelligence section. They left the premises shouting threats.

In fact, for their own sake Samuel never told the family where he was. And he had to be extremely careful about visiting his home. Night time was best. Even then it was risky. He actually used a different type of walk when nearing his house, for a person's walk could identify him to the neighbours.

Samuel's mother, Mamorena, worried ceaselessly about his safety. If he was caught she knew terrible things could happen to him. Some, she heard, had even died while with the police. Increasingly it bothered her. One morning she woke with a plan. She must get him out of the country as soon as possible. A friend would help her to smuggle him into Lesotho.

A family friend, Jacob Moeti, ran a funeral service in Lesotho near Leribe. Without telling the family, she told him what she wanted to do. The plan was that Samuel would come with his mother, by private car from Johannesburg, and meet Moeti with his hearse (and empty coffin) at a place outside Senegal in the Free State.

It happened as planned. The friends met and quickly changed vehicles. The private car headed back to Johannesburg. The hearse moved off in the direction of Lesotho. Muted, nervous conversation continued between Moeti and Mamorena until they arrived near the Maseru border post. Here they stopped as if to stretch their legs. Samuel climbed into the back of the hearse and lowered himself into the coffin. Fortunately Moeti had opted for a large size. He had difficulty arranging himself within the coffin but eventually succeeded. He replaced the lid. It was common enough for deceased Basotho from the Republic to be brought home to Lesotho for burial. Samuel, in the black, suffocating heat of the coffin, held his breath – he inched the lid open to get some air. Soon they arrived at the customs, slowed down and parked. He heard the driver's door slamming closed. Silence. Just silence. He was swimming in sweat.

South African border posts during the time of apartheid were a law unto themselves. The inmates – what else can I call them? – were people of proven zeal in defending their country's policies. They scrutinised meticulously the credentials of all who passed through their hands. They checked names against their own lists of undesirables kept underneath the counter or on their computer screens. They searched cars for arms and bombs and *Playboy* magazines. They strip-searched many, including nuns. They deliberately delayed some for questioning.

Samuel could hear nothing except for periodic banging of car doors. This was followed by silence. Time stood still. Some shouting in Afrikaans in the distance he vaguely remembered. But the midday heat of his enclosure was something else. His mother, Mamorena, the chief "mourner", sat staring ahead of her in the front seat, her motherly instincts triggering off surprising reserves of steely self-control. She was within minutes of outsmarting the apartheid security machine. Unknown to Samuel a customs policeman was menacingly circling the hearse. Suddenly the vehicle heaved, a door slammed and the engine burst into life. Moeti sighed to no one in particular, relief not yet showing on his face as sweaty hands steered the vehicle towards the Lesotho side of the border. As the old banger bumped across the ancient Caledon railway bridge to Lesotho, Samuel wanted to escape the suffocating coffin. The driver barked an order to stay low, as the danger has not yet passed. The Lesotho customs officers knew Mr Moeti so the perfunctory stop there was of short duration. A lurch forward and the "funeral" was on its way. Four minutes later there was another stop followed by silence. A voice questioned, "Sam, what do you see?" as the lid was raised from the coffin and the curtain partially pulled across. "I see a big hut like a Basotho hat," referring to the Basotho Hat tourist shop in lower Maseru. Moeti told him to climb through the front partition into the driver's cabin. He found his mother outside standing beside the open door weeping with relief. For the time being his injury was forgotten. They embraced.

Two Irish Aid workers driving a dust-covered Land Rover with NGO markings passed the stationary hearse and remarked that there seemed to be some peculiar sort of movement behind the curtains where a coffin normally would be found. They sped on towards the border en route to Bloemfontein for supplies, preoccupied with the news that an Irishman had just won the Tour de France.

Chapter 40

Now we come to the mid-eighties just after the adult/youth uprising of 1984. Although new community leaders were emerging it was a very dangerous time in South Africa to be a resister. Repression reached new levels of viciousness and depravity. Being professionals, they came in the small hours of the morning when humanity was at its most vulnerable. It was 3 September 1985, three months into the state of emergency and one year to the minute since the beginning of the Vaal uprising. The timing was impeccable. It was the usual swoop before a big date. Net the political movers and "rest" them for a while – more, if necessary. They bundled Thami Zondo into one of their cars, arrogantly ripping the TV cable from the house wall as they left. He had known that it could happen at any time, the signs were always there. It was his second detention in a year. It was, however, still a shock. The DPSC of which Thami was a member knew they were under close state surveillance. So they expected the midnight bang on the door at any time. They even joked about it. Thami Zondo had been asking questions about the disappearance of Tahleho Francis Korotsoane[14] in police custody – perhaps too publicly. The state now acted decisively. They had removed him from his family, the DPSC and this, the police hoped, would be a lesson to the remaining members of that interfering organisation. They brought him to the Leeuhof cells.

There his drooping spirits lifted when he found fellow comrades from Sebokeng – "Tommi" Maleka, Slovo Majola, Themba Goba, Shaka Radebe and Toy Manqa. At least it wasn't solitary confinement.

He settled down to life in detention as best he could. His mental agitation gradually subsided. He began to learn the ins and outs, the dos and don'ts of prison life. Being a political detainee automatically separated him from other prisoners. He, as a political prisoner, had

[14] He was one of the many people arrested by the Security Branch and who was never seen or heard of again.

different status and little in common with those in jail for criminal offences. The latter had great respect for the former.

Time for Zondo began to slow down. Days began to drag. And still nobody came to charge him for any offence. He grew righteously angry. And when a poet with a will of steel grows angry the state has a problem. The urge to express himself, to express his anger grew in intensity.

Then he remembered a book he had read on Bobby Sands, the Irish Republican Army prisoner who deliberately starved himself to death as a protest in a Northern Ireland prison years before. Zondo had read his story and found it inspiring, never realising that one day he might be confronted with a similar choice. His fellow detainees listened eagerly as he told them the story of Sands. And they were a little in awe of him when he told them he was about to embark on a hunger strike.

On 28 September 1985 he started – to the initial dismay of only the warders. Dismay led to concern among the Vereeniging prison authorities when he continued into the second week. His health began to fail.

After a while they removed him to the prison infirmary. While he was there the authorities continued to try and persuade him to be "sensible" and resume eating. The prison chaplain, a Dutch Reformed *predikant*, came one day armed with Romans 13 on obeying legitimate authority. Zondo listened politely to the earnest man of the church. He had a feeling that Paul's advice to his fellow citizens wasn't the issue here. He said he would ponder the matter.

Police threats followed, " You can be charged for a hunger strike, man," they told him with growing impatience. By the end of the second week the authorities promised to release or charge him if he stopped the hunger strike. But when they discovered that hunger strike fever was spreading among political detainees at Leeuhof, they removed Zondo to Groenpunt prison south of Vereeniging. Taking them at their word he resumed eating – to no avail. They didn't release him so he stopped eating again.

Captain Botha was a likeable, easy-to-talk-to member of the prison staff. One day Zondo asked him to relay the following message to the

State President, PW Botha: "I will stay on hunger strike until the last drop of my blood drips down your hands." Botha conveyed this message to the Security Branch. They came running, fuming, and demanding that Zondo put his grievances in writing – which he did. They studied and discussed his notes in Vereeniging. They made a plan.

Some days later, Security Branch members, Lieutenant Colonel le Roux, Captain Steyn and Lieutenant de Klerk[15], came to visit their prisoner again. Captain Steyn was the one, Zondo recalls, who had kept his father Michael under surveillance ever since the 1960 Sharpeville massacre. It was obvious by their tone of voice they meant business. They needed a reason why he was in jail. And they wanted him to know this reason. The captain, with his foot on the prostrate patient's bed, accused him of fomenting unrest and disturbances in the Sharpeville area, and specifically with the DPSC of organising the "Black Christmas" protests the previous year. Voices were raised and annoyance simmered.

The tall Le Roux burst in, "Listen to me. Now listen to me. You've caused fire in the country."

"What?" exclaims Zondo, aghast. And in his weakened condition the only way he can show his indignation was to turn from the three policemen and face the prison wall. Frustrated, Le Roux threw up his hands. *"Los hom. Hy is 'n hardegat,"* (Leave him. This is a difficult asshole), someone mutters as they leave the prison infirmary.

All being quiet again, Zondo turned from the wall, a sickly smile on his face. "Hey man, taba ea hao e tswana le ea Bobby Sands" (Hey man, your story is like that of Bobby Sands) whispers a sympathetic warder that evening.

Zondo recalls another strange incident. He was three weeks into his second fast when one fine morning a Dr van Zyl came to see him, accompanied by a white female warder. The smiling doctor without engaging in any preliminary medical examination offered to give Thami an injection to make him feel better. Zondo suspicious, replied, "If you are going to give me an injection while I'm on a fast are you aware that you'll be poisoning me?" The smile faded from the doctor's face. "I was only trying to help you," he maintained and left.

[15] First names of Security Branch members were not always known.

One morning Thami heard that political detainees refused to return to their solitary confinement cells, out of sympathy for him. Satisfaction welled up inside him. His strike was making a difference.

By now state officials was becoming worried. What if this stupid idea of his spread to other prisons, they asked? Already, fellow prisoners were joining him. And the world media was receptive to a story like this. Something desperate would have to be done. The local police knew the situation was getting beyond them. "Cheeky fucking bastard," they ranted among themselves. Finally they asked for help from headquarters in Johannesburg. Johannesburg knew that hunger strikes, if not handled properly, could lead to serious complications. Machinery was set in motion to defuse the situation.

Soon after the Minister of Justice, Johan Coetzee, sent Judge C Steyn of the appellate division of the Bloemfontein Supreme Court to intervene.

"Is it a crime," Thami Zondo asked him, "to work at social welfare?" (i.e. the work of the DPSC). "No, it's not a crime." The judge was impressed. He promised to report back to the Minister immediately. Two weeks later Lieutenant de Klerk of the Security Branch released Zondo.

It was only later that Thami Zondo heard that his voluntary fast had triggered further illegal fasts around the country. For the first time in recent South African history the refusal to eat food had became a potent weapon for resistance.

Chapter 41

Mrs Hlophekile Makhema, a domestic helper, was in the shopping mall at Amanzimtoti, south of Durban, when a bomb exploded in September 1986. It was 8.45 a.m. and Hlophekile had been sent to the shops to fetch a fabric softener. She had her Sasolburg employer – Mrs Beverley Venter's – two children with her. Alice, 2 , had run ahead when the bomb went off. She died instantly. In the ensuing mayhem, the elder daughter and Hlophekile sustained serious injuries. Both were hospitalised. The family was devastated by the death of their beloved youngest daughter.

Recalling the tragedy, the domestic assistant remembers that she fell to the ground, became disorientated, and "rubbing my face, which was full of blood, my eye came out in my hand," she said. One morning much later, her employer told her, "I've bought you a glass eye," and told her to fit it in – which she did with some difficulty. That's how Makhema describes it. Since the explosion Makhema seems to have suffered from a mental condition. She also became aware of a *"Moea"* (a spirit relating to her ancestors) within her.

Tension developed between employer and helper over small, incidental things. Relations became strained. In exasperation, one evening, she said, Beverley Venter burst out: "I've spent R300 on that eye of yours. Give it back to me." The helper asked her employer what she would do with it. "I'll give it to my family," she replied. But Makhema refused to return the eye. Then, she said, an angry Venter shouted, "I did not bomb you. You were bombed by your own kaffirs."

Endless court cases about the bombing served only to intensify the stress and trauma in the Venter home and between family and employee. Disputes over payments followed.

One morning, a particularly difficult exchange took place and ended up at the local police station. Much argument followed with the police appearing to take the side of her employer. Infuriated, Hlophekile

Makhema ripped her new glass eye from its socket, slapped it on the charge office counter and soon after walked out of the Venter household. Later her employer returned it to her and to this day Hlophekile keeps it in a box, unable to use it owing to medical complications.

Like Makhema and Venter there are thousands of other silent casualties of the struggle for democracy.

~

As chaplain, I visited Vereeniging prison weekly. While other inmates busied themselves at regulation chores, I held a service for those interested at a corner of one of the large prison squares called Angola. A noisy prison yard was not an ideal situation No nice sanitised, incense-smelling church to create the right atmosphere for God-affairs. The mood didn't lend itself to the mystical and mysterious. Then one day I realised with a jolt that God had burst into the lives of many political prisoners, like Francis of Assisi and other world heroes of all religions, and was doing so even today, during their prison days. For some the silence of a cell has become the classroom of the divine. I shared this insight with the prisoners and they grew strangely silent. That day they really listened.

Apart from meeting prisoners, the visit enabled me to monitor where political detainees were kept. Often they were in the "Angola" awaiting-trial section but kept apart from the ordinary prisoners. Therefore I would "arrange" the service so that it could take place under the window of the detention room overlooking the square. Thus "mapantiti" (ordinary prisoners) attending the service would stand or squat as a group, facing the prison square with their backs to the detention room windows. In this way I could communicate with the detainees behind the windows, giving them information from the outside and in turn bringing messages (for instance from Saul Tsotetsi) to their families or legal representatives. My congregation understood as they respected the detainees above.

At the women's section I visited Sister Christine Obotseng once a week. A nun of the Companions of St Angela, Sister Christine, and two other young female detainees had been transferred here and were to be here for the next five months. The nun was arrested while escorting youth home after a meeting in the parish church in Kagiso, accused of leading "an illegal march".

All received communion and, because they were Emergency detainees (under Section 3 of the Emergency Act), a black female warder closely monitored our conversations. A certain craft was necessary to give them messages or news from the outside world. This was done by luring the female warder into our conversation which then wandered gently over the necessary areas of interest to the detainees.

Sister Christine's health broke during her imprisonment. She has never completely recovered. Little did I know what was happening behind the scenes. Sister Christine recalls some of it:

> "One day, during the late morning session of 23 December 1986, the political prisoners were assembled in the small prison hall which also served as the place for religious services. As we sat there, two white security police started addressing us by asking us whether we knew why we were imprisoned. Most of us were highly annoyed by this type of question, because we could not understand why they came to pose such a question to us after we had been six months in detention.
>
> While we were still puzzled by this arrogance, one of the two policemen suddenly turned to me and said: "Sister, what's your name?" I instantly got angry and just stared at him without uttering a word. He then posed the same question to one of the girls who happened to be an ex-pupil of ours at St Peters. Her name was Segakweng. I think the question found her unguarded and, unthinkingly, she answered "Sister Christine". "Christine who?" "Obotseng," came the reply. Then he continued in Afrikaans saying: *"Daar is ander bobbejaan onder julle wat ..."* (there are certain monkeys among you who ...) Before he completed the sentence something within me at once seemed to say: "This man is insulting us and I for one am not going to listen to such offensive people." I got up at once and left, followed by

192

Patricia Nzwane of Kagiso 11 and Nobantu Nkosi from Randfontein. The three of us remained outside until the meeting was over after which we returned to the cells with the other detainees.

Early the next morning the three of us were told by the warder to take all our belongings and go to the reception. (Of course this move did not surprise us much. We expected a reaction from the security police, in response to our previous day's behaviour.) When we arrived at the reception, we found two security police, one black and one white. We never got to know their names. Our fingerprints were taken. As I stood next to one of the policemen I noticed that he was writing: "Transferred from Johannesburg prison to Vereeniging prison." It was Christmas Eve.

When we arrived at Vereeniging, south of Johannesburg, the three of us were placed in one cell. One day after three months the warder, Ms Smith, told us that we had to move out and go to single cells. This meant solitary confinement. This was just too much for us to accept. We could not face single cells again. The stress was too great. We knew from the past. We resisted. Ms Smith realised that we didn't want to shift to the single cells. She took a hosepipe and sprayed us with water, right inside the cell. We reacted with fury. We grabbed her and struggled to dispossess her of the hosepipe. Eventually one of us got hold of her, tightening our grip around her hands, which were still gripping the hosepipe. She became helpless and was now suspecting that we were about to spray her with water.

As we were hosing her with water a black warder entered the cell. Smith shouted: *"Druk die klok. Hulle wil my doodmaak!"* (Press the alarm. They want to kill me). Then a certain Mr Labuschagne from the male prison department came to her assistance. When he came in he pulled Ms Smith and tore her from our grip. He then grabbed me and tried to kick me. I grabbed him by the jacket and held on to him.

The floor was a mini-pool so we both slipped and fell. From the floor we were a sight for a fly on the wall!

The number of warders had now risen to six. They stood there and watched. I continued to argue but he again grabbed me and pushed me. I was a bag of emotions, anger, humiliation and frustration. I felt like crying, but something within me said: "Don't. You cannot afford the luxury of being seen to shed tears in such a situation. You cry, then what?" I became victorious.

Tears were blocked through exercising my will. I continued to argue with Mr Labuschagne but that did not help me. He eventually managed to forcefully put me into one of the single cells where we remained until we were taken back to Krugersdorp prison to be released …

But the time I really felt helpless, frustrated, bitter and powerless was when Sisters Mary Modise and Anne Mayhew came to see me at Leeuhof prison in Vereeniging, and broke the news of Sister Raphael Molokwane's death. Sister Raphael had been detained originally (19 June 1986). I pleaded with the warders to request the prison officials, i.e. whoever was the rightful authority, to grant me leave to go to her funeral. The answer was "No, that is impossible." I even begged them to accompany me to make sure I came back to prison and that was met with a flat refusal. This is one experience that pained me very much during my detention."

~

"*Amandla!*" they cried.

"*Aluta continua!*" they chorused.

"*Phanzi ngo Botha!*" (Down with Botha) they screamed with renewed passion.

It was 1.30 p.m. on Tuesday, 20 March 1988 at the African Methodist Episcopal church in Zone 11, Sebokeng. It's hot outside but hotter and very humid inside the building. Emotions were running high. It also happened to be an illegal gathering to mark the eve of the 1960 Sharpeville massacre.

The subject of the meeting was the launch of a new students' organisation called Vaal Students Congress (VASCO). The previous organisation, COSAS, had recently been banned.

Peter Doctor Malinga, a member of COSAS, told me years later:

"The message we wanted to send the government was that the banning of movements and organisations wouldn't solve our national problems. Instead, it will create more. They can keep on banning, but we will keep on launching. They cannot wish away the fighting spirit of the masses. By launching VASCO we were going to further the aims and objectives of COSAS."

Jacob "Ree" Masangana was duly elected Chairman of the new youth formation. Just then a shout went up from a lookout, "Ke bao!" (It's them!) – a warning that police were arriving and taking up positions. Pandemonium broke out as people stampeded in all directions, through windows and doors, over walls and wire fences, into private yards and homes, short-cutting to other streets.

Malinga, seeing the church entrance blocked by a police Casspir, hurriedly skirted a few fences and found himself running in a "back-opposite" street in the general direction of the Sebokeng post office. Rushing into someone's house (today they are his in-laws), he was greeted in no uncertain terms by the owner: "You fucking comrades, you start problems teasing the police and then you run away. Get out of here!" On the run again, Malinga ducked into a corner house "where I passed everybody in the kitchen straight down to the main bedroom and got myself under the bed which was about 30 cm from the ground. I thought I was safe until I saw shiny boots in front of my nose."

"*Kom uit daar onder die bed!*" (Come out from under the bed).

"Before the astonished household and neighbours I was bundled off to the police detention centre outside Vanderbijlpark," he recalls.

Later in the evening, after continuous questioning, the branch officers got an inspiration. Probably it was planned. Call in the monkeys, they said. And they did. They brought in a monkey as part of their interrogation programme. The sequence went like this. Malinga was told to sit at a table where food was placed before him. The monkey was also standing on the table and was addressed by its master in the following words: "*Vullis, vang sy ballas, want hy wil jou kos eet*" (Vullis, catch his

195

balls because he wants to eat your food). At this prompting Vullis came straight for Malinga's private parts upon which the schoolboy screamed, *"Vullis, ek vat nie jou kos nie"* (Vullis, I'm not taking your food). Feigning anger, the police forced the detainee to call the monkey *"Baas Vullis"* (Boss Vullis). By this time Malinga was too exhausted for further questioning.

As is customary during interrogations a "gentleman" Security Branch officer usually enters the scene – the others having left – and proceeds to quietly coax information from the subject. And then, on cue, in steps a black officer called Moagi and ever so "compassionately" asks what plans the youth had for the next day's commemoration of the Sharpeville shootings of 1960. Offering Malinga financial assistance for his schooling, Moagi inviteed him to work with the Security Branch.

Malinga, exhausted, pretended to play along with this slightly built, bespectacled, softly spoken security officer. He was told to attend the gathering at the Reverend Lord McCamel's Church next day in Evaton and bring back as much information as possible about the speakers and their speeches. They would meet, Moagi said, under the tree next to the police station. For his first "informer" payment the branch man gave him a solitary R1. I wonder what amount of information was worth R1! – perhaps to report that the moon was round? Finally, the SP man dropped Malinga off at Sefatsa's filling station at Sebokeng. Needless to say, the mission was never accomplished. "I thanked God when I saw him driving away from me," recalls Malinga. They never met again.

~

Shele Papane was arrested at his Sharpeville home on 10 April 1986 and accused of involvement in the burning of a town councillor's house. Three Security Branch officers called Piet Cilliers, Koos and Mthonga (who later killed himself in a family quarrel at the Sebokeng police station) accompanied him from his home. As they did not want him to know where they were bringing him, Koos violently elbowed Papane into a crouch in the back of the police car. In fact, they were bringing him to a Vanderbijlpark internment centre, popularly called the "White House", situated at the corner where the Golden Highway begins. It was formerly a disused factory and later taken over by the police. Papane

196

was bundled into the centre and thus his forced humiliation began. During continuous systematic beatings administered at this place by both Koos and Piet, he was instructed not to speak English and not to address the police as "*Meneer*". Koos explained patiently, "A meneer is a kaffir *predikant*" (a sir is a kaffir priest). Which is news to all vicars, priests, *predikants* and *abafundisi* – male or female!

In the shower room of this building one of the men sat on Papane's back (earlier he had been stripped of his trousers and underclothes) while another worked on him. "They put something on my buttocks – it buzzed like a welding machine." "Praat!" they shouted, hoping that he would admit to burning the councillor's house. During this torture, a canvas bag had been tied around Papane's head.

Then Koos, who had been sitting on him, got a bright, biologically induced idea. He urinated on Papane before recommencing the shock treatment. To this day, Papane hasn't forgotten the degradation of this despicable act.

And then they had another idea. They told him to sing, "*Ek is PW Botha se kaffir*" (I am PW Botha's kaffir). "I did as they told me. Then they said that I was not singing loud enough and shocked me on my back and made me sing again."

Piet and Koos asked, "*Ken jy rugby?*" Now, blindfolded, the victim became a rugby ball. "Then they kicked my forehead and I fell onto the ground." Papane has not been able to like rugby since that day.

He continued: "Once I had fallen, they demanded that I stand up again. My shoes were off and I only had socks on. I don't know when my shoes came off. I was still suffering the burning after-effects of the shocks, making my whole body vibrate and shudder. One shouted, 'Moenie beweeg nie!' (Don't move!). He kicked me in my ribs and I fell onto the ground from the impact. I could not stand again; my whole body was in pain. I crouched on the floor and had to grasp my knees with my hands to stop my body shaking so as not to offend him. This because they kept telling me not to move. I was then kicked on my back."

The interrogation continued for another two hours and he was regularly kicked when he tried to answer allegations that he was a trained terrorist paid by the communists. Tiring of their efforts, the policemen pushed bread into his mouth and afterwards a cigarette (he doesn't smoke) was shoved between his bloodied and swollen lips. It remained there until it burnt out.

"*Piet, laat ons die vokking goeters los*" (Piet, let's leave these fucking things – referring to Papane and another person arrested with him). The other answered, "Ons gaan in die kak wees, kyk hoe lyk hulle nou" (We'll be in shit, look at their appearance). It was time to release Papane but first they had to clean him up and make him a little more presentable to the public. To this end, he was brought, again blindfolded, to Sebokeng police station from which he was admitted to the hospital next door. Although he was treated by two doctors and given a prescription (the police ignored it) his buttocks became inflamed and septic within a day.

On Saturday he was returned to the interrogation centre for prolonged gruelling concerning the burning incident. This time, however, they made him write a lengthy statement to compare his handwriting with that found on threatening letters originally sent to the councillor whose house had been burnt. Next, Papane was ordered to copy them using his left and right hand. Fearing the police would frame him he was careful to date and sign each page.

Finally, after explaining exhaustively his alibi on the day of the crime, he was released. Innocent. That evening he came to me at the church in Sharpeville and showed me the scars, burns and lacerations on his body. He was smiling, as usual. After such a horrific experience!

These were the days when from the State President down, increasingly shrill orders to neutralise growing opposition to the government were filtering through to all branches of the security services. And Shele Papane was a leading member of the DPSC in the area.

That night Piet got drunk, Koos fought with his wife, and Mthonga had a nightmare.

~

Cases of sexual torture included … the insertion of objects such as batons into bodily orifices – TRC, 1998

Jan Oupa Mofokeng is small, thinnish, and unnoticeable in a crowd. He comes from Evaton, south of Johannesburg. He is a passionate person who early in life gave himself over to public life. Unhappy with the lack of political change he left the land of his birth in 1989 to join the military arm of the ANC. His training as an MK cadre brought him to many countries. He returned with renewed hope to a changing South Africa in 1991 and re-engaged in public life.

On Sundays he worshipped with his family at St Peters Apostolic Church. Thus it was not unusual when he took a 13-day trip (from 15 to 28 December 1993) with church members to Confimvaba in the Eastern Cape.

Our story opens while he was away on this trip. The notorious Vanderbijlpark Murder and Robbery squad sent their men to his home in West Street, Evaton where they behaved in a very aggressive way with members of the family while declaring that "exiles were criminals". When Oupa returned from Cofimvaba he went to the police to find out what was the matter. They accused him of surreptitiously passing a handgrenade to a prisoner-in-transit at Sebokeng courthouses. He was shocked – a serious accusation indeed.

During a visit to his home on the same day the police assaulted him, and squeezed his penis with a pliers for about five minutes. They decided to take him with them. Leaving Small Farms in the police car they came upon a barking dog, shot it dead and hoisted the dead animal onto Oupa's lap. And off they went again, all three of them, Sergeant Taylor, Major Cilliers[16] (both former Vanderbijlpark Murder and Robbery Squad officers) and one identified by the newspapers as Tiekie Sidney Chaka.

Nearing Golden Store (on the Golden Highway) they stopped again, parked the car, and told Mofokeng to strip. Holding him firmly, Cilliers proceeded to circle his penis with wires, inserting one through the entrance of his member. Then they attached the other ends of the wire to the car battery and turned the engine on. Mofokeng screamed in agony.

After some time all got into the car again, covering Mofokeng's head with a black cloth tied at the neck. By now he was almost fainting. In the car they regularly twisted his testicles during the 15-km journey to the infamous police interrogation centre outside Vanderbijlpark at the start of the Golden Highway.

At this centre, for the next 40 minutes they continued to interrogate him about the hand grenade incident. They pretended to hang him from

---

[16] First names of Security Branch members were not always known.

a rope, and attached electric wires again to his penis, thigh and ear. It was all part of the crude softening-up process preceding a future confession. But the process was far from over.

The dead dog was again produced. Other CID were in the vicinity wondering what was going to happen next. There was an air of expectation as Cilliers instructed "Chaka" to tell Mofokeng to have sex with the lifeless animal. "*Tsamaya u kota ntja eo*," (go and have sex with that dog) he was told. Mofokeng, naked, disorientated, blood flowing from his wounded penis, had no choice but to obey. "*U kota ntja hobane lona maexile le kota dintja hlatheng*" (have sex with the dog because you exiles are used to having sex with dogs in the veld) bellowed Chaka. Laughter rocked the large room as Oupa Mofokeng was forced into an act of bestiality. Official depravity of another kind.

In the following year Mofokeng was kept in jail at a Johannesburg prison at Diepkloof and in other parts of the Vaal Triangle. According to his account during this time he refused free bail, the offer of a house, a BMW, and furniture to the cost of R60 000 if only he would forget that his ill-treatment had happened. He also refused to join the CID. These refusals annoyed his captors.

One late night the police took him from his cell and brought him to the Sebokeng courthouse, scene of the crime of which he was accused. It was about 10.30 p.m. They wanted, they said, to check the metal detector equipment at the site of the original transfer of the hand grenade.

Again they ordered him to strip. They forced him to bend over as they inserted a rubber-tipped five-inch rod the thickness of a broom handle far up his anus. In this position (bent over) and condition (bleeding from the anus) for the next three hours they taunted him to demonstrate for them the physical exercises and training he did as a member of MK, that is frog jumping, squatting, and so on.

Some time later Jan Oupa Mofokeng was released, charges having been dropped against him. In an out-of-court settlement he was offered R73 000 in compensation. The person who had given the hand grenade to the prisoner-in-transit was arrested, tried, convicted and jailed for 32 years. Mofokeng, who is married, still suffers from severe post-traumatic stress disorder.

Chapter 42

The church has the duty to proclaim the liberation of millions
of human beings ... the duty of assisting the birth of this liberation,
of giving witness to it, of ensuring that it is complete –
Pope Paul VI, E.N. 30

"Twenty-five churchmen and six churchwomen were each fined
R50 or ten days' imprisonment suspended for three years yesterday
by Mr BB Haasbroek in the Sebokeng Magistrate's Court. They were
convicted after being found guilty of trespassing on public property."
A newspaper carried this story on 20 January 1992.

Our appearance in court followed trespassing charges against
members of the Vaal Council of Churches during negotiations over
the supply of water and electricity to the Vaal townships.

Actually, when we left our homes that morning it wasn't in search
of protest. We were simply intervening when all other local means
of mediation had failed. The crux was the imminent switching
off of electricity in the townships because of non-payment of
electricity bills.

A small delegation had spent fruitless hours that morning appealing
to the town clerk, Nicholas Louw, not to go ahead with this type of
"punishment", while the rest of the clergy, including Bishop Peter Lee
of the Church of the Province, had been forbidden entry at the front
gate of the administration buildings on Louw's instructions. Around
midday, after another discouraging report from the meeting with the
town clerk, I suggested that we infiltrate the administration complex
by slipping past the security guards in ones and twos and meeting
outside the Transvaal Provincial Administration (TPA) offices. It
worked. We came, we met and we stayed in the TPA offices' foyer
while discussions moved into higher gear.

It was here we were arrested later that same day.

We had refused to leave the TPA offices after they closed at 4.00 p.m. We had wanted to believe that the office of the State President, FW de Klerk, was in the process of replying to urgent faxes sent from the TPA earlier that day. We were content to wait. We sang hymns to pass the time. We were perfectly aware that a balance had to be struck between a mere trespass offence and the greater good of the community we served.

We hadn't long to wait. At 4.15 p.m. big white portly policemen in camouflage dress rushed up the stairs to our level, turned, and observed keenly a motley crowd of church people calmly occupying the TPA's large foyer. My pigmentation momentarily unfocused them. But they recovered, and formally declared that we had broken the law. It was a strange moment for us clergy to be harshly addressed by policemen. Our sense of security, our clerical image of ourselves, was instantly under threat. There wasn't a church in sight to run to. We stared at the police blankly and they stared back at us, some a little nervously. They were a bit embarrassed too. But we had come so far and knew there was no turning back.

We were pronounced arrested, and, singing hymns, bundled into a *kwela-kwela* police vehicle and transported to the police station. The experience of being squashed into a police lorry like common criminals for three hours was a shocking and alienating experience. It was a lesson of closeness with the countless millions of apartheid's victims. The yellow police vehicle, so familiar a symbol of oppression, forced me to think back on the criminalised thousands, their ghosts seemed to pervade the austere interior, who had been shoved through these steel doors over the years. We were still singing. But there was no incense, candles, vestments, altar servers or congregations to accompany our deadly serious harmony. And the makeshift mobile church was a trifle claustrophobic.

Clergy forms hovering in the dark interior or clergy faces peering from behind the steel mesh of a large police lorry provoked much talk and even some self-questioning among the mainly black police personnel at Sebokeng police station. A few seemed confused or embarrassed. Some were our parishioners. Going off-duty we knew that they would spread the word around the townships.

We were released from the truck in groups of four to be led under guard to the police office to be charged. It took nearly three hours to complete the job. We asked among ourselves why did they not bring us all together into the charge office? Perhaps they wanted to teach us a lesson. Or maybe they were afraid the priests would run amok.

When finally it came to my turn to be charged the desk sergeant looked at me quizzically. He hesitated. He wondered how I, a *leghowa* (white person), got into this mess with these blacks. He smiled resignedly and began to write. Seeing him stop and shake the biro questioningly over a blank square in the charge sheet I told him to write "Celt" under the heading "Tribe" and named my "Headman/Chief" as Charles Haughey, the then Irish Prime Minister. This completely confused the policeman who had never heard of "Chief" Charles Haughey (only Chief Charles Sebe, a homeland headman) or a tribe called the Celts. I was beginning to enjoy the incongruity of my situation. The African officer scribbled "black", probably from habit, in the race category. I corrected him. And who could blame him? I was the first white he had ever charged and the first white to be charged at Sebokeng. (Much later it hit me that they might apply segregated imprisonment in my case as we were prepared for imprisonment rather than to pay fines. *That* I could not accept. Imagine being led off alone to a nice clean sanitised lily-white Vanderbijlpark prison cell.) We were ordered to appear in court on 23 July. Time 8.00 p.m. It had been a long day.

After our first court appearance (23 July 1991, remanded until 21 August 1991) the 30 robed clergy and people from various churches filed out of the courtroom, and hymn-sang their way down the crowded corridors of the courthouse. We passed black and white uncomprehending clerks and, with more church members joining, proceeded down the street to the Administration offices. Something new was afoot, they thought. Entry *en masse* was affected (I think that the security guards are still scratching their heads!) and once again the well-appointed upper chambers of the Transvaal Provincial Administration were invaded and occupied by a noisy though disciplined group of church people. For the white officials, however, it must have looked as if the clergy was on the rampage again. A feeling

203

of quiet consternation pervaded the carpeted corridors of the TPA as black assistants peeped from busy offices.

The purpose of this latest protest invasion was to advise the town clerk once again not to commence a new round of switching off township lights but rather to return to the negotiating table in good faith. Having said our piece in quite an emotionally charged atmosphere we departed just in time to avoid a second arrest as the all-white riot squad assembled at the bottom entrance. Louw's office had once again called the police.

But not before we had a short kneel-down prayer service blocking the main entrance gateway, as police Casspirs, like giant moon machines, manoeuvred into place behind and over us, I think to encourage our departure!

"Will no one rid me of this turbulent priest?" sighed King Henry II of England (1133-1189). The same sentiments must have occupied the mind of the Lekoa town clerk as he sat back in his plush chair, pulled deeply on his Rothmans cigarette, and wondered how to report this latest lapse in security, and altercation with the churches.

These were serious and grave times, times when priestly blood pressure often flew out of control. When normally sedate presbyteries suddenly went onto red alert to accommodate unscheduled meetings with unscheduled people.

But there were funny things too. I thought so anyway. During our court appearances we were cautioned a few times to stop the hymn singing while awaiting the arrival of the magistrate. We were interfering with the proceedings in neighbouring courts, they said. How can a clergyman stop singing his songs? We sang on regardless and they removed us from court at least once for disrupting the proceedings. It was also surprising and emotionally demanding for the people to see their conservative and pious priests openly defying authority. To see their priest, for the first time, in the totally vulnerable situation of being arrested. What a peculiar un-churchlike spectacle. What went through their minds, I wondered. The answer to that became clear when parishioners filled the courtroom to capacity for the five-month duration of our trial. It tickled me too that I was the first white to be tried in a black court.

Our dress code also ignored court conventions. We wore colourful liturgical dress for all five appearances after our arrest, a touch of ecclesiastical pageantry. Our wardrobe was enhanced by the fact that among the other 16 churches whose members were arrested, we had three bishops, an Anglican archdeacon and executive members of the Vaal Council of Churches.

The magistrate's court of Sebokeng was our altar and our pulpit. We had to be properly dressed for such occasions forced on us by the state – indeed, we felt that we had to turn the occasion to our advantage. Surrounded by milling crowds in crowded corridors it was important to send public signals of peaceful defiance whenever the opportunity arose.

We knew our people and our people knew us. They understood our message.

The town clerk was asked during the trial why he found it necessary to call in the riot squad to arrest the clergy. He replied that it was a precaution in case someone was carrying an AK-47. I wondered if all town clerks took such a dim view of priests and ministers?

After our fourth appearance on 4 November 1991, we were conducted to the charge office for two hours of noisy reluctant fingerprinting. Clearly somebody in the Vaal legal system didn't like us.

We were determined to use this deliberately drawn-out trial to reach the minds and hearts of state employees – to assist them to question their long-held loyalties and thus prepare them to cope with new allegiances in the future. The black police fingerprinting their own priests and ministers seemed deeply embarrassed. They were very apologetic. They had been told to do it by the whites they said. We understood.

Once fingerprinted, and being people of the cloth, somebody proposed prayer. Now serious criminal work, humour and religion combined to forge a new form of dissent. We joined hands in a circle, insisting that male and female police officers join us. The 25-minute prayer meeting resounded throughout the police station with hymns punctuated by impromptu homilies of a bloodcurdling anti-police anti-apartheid nature by some of our church ladies. All work at the two-storey police station seemed to come to a halt. Ordinary decent black policemen and women seemed confused, placed in a situation where their loyalties were blurring.

Impromptu public prayer became a feature of our discontent. Before entering the courthouse for each of our five appearances, we formed a large circle with supporters among the street hawkers, and prayed and sang hymns. This was public witnessing geared to send reminders of political deliverance to the surrounding crowds.

Chapter 43

On the day of our trial, 12 January 1992, the public gallery was crammed with visitors, activists and trade unionists monitoring the trial. Camouflaged riot police rubbed shoulders with colourfully cassocked ministers and lay leaders from the Methodist, Presbyterian, Anglican, Zionist, Catholic, Dutch Reformed and Apostolic Churches. Outside the court police vans were parked ominously all day in case of incidents, and more arrived in the late afternoon to whisk us away when convicted.

Our advocate, Gys Rautenbach, knew we were prepared to be convicted and jailed by nightfall. He had been instructed so. He remembers being uneasy about it. His interest, his learning, his profession, his instinct was to help people *avoid* going to jail.

The trial got under way in an atmosphere of tension and anticipation. The magistrate was clearly unhappy that the clergy had pleaded not guilty. Why could they not have paid an admission of guilt months ago and got it over with?

Rautenbach urged the magistrate to impose a fine on all the accused. Alas, it was our plan not to pay any fine. And he knew this too. Thus refusing to pay a fine we would be bundled off to prison – and create a stink in our church communities and further afield.

But there was a twist. During the many adjournments it had crossed my mind that before the case ended the churches must use the opportunity to explain their position. I felt the big picture needed exposure. My colleagues in the Council of Churches enthusiastically supported the idea. I composed a speech highlighting the unhappy relations between the church and state in the region. (I knew that for many years the apartheid administration of the area had consistently refused us a church site in Bophelong.) Perhaps it was an oversight that we did not inform our advocate of our intentions.

We came to court ready to explain ourselves to the world. We decided that our secretary at the Council of Churches, Reverend Isaac Kolokoto of the Dutch Reformed Church, would deliver the address. During the exhausting third recess there was high drama when Reverend Kolokoto, Reverend Moerane, SACC activist Saul Tsotetsi and I informed advocate Rautenbach of our intentions to deliver a speech. Understandably he became agitated at this late intervention. Quickly he scanned the five-page speech and lapsed into a state of apprehension. He strongly advised against our course of action.

But we were luminously clear about what we must do. Clever human arguments would have to take a back seat – at least for this final section of the trial. We knew we must grasp this crucial moment. We did not expect legal people to understand that this case had prophetic implications beyond the scope of their work. That is why we had earlier passed over young local lawyer Peter Mahlung. Most legal people live and practise outside the province of Biblical prophecy. Understandably, conscientious (or Christian) witness is not necessarily their domain. They normally deal with criminals and we didn't think we were criminals. We were leaders of a community who had to lead by example in critical times. People expected nothing less.

Rautenbach threw up his hands and resigned himself to the inevitable. The address that caused the uproar during the final moments of our trial before sentencing follows:

"Your Worship, Members of the Public, unlike churchmen of the recent past who have involved themselves in party politics, such as joining the National Party, the Conservative Party, Homeland parties etc. we stand before you today as members of no political party with no political axe to grind.

The riot squad unit of the South African police arrested us on June 3rd at the administration/TPA offices at Sebokeng. We came there simply to impress on the local authorities the dangers inherent in switching off the township electricity and further to send a strong signal to these same authorities to take the initiative in breaking the deadlocked rent negotiations between themselves and the VCA.

It was not a planned affair but assumed a certain urgency, we
believe justly so, as the hour for switching off of township lights
approached and passed on that fateful day. Profound Christian
concern motivated our subsequent actions. We plead guilty of
active non-violent peacemaking. We have, with our people,
experienced the jackboot application of evil and immoral laws
during the years of apartheid.

We believe too, passionately, that people are more important than
laws; that love, not law, is primary in the eyes of God.

We associate ourselves with Christ who spoke harsh words to the
leaders of his day who applied and interpreted laws at the expense
of love and concern for the poor. We must not – we dare not stand
aloof from the grief and anguish, the joys and hopes of the people
we serve. The church after the example of Christ must reach out
to the poor and dispossessed.

To do this in the Vaal Triangle the church has had to pay the
price. Indeed this case, to be seen in proper perspective, must be
situated in a context which clearly demonstrates the fractured
state of relations between township churches and the state
administration. This, in spite of efforts by employees of this board
(Lekoa Town Council) to woo the churches. The organs of
oppression and the agents of religion make bad bedfellows!

We will not forget that September day in 1984 when the chief
director of the Orange-Vaal Development Board declared, as
reported in the media, that the "burning of shops and the driving
out of community council members was planned … with the
wholehearted co-operation and direction" of church ministers.

We will not forget the letters and notices sent by the Orange-Vaal
Development Board to churches in 1984 designed to intimidate
church ministers so that they wouldn't allow their churches to be
used for meetings where residents discussed their problems.

The Van der Walt Commission of Enquiry (1985) told the world
that the widespread corruption among certain employees of this
board was a serious cause of the riots which engulfed the Vaal some
years ago, leaving at least seventy-five dead.

Was it not from the same Orange-Vaal Development Board that the covert campaigns (youth camps) for the "hearts and minds" of our youth emanated during the 1985 to 1987 period?

Was it not Nicholas Louw himself, who in 1984 refused entry to a white colleague of ours when he arrived for negotiations as a member of a people's emergency delegation – a decision clearly based on the discriminatory philosophy of the time?

We, as servants of the people of God, seeking to be "instruments of peace", have in the recent past been maligned ruthlessly both by visible and invisible, colluding right-wing forces linked to local and national organisations (e.g. *Signposts*, IFF, local anti-church leaflet campaigns).

We will continue, in the power of the Spirit, to resist any "peace" or "truth" manufactured or engineered to serve the purposes of a prevailing ideology (apartheid). Christ is truly "our peace" (Ephesians 2:14).

We will continue to resist subtle local efforts (e.g. this trial) to discredit the church's solidarity with the poor (Luke 4:18) who in the eyes of Jesus are blessed (Luke 6:20).

The Sebokeng Administration Board, past powerhouse and local executor of grand apartheid, and site of our arrest, is destined to remain a mute testimony for future generations to the degradation and devastation wrought by that divisive ideology.

It may be noted that a priest – Peter Shanahan – serving in the Vaal Triangle was deported in 1970 with, as the records will show, the "common cause" participation of the then administration authorities. Further harassment of church personnel reached new heights in the middle eighties when four prominent clergymen were arrested, two of whom (Lord McCamel, McCamel Church of God, and Reverend Geoff Moselane, Anglican, were subsequently involved in the now infamous and aborted Delmas Treason Trial. The Reverend Luther Mateza, Presbyterian, and Reverend Washington Malumbazo, African Presbyterian Church, were among those arrested.

Indeed we are of the opinion that the only decent, Christian option open to all former unrepentant field managers (development board officials) of the heresy of apartheid is to resign immediately or go on early pension!

This court sits in strange, peculiar and unhappy circumstances. Circumstances dictated by a bleeding nation desperately seeking to escape from its past greed and sinfulness. We, the voteless leaders of thousands of Christians in the Vaal Triangle, may well be judged guilty by this court. We will thus be criminalised like countless millions of apartheid's victims. We were honoured to walk in such company.

And you Vereeniging and Vanderbijlpark (see Matthew 11:21) (and Meyerton and Sasolburg)! Haven and refuge of apartheid's secret and overt security machinery for over four decades of wasted public resources. You sent your husbands and sons to arrest, detain and imprison us when our righteous anti-apartheid rage spilled over in 1960, 1976 and 1984. You voted into power, locally and nationally, politicians who ensured that you would remain blinkered and blinded by your own small-minded and petty affairs. You accepted our money but never us (in 1984 black buying power in the Vaal area was at least R200 million). For the record, local priest Benen Fahy had offered Mayor Mahlatsi a plan in 1983 to retrieve "black" money from white towns for the upkeep of the townships. As your police Casspirs and police Hippos trundled from your centres to our centres, your sense of security was assured. And when 31 church people were arrested on June 3, 1991 you still did not seem to care.

We weep for your silence, the comfortable silence of a domesticated Christ. And yet, as Christians, as church people, we are compelled to discern the "signs of the times" (Luke 12:54-59). The Spirit is powerfully at work in our land today. Ever sensitive to our call we as church leaders strive to be willing and active if weak agents of that Spirit. We believe that this Spirit is calling all Vaal Christians to repentance, reconciliation and finally fellowship – in a renewed context of justice, love and equality. We await genuine Christian gestures and overtures from our fellow Christian sisters and brothers of Vereeniging and

211

Vanderbijlpark. The scandal of our division has gone on for too long. We have sinned, have we not?"

Reverend Kolokoto stepped down from the dock. The silence was long and deep.

The magistrate, Mr BB Haasbroek, in passing judgement after the third recess of the day-long trial, indicated that the penalty for a case like this was R2 000 or two years' imprisonment. But after noting everything that had been presented, especially the address of the clergymen from the dock, he sentenced the churchmen and lay leaders to R50 or 10 days, suspended for three years. Did he sense that we were going to refuse to pay any fines he might impose, we wondered? Haasbroek went back to his chambers.

We briefly considered appealing, as a suspended sentence was seen as inhibiting the work of the churches in the area. In the end we decided to ignore the court ruling as quite irrelevant if not a bit impertinent.

The names and titles of the clergy who were arrested:

Marcel Ntoane, 49, Sacred Heart Sodality, Movement of Christian Workers – Emmanuel Catholic parish, Sebokeng.

Anna Zwane, 50, Lay Preacher, African Methodist Episcopal Church.

Selina Mokoena, 54, Sacred Heart Sodality, Nyolohelo Catholic parish, Sebokeng.

Maria Mohapeloa, 74, Emmanuel Ethiopian Church in South Africa.

Rosa Mokoena, 64, St Anne's Sodality, Emmanuel Ethiopian Church in South Africa.

Paulina Selebeleng, 39, Mother's Union, St Michael's Anglican parish, Sebokeng.

Job Macatshwa, 65, New Nazareth Good Nation Apostolic Church in South Africa.

Reverend Isaac Kolokoto, 36, NGK, SACC (Vaal) Organising Secretary.

Reverend Peter Moerane, 37, St John's Apostolic Church, SACC (Vaal) fieldworker.

Reverend David Dinkebogile, 37, St Cyprian's Anglican parish, Sharpeville.

Reverend Sipho Chalete, 29, Apostolic Faith Mission.

Reverend Johannes Skhosana, 28, Apostolic Faith Mission.

Nimrod Moss, 66, Ethiopian Church in Zion.

Phillip Cindi, 24, Lay Preacher, African Methodist Episcopal Church.

Reverend Patrick Noonan, 49, Franciscan, Emmanuel and Bophelong Catholic Church.

Reverend Ndzane Mali, 65, Mountain Apostolic Church in South Africa, SACC (Vaal).

Reverend Herbert Koaho, 57, NGK Sebokeng, SACC (Vaal).

Ernest Skosana, Lay Preacher, Methodist Church of South Africa.

David Tsotetsi, 44, Minister of the Eucharist, Emmanuel Catholic parish, Sebokeng.

Sam Ntepe, 42, Bishop, Christian Assembly Faith Church.

Reverend John Mqebwasa, New Holy Catholic Church.

Stephen Motloung, 64, Minister of Eucharist, Refenkhotso Catholic parish.

Israel Qwelane, 47, Archdeacon, St Michaels and St. Lawrence Anglican parishes, Sebokeng/Evaton, SACC (Vaal).

Reverend Jacob Moleli, Robinson African Methodist Episcopal Church.

Archibald Monyake, 25, Lay Preacher, Anglican Church.

Bethuel Lehoko, 27, Lay Minister, Anglican Church, Sebokeng.

Andries Mngomezulu, 73, Bishop, Foundation Apostolic Church in S.A.

Frans Tokota, 72, Bishop, Prayer of God Catholic Apostolic Church in S.A.

Casbah Tau, 33, Lay Minister, Nyolohelo Catholic parish, Sebokeng.

Soloman Tana, Chairman, Justice and Peace Committee, Vaal.

Karabo Molefe, International Assemblies of God, Sharpeville.

Chapter 44

Theresa Ramashamole was the only female amongst the Sharpeville Six. Some time prior to her release in December 1991, after years of communicating through glass and a type of pipe fitting, I was told by her mother that a "contact" visit was now possible. I went to see her at Johannesburg Prison in Diepkloof, Soweto.

I understood that Theresa was not getting on well with her warders. While at Pretoria Maximum a male warder was alleged to have broken her arm during an altercation.

After some time I was politely ushered through steel doors and eventually into a room in which sat Theresa and a very stern-looking and plumpish female warder. We embraced for the first time since she had been arrested seven years earlier. It was a strange emotional moment for me when I considered the long years of bizarre trauma she had faced since. The stern warder remained seated facing both of us and was obviously obliged, indeed determined, to listen to our conversation. Orders, I supposed. After some casual remarks of greeting we seated ourselves in a sort of threesome. I began to speak in Sesotho and was soon informed by you-know-who that the exchanges were to be in English only.

It was becoming clear that Theresa was not herself – her smile was wan, zombie-like. She looked tired and was clearly under pressure, if not depressed. Unlike her usual self, she appeared unresponsive, which spoke volumes. The message was clear. I had to think of some way of communicating with her before leaving. The inspiration came just when I wanted it.

The medium was prayer. And why not? It would be expected. The *moruti* (the minister) is expected to pray. As the warder indicated that the time was up, I jumped up, advanced towards Theresa and suggested that we have a closing prayer. Seeing my virtuous priestly intentions, the warder duly closed her eyes, bowed her head and waited. Laying hands on Theresa's head and shoulders, I exclaimed, "Heavenly Father we place ourselves before You," and I reverted to praying in Sesotho, assuring Theresa that I understood and knew about the predicament she was in just then. And just as suddenly, I reverted to English, "Jesus we love You and praise Your Holy name." And then it was back to Sesotho, "Theresa, I hear you might be released soon," and immediately to English again as I nearly swooned in prayerful fervour. The warder wasn't about to interrupt a church minister prayerfully breaking the language rule.

Theresa, demure, eyes closed, listened intently and enjoyed the prayerful deception. I prolonged the prayer as much as possible, alternating between bouts of praise for Jesus (English) and encouragement (Sesotho) for Theresa. Finally I ended the invocation and the warder's head gradually eased up, bathed in beatific light and a confident born again smile. Theresa and I beamed knowingly as we embraced and parted. The visit was over. God loved it!

Since the prison officers refused to give me information about rumours that Theresa would be released soon, it struck me to try another ploy. I made my way down to the visitors' section where I was fortunately recognised by an African uniformed clerk as a priest of her own church. I asked her in Sesotho, over the shoulder of an officious white clerk, if Theresa's file was there. She went away to check, assured that her white superior hadn't understood our conversation. I watched her rummaging in a filing cabinet. She came back and told me it had been removed, a definite sign that Theresa was due for release. Praise Jesus! I wanted to hug her for breaking security regulations so professionally. I was quietly exhilarated as we tailed off our chat, which by now was safely back on church matters. A tiny victory over the system, I thought, as I searched for the car park. I fumbled for my car keys. I had news for Theresa's mother.

That clerk wasn't the only person in government employment to assist us illegally in those days. Thlathla was another.

Chapter 45

Noko Anthony Thlathla, a policeman and well known figure in Vaal church circles, knew his life's options were narrowing prematurely as the last years of apartheid dragged inexorably to their final consummation. Northern Transvaler, boxing enthusiast, Bible teacher and brother of a Black Consciousness activist, Thlathla was compulsively cheerful. This quality certainly helped him keep his head above water during those dreadfully stressful times – especially as a policeman. Indeed he would have thankfully retired from the force in the early 1980s but for the fact of his upcoming pension.

Eventually, in the best interests of his family, he moved from Sebokeng to the safer and quieter suburbs of Vereeniging. Even there, informally, people came to him with family problems or for legal advice. He was that kind of person.

His life's journey became increasingly painful as he wrestled with his Christian conscience on the one hand and the ideological dictates of his job on the other. A regular church attendee – many Christian police and army personnel avoided church during the last years of apartheid – he was often obliged to sit through, if a little ruefully, Masses where Christian social teaching was constantly alluded to.

Nevertheless, he would not allow alienation from the church to set in. Was it his Pax Institution grounding in the faith or his Barolong ancestry – or both, that made him different from others?

As I said, laughter was part of his life. One Saturday evening in 1979 he attended a Church Justice and Peace meeting in Johannesburg. Introducing himself as a member of the police force he brought the house down with laughter at the incongruity of the situation. He actually joined in the hilarity that followed. At the time he was representing the St Joseph's parish at Boipatong. He was saved, he once told me, with that familiar burst of laughter, on a few occasions from the hands of marauding, angry political mobs targeting his police van, by declaring himself a church member.

During the 1980s he was to be found each Sunday morning teaching Bible and religious formation in his Zone 14 parish after Sunday services. Then it was off to his second-floor office at the Sebokeng police station. It was from this second-floor office in the political hurricane years of the early 1980s that he, more than once, secretly furnished the clergy with the charge sheets of those detained in mass arrests. This enabled the churchmen to get legal assistance for the detainees. During the detention of Litau Litau, an old Sebokeng activist, Thlathla more than once secretly visited the prisoner's home to get a change of clothes (unironed, rolled in a ball, in supermarket plastic bag, for easier transit and least detection) to be smuggled in to the section-29 detainee.

One morning in 1994, I sat pondering for some time the bullet-marked Station Commander's office where, on 5 October that year, Noko Anthony Thlathla was shot dead while mediating the domestic problems of a police couple. Two other policemen died in the same incident, including the killer himself, a policeman – by his own hand. Thlathla was buried in his Secular Franciscan habit (he had been a member of this lay order dedicated to living according to the spirit of St Francis) just three weeks after the murder of Father Thabo Mokomele (OFM), his spiritual assistant.

Chapter 46

Bureaucrats were always the most important people in our country. That's a lesson I learned soon after arriving in South Africa. During daylight hours if you were white you had to get a permit under the following law (Government Gazette 14/6/68 No 2068 Q15729 Paragraph 19):

Section (1):

"Any person, other than a Bantu, desirous of entering the Bantu residential area, shall, prior to or on arrival, apply for an entry permit at the office of the superintendent, his assistant or such other officer of the Council as the superintendent may designate."

However in Section (6) a little-known paragraph had the following information:

"The following persons shall be exempt from the provisions of these regulations: Ministers of Religion, registered medical practitioners, nurses and midwives, in the lawful following of this profession or calling, and Missionaries who are marriage officers."

I was a so-called missionary and minister of religion but not a marriage officer. I hoped they would be happy with that.

I needed permission another time. In 1972, a fellow priest and I wanted to see an African show at the famous Wilberforce AME Training College in Evaton. It was Gibson Kente's musical hit *Sikhalo*. A black policeman had once earnestly questioned Father Dominic Hession at Sharpeville for attending a performance there. The policeman had called him out of the hall to demand his permit to be in the black area at night. Was he not afraid of being in the township at night, the policeman wanted to know. The same seriousness applied to blacks in white areas after dark.

Looking back I'm embarrassed that I asked for a permit to go to that show. I now confess my timidity. Somebody out there give me absolution! We knew a bureaucrat's piece of paper might save us hassles. This was our reasoning. We were still learners. Captain Botes (a friendly chap who once wanted to be a preacher himself) of the South Africa Police gave us the following note for an after-hours visit to the township:

S A Police Residensia   11/2/1972
To Whom It May Concern
This is to certify that the S A Police have no objection to
Fathers Noonan and Hession of the Roman Catholic Church
to enter and be in the area of Sebokeng to attend an African
play in the Bantu township on 11/2/1972.
Signed: Capt. Botes

He graciously rang the feared Mr Kruger of the Management Board at Sebokeng for a second permission – and confirmation of the first:

Bearer hereof permitted to be in the area of the
Management Board of Sebokeng on 11/2/1972 to attend an
African play in the Bantu township.
Authority granted by Mr Kruger of the Management Board
of Sebokeng.
Signed: Capt. Botes (South African Police)

Even now I feel nostalgic when I hear songs from *Sikhalo*. I vividly remember being moved by the passion and emotion with which the songs were sung and the story was told. The whole experience (including the permits) was, I think, a watershed for me. Thank you, playwright Gibson Kente, for the memory.

The story I am about to tell is all about impact – the human environment's impact on me and my impact on my immediate surroundings. My mythologies, religion, family, Irish inheritance and South African citizenship, as well as my day-to-day experiences, no doubt colour my perceptions and observations in the telling. And why not? Can it be otherwise?

~

Dear Reader, I would like to take you on a drive through the dirt roads of Sebokeng and Evaton in the late 1970s. There is so much to say, to unload. I'm white – pink, more precisely, having been raised with a mop of red hair. I have been living and working in these black ghettos for over thirty years, the "end years" of the old, unforgettable South Africa.

Let's start our drive in Evaton.

In the late 1970s the Vaal townships under the paternal guardianship of Chief Director John Knoetze are seen as a political success story for his administration board. Politicians from Pretoria come to see for themselves and depart suitably impressed. Earnest-looking white employees of the board are regularly seen scurrying around the townships in their white bakkies. There is a hint of the messianic about them as they supervise building and construction sites. Do they need to fill their petrol tanks daily to do that? – the cynics ask, implying that there is a lot of corruption in white administration circles. Perhaps. I hear the distant voice of Elijah Moremi, a restricted person in the late 1970s, describing the corruption of officials in the administration of the townships. He suffered for knowing too much about how the Sebokeng managers feathered their neatly developed nests. He was so passionate about that.

Sometimes as white officials pass there's a nod of racial solidarity, white-to-white acknowledgement. An ethnic group instinctively acknowledges its own. I find myself unable to respond to this. I reason that I don't need the acknowledgement. It leaves me with a funny hollow feeling pondering the peculiar, exclusive world the nodding white driver inhabits. Other times their faces register sudden shock, as if I shouldn't be in their township without their permission.

Mr Johan Maritz, the Zone 12 superintendent, however, is an amiable sort. He is proud of his Zone. Proud of his friends, the dry cleaners at the shopping centre who offer cups of tea to carefully guided tourists who in the 1970s stopped to view the Bantu in their natural habitat.

He is smart too. Knowing that whites have to be out of the townships by four in the afternoon, on occasion he asks Father Dominic where he can contact him at say five or six o'clock in the afternoon, thus letting the reverend know that he should be out of the area by four o'clock.

Business booms in the dingy semi-barred-up shops of Evaton, where once the Russians and Msomi gangs roamed the streets. High-up white administration board officials have developed excellent working relations with many of these township business people. These businesses have become outlets for private farming produce of administration board officials. On Adams Road near Central I pass a shop reputed to sell Kruger's hens. Hens are big business and board men are rumoured to use the local shops for their foul play! Steenkamp, the Superintendent of Zone 7, owns a café in Boipatong and, like his colleagues, calls in regularly to see how things are going.

We pass the old hall at Small Farms and note the windows covered in black plastic refuse bags. Some "skop, skiet en donder" film no doubt featuring today – until the projector breaks down. It always does.

Posters outside the church include: Guinness; Miss Lovely Legs competition on 10 August; Holy St Patrick v Joshua XI next Saturday; Bruce Lee film 3.30 and 6 p.m.; beauty competition for grandmothers; fundraising events for a new church; a youth conference; an ordination to the priesthood.

Some shop owners are community councillors. Good men, decent men, portly, affable, the type of person the board could deal with. Yes, many marriages of convenience and profit were solemnised at this time between white administration officials and sometimes-fawning township shop owners.

As I leave Evaton for Zone 3, Ma Modise waves to me. I remember when one evening in July 1978 I visited the family, she told me that on that very day she had paid out the last of the family's savings (R800) on fines because she hadn't got a permit (section 10) to be in the area. Things like this kept my anger well oiled. Sometime later, through the use of her son's next meagre salary, she was able to buy the section 10 and with obvious pleasure showed it to me.

Ah, but let us move on.

Chapter 47

Was it in the late 1970s or early 1980s that the next part of my story begins? I am not sure, but I do know that apartheid was in its noisy, arrogant heyday when I quietly began to live in the townships to the astonishment of the local administration board and their friends in security. Now a white "illegally" living in the township or even, for that matter, dallying after hours was always a source of concern for the authorities. And lurking in the background was the ever-present murky issue of the Immorality Act, so loved by curious police constables and captains in their bizarre search for hot semen-drenched sheets! (South African police regularly raided the bedrooms of inter-racial frolickers and tested the temperature and contents of the sheets for evidence against them in any future trial.)

"We know the white Roman *predikants* (Catholic priests) are staying in the townships. Fucking kaffir boeties!" one policeman was heard whispering under his breath one morning after an inquiry from a priest. So I began to live in the township, and then so did other priests – like Edward Lennon.

The state did not like it; the church, cleverly enough, did not ask any questions. And my religious order, very wisely, said nothing. But God smiled. It was another personal watershed.

People reacted in different ways to our white presence. Some were mystified at first, especially members of other Christian communities. Conversations might have gone like this: "Staying in the location, eh, right here in the location ... right in Sebokeng/Sharpeville, *Modimo!*" exclaimed Ma Matela to her neighbour Ma Masipha one morning on the way to a spaza shop.

"Man, ke tla re'ng? Ke dipolitiki." (What can I say? It's politics.)

"I'd say it is," agreed Ma Masipha as she called her child to go to the shops for a colddrink.

"And their wives, have you seen them yet?" a third neighbour intervened from her garden fence, having heard the story earlier.

"Atjhe, how will their children play with ours? Don't whites speak Afrikaans? Maybe they'll learn Sesotho. Hey ye ye ye ye ye. I really don't know," mused Ma Matela at length.

"Let me ask Mathabo tomorrow. Isn't she a Roman?" allowed the third neighbour.

"I wonder will they go to our stokies and spots (self-help parties and shebeens) too?" Ma Masipha enquired again, looking nervously in the direction of the church.

"I don't know," replied the neighbour, adding, "Maybe they'll marry blacks too, if they're not married." Laughter all round.

Parishioners loved it and talked about it a lot amongst themselves. Those on the margins of our congregations expressed a little worry for our safety. How would blacks take to whites living in the neighbourhood? they asked. Those closer to the centre of church life, however, happily handled questions and enquiries, all of which raised social consciousness and provoked questioning of the policy of separate development. And that was healthy.

Living in the townships illegally was a public statement on our part, which was celebrated by the parishioners. In the process, it heightened their awareness of being victims of a pernicious policy. We deliberately never spoke about it publicly in church. We did not need to. The process was more effective than any one-off anti-government statement.

Our immediate neighbours talked among themselves about it – some were a little worried that it would attract police attention. Others among them were confused that whites wanted to break "their own laws". This smaller group, who had unconsciously internalised what apartheid expected of them, tended to equate government policy with divine law!

~

A memory from this time: outside the gates of the churchyard teenagers playing football part and stop playing as I steer past the two beercan goal posts, narrowly avoiding the old tennis ball that has rolled to a halt near the front wheel of the van. During the football lull some wave as others not yet familiar with me study my presence against the background of the church, and rightly so, as my alien whiteness sticks out like a sore thumb. Their young minds are racing to make sense of this unusual appearance, given the accumulating baggage they are carrying about whites. For years the first whites that township children ever saw were police raiding their homes at one in the morning, arresting their parents for pass offences and carting them off to police stations to be fined because they did not have Section 10 (legal rights to stay or live there). The "Black Jacks" (raiding police) were good at their jobs and some of them loved the power it conferred. The youngsters playing football on the street know things like this as I slowly drive past.

~

Small children, however, always wanted to make a fuss of me. They often waved and shouted, "Father", and if it was near Christmas, "Fada Kismas". In some neighbourhood streets it becomes a chorus of "Fadas" from little toddlers, and I used to feign surprise to make them laugh – a bit embarrassed by their noisy charming spontaneity. But this only wound them up for the next time I passed. These regular and seemingly insignificant street encounters, sifted and diffused by the kids, helped to cement and enhance my developing relationship with the local community. They elicited and nourished in the broader community a climate of acceptance and trust.

My impossible challenge of course was to continually redefine my white existence in the townships so that it became as invisible as possible. No, not that I became invisible which was quite impossible, but that my whiteness shouldn't become a hindrance to my calling as an agent of hope in a situation of much hopelessness. Any attempt to become racially invisible in a so-called black area was a little presumptuous. Especially in a society designed and engineered specifically to isolate and promote differences among its populations.

My own parish community, knowing me more intimately, was the chief catalyst of my indigenisation on the local level. The parishioners actively marketed me in their homes, their neighbours' homes, their shebeens, taverns, night clubs, shops and spazas. I got used to heads turning curiously when I walked into a township shop for a newspaper or a packet of chips, or a freeze in time at the post office – my diary tells the story:

> *I'm collecting the post one day in 1990. As I enter the post office and join the queue at Masoheng, next to the hostel, all look around and someone greets me knowingly. I return the greeting in the local language and a new signal goes out that the Roman* moruti *(Catholic priest) speaks Sesotho. People relax noticeably and the teller, momentarily distracted, looks up from his triple-page receipt book and gives a friendly nod. A chat with an old friend, Father Photolo – the Anglican priest coming to collect his post – follows. And a greeting from someone who says he wants to come and see me about something.*

Chapter 48

Within the structures of the faith community my role as a priest was to sow seeds for the transformation of society in the Spirit of Christ, building, uniting and maintaining unity in a community of hope, liberation and Christian self-determination. I was a faith worker, listening and learning from others as we mutually sought to unearth and interpret the active presence of God in our cultural environment; a person of religion who searches for God's point of view in local situations.

As a priest, an expatriate embedded in my own culture, I had to unlearn all my Euro-centric assumptions. That was difficult. And I was a slow learner. In the area of community development I had to learn to stay in the background, to enable the leadership role of the people to emerge, to express itself, to develop and finally to take charge. It was important, indeed crucial to discern change within a group – change that was in line with that group's frame of reference.

During church meetings as a white priest I needed to refrain from fulfilling a perceived South African white role of dominating, deciding for, telling or directing the participants how things should be done. Again I was a slow learner. A *City Press* journalist put it succinctly when he said, "for one whose mind had been conditioned to apartheid the appearance of a white liberal was something similar to the appearance of God." My fellow black church ministers, even during the black consciousness years of the late 1970s, never hinted that we were at any time unwelcome – ever! Nor did the people either – at any time.

With delightful irony our white presence at some community gatherings served to give the quest for radical political change some legitimacy in the eyes of a certain type of otherwise conservative or timid black citizens born and bred into the "white is right" mould. It prodded them into questioning their stance in relation to changing society and thus perhaps broadened the support base for change. By the time of the Delmas Treason Trial in 1987, conservative church "*manyano*" (church women's organisations) were flocking to the trial court. The treason trialists and their legal team noted with singular satisfaction this community-based support for their important cause.

A smaller role was to allow our African church colleagues to make use of our "whiteness" for some particular urgent and immediate end not that it always worked. An example was appointing Father Edward Lennon to a people's delegation to meet the white-controlled Lekoa Town Council during the heat of the uprising of 1984. As it happened Nicholas Louw, the all-powerful town clerk, refused him entrance, insisting that a white couldn't be on a black people's delegation. Surely Louw was fiddling with racism here. Today it's called using the "race card" when trapped in a corner of one's own making. And how did the Indian and white conservative business people of Vereeniging feel when in 1990 they saw two white priests in the front row of a teachers' protest march surging through their town?

State security people hunched and bunched in their white, dark-windowed security cars (identifiable by their numerous aerials) knew that some of us township priests were foreign nationals and that one had been effectively deported in 1970. But the police were badly shaken when we discovered, in the late 1970s, their smear campaign to discredit us. The people had told us that the Security Branch was planting nasty whisperings about us in Sebokeng township.

The normal day-to-day running of our parishes – our traditional ministries – demanded attention and indeed enabled us at all times to retain intimate contact with the community. Pastoral service such as home Masses (devotional or religious celebrations in homes as distinct from church), healing and hospital ministry, baptisms and marriages with their appropriate preparations, counselling, skills training in do-it-yourself caring for others, all served to keep us rooted in the broken lives of the people.

But all this was about to change.

Christian fellowship, solidarity and calling redefined itself at this
time and took on new, unprecedented forms after the critical uprising
of the 1980s in the Vaal Triangle. The churches suddenly leaped to the
fore, organising and participating in political funerals, regular
attendance at inter-church clergy meetings, community meetings,
sermons aimed at progressive opinion-makers and conservative
Christians alike, private meetings with political strategists and
community leaders, irritating the state by making church property
available both secretly and publicly for anti-apartheid meetings,
displaying awareness-raising posters on church walls (until they were
removed by the Special Branch), discreet and public empathy with the
ideals and aims of AZAPO, the UDF, COSAS and other community
organisations. This activity of the churches raised consciousness of our
Christian service role in the black community to a level hitherto
unheard of. It also brought new responsibilities on our part and new
expectations on the part of the people of God. The apparently new role
of the historic churches was profoundly unsettling to the "plantation
politics" of the black local government structures, some of whose
stakeholders saw themselves as upright members of various
conservative Christian denominations.

~

The churches, which were strategically located throughout the Vaal
townships, became accepted centres of opposition politics. For us
church ministers it was at times highly unnerving, as members of the
former VMSG will surely attest. This extraordinary grouping of
churchmen, whether we liked it or not, was to be instrumental in
ushering us into high-profile community leadership during the darkest
(or greatest) hours of Vaal Triangle history. For me it was a profound
moment of passing over, an initiation, a rite of passage to a new
consciousness of self and of people's perceptions of me. It was another
step in my declassification, my assimilation, my incorporation.

Frankly, I had to ask myself many years ago how I could live at
peace with myself while daily breathing the suffocating fumes of the
government's unchristian policies. Given that apartheid was in direct
confrontation with authentic religion, all church leaders – of all

religions – had to face this crucial question in the privacy of their hearts. What I have outlined here so far, is my not-so-brave, clumsy reaction to the question. My church peers used to observe sagely: "Do the best you can in the circumstances you find yourself in." But what is the best for God, I thought? Who can define it? The Old Testament prophets got into bad trouble when they tried. And do we Christian mortals, left to ourselves, always seek out circumstances in life best suited to promote the project of God? Not always. Often the Spirit cannot blow where he wishes because of our manipulation of circumstances.

It had always been my instinctive intention, my basic instinct, to use my privileged church position in the townships to undermine and subvert, in various ways, the established disorder of the day as it impinged on the communities I was close to. The chief vehicle for this process was the weekly celebration of Mass where the Good News of salvation was proclaimed – often in and through the vivid liberation spirituality of the Bible and localised by the social teaching of the church over many years. My colleagues in some other churches felt the same way.

My strength as a priest I knew was my direct insertion into the community and the people's acceptance and deepening, even at times, frightening, trust in me. I would use that trust to promote the powerful Christian calling to search out "the Way, the Light, and the Truth" in all its ramifications right down to pot-holed street level. These sentiments, this urge or feeling was not something particular to me. It was the common experience of many religious and Christian leaders who dared like St Francis to reach beyond the accepted man-made parameters of their special calling.

~

My involvement with people at this level hadn't been something I suddenly decided to embark on when I arrived in South Africa. It wasn't a dormant feeling blossoming on encountering evil. The seeds of what I would hope tentatively to call a maturing compassion, seem to have been already in place before I arrived. My father caught me one morning, at 17, sticking anti-apartheid orange stickers on the walls of the family store overlooking the River Liffey in Dublin, Ireland. He had bought South African oranges that morning. My behaviour did not impress him. When I left he tore them down unceremoniously and wondered where I got these ideas.

I remember vivid photos splashed across Irish newspapers in the aftermath of the 1960 massacre at Sharpeville. Perhaps that ignited something in me. I was 18 at the time, not ever realising that I would be living in Sharpeville when the liberation struggle took another giant step forward (in the 1980s) into the future.

Indeed I can well remember the scene – a clue to my early perceptions of life in South Africa – when, with all the mystified, innocent air (and dishevelled hair) of arriving immigrants, some priests and I touched down at Jan Smuts Airport in January 1970. A little apprehensive, I wheeled past the sour-faced custom officers with a brand-new copy of Brian Bunting's *The Rise of the South African Reich* hidden deep in the copious pockets of my brown Franciscan habit. Not all thought that was a bright idea. Later I learned to conceal books and videos critical of South Africa in soiled underwear. It always worked.

But I've wandered too much. Back to my confessions, back to our drive through Sebokeng.

~

As I turn into the Pepa Ngwana section of the township, giggling schoolgirls note my passing with the shared observation "Ke Father oa Roma" (It's the Roman Father) as they straggle home in knots of black-and-white school uniforms. Entering another block you hear it before you reach his place – Bra Joe's place that is. His two big amplifiers pulverise the block with throbbing hypnotic rap played over and over again. Doors thrown open, it's stoki time. Four inebriated clients shout and wave a prolonged all-is-well-in-the-world greeting as I pass: "Hyt Gazi."

It's four o'clock in the afternoon and the midday hours of quiet are giving way to sounds of new life as weary homebound commuters, mostly at this time domestic workers, laden with plastic food bags, criss-cross the length and breath of Sebokeng and Evaton. The staff

230

from day-care centres, pre-schools, kindergarten and bridging schools
make their way home too. A new familiar vibrancy settles over the
sprawling ghettos as numerous local football teams flood into open
grounds for an hour's gymming before dusk. Since it's Thursday,
women's day, I pass women of different churches winding their way
homewards the black and purple of the St Anne's Sodality (Catholic),
the red and black for "Amawesele" (Methodist), the blue and white
uniform of "Amazayoni" (the Zionists), the black and white of the
Women's Union (Anglican) and many more.

Back in the churchyard at Zone 14, with my engine switched off
and still seated, I spend a few moments in silent rumination. A lean,
scraggy, township hen wanders into sight and I remember the words of
Norman MacCaig, the Scottish poet:

A hen stares at nothing with one eye,
Then picks it up.

Chapter 49

*Right-wing Christianity is being promoted with vigorous and
expensive campaigns in all our churches and in almost all Christian
traditions: Catholic, Reformed, Lutheran, Anglican, Evangelical and
Pentecostal ... right-wing sects are promoted in order to undermine
and divide those churches that take the side of the poor* – The Road to
Damascus, *p.14. ICT Skotaville, 1989.*
*In terms of the Bible we as Christians are told that it is our duty to
fight the anti-Christ in whichever way we can* – Convicted murderer
Clive Derby-Lewis to the TRC, 1998

People sell their souls in different ways and for different reasons.
Some are said to sell their souls to the devil and have become
satanists. There are, however, less dramatic reasons why people sell
their souls. Some do it for reasons of fear for the future; others for
financial reward. Only a few believe they are being used or bought
over by, for example, a political regime or ideology. During the final
years of apartheid the South African security system depended very
much on secret agents (sometimes called "moles", "sleepers",
informers or *"dimpimpi"*) to provide them with the necessary
information to carry out its work. Take the story of a man I will call
Abel Maluleke.

It was because of people like Abel that popular leaders were arrested
in the first place. Abel Maluleke was from a village in what is now
North-West Province. He came to Daveyton way back in the late
1970s, and stayed with his grandmother. He matriculated, got a job as
a salesman in a furniture retail firm, married, and divorced six years
later. His three children stayed with his ex-wife. He was gifted at his
job and worked hard for his monthly commission. He met and married
a second wife and they settled down in Sebokeng. It was 1985.

Apart from Sepedi, Abel had a clear aptitude for both English and Afrikaans, which he naturally used to promote his career. Given the nature of his job he was well known and had easy access to the social life of the township. Some envied his expensive possessions, especially the furnishings of his home. His up-market car, too, caused eyes to turn.

But there was another side to Abel (he never used his Sepedi name). He had a dark secret. For in the past he had been a paid informer for the Security Branch.

Nobody knew about it, he thought, not his wife, not his parents, not his children. And now apartheid was all over and he was left with the memories, guilty memories which were fuelled every time he heard mention of the TRC. He couldn't bear to look at the Sunday night TRC report on television. To think, as some would if they knew, that he had been part of these obscenities, however remotely. Ironically his wife, Florence, wouldn't miss the TRC report for anything, and insisted that the washing up be done before the weekly programme commenced.

There had, of course, been whispers unknown to him. Hints really. Sometimes strange, bland people had visited him. His wife noted that they were not buyers or bargainers, but said nothing. His brother at Boipatong had heard vague rumours. Since they were few and far between, he had dismissed them.

Abel sometimes wondered how to deal with a situation like this without making matters worse. In his quiet desperation he must remain vigilant. Periodic flashbacks gave him panic flushes and he was relieved that nobody seemed to notice, although sometimes when people appeared to stare at him at taxis he felt a wave of exposure.

Never in his wildest dreams did he think that a new South Africa would materialise, led by the very people he had informed on. His wife noticed a certain furtiveness when visitors came to see them. At times she found him peeping through the lace curtains.

Thousands more touched or untouched by the TRC proceedings were like Abel, living in the shadow of their past cloak-and-dagger existences. Some were defiant, their consciences dead. Others suffered silently, guarding their memories for dear life, fearful that their past might catch up with them. Terrified that a face in a crowd might confront them. That someone would hear something. That their children might be labelled some day. Or worse, that they might be accused by their own children. Had he really sold his soul for money? How many had suffered because of him? he wondered. Best to try not to think about it.

He decided to seek out his former handlers to discuss relocating to another area where he hoped he would be unknown, and perhaps start again. Did he not know that they had quietly joined the new Crime Investigation Service, taken up farming or had moved to some coastal retreat to live on their memories – or nightmares?

Abel finally withdrew from his former occupation. He moved house and began to attend church after many years' absence. But there were others also ready to sell their souls. They were South Africa's noisy Christian right.

~

Like sex magazines at the corner shop the magazines and pamphlets came in transparent plastic wrappings. The covers titillated, giving only a glimpse of what was lurking inside. Others came in pre-paid good quality envelopes that I wanted to keep for further use. The senders really did want to bring certain members of the clergy back to the straight and narrow. And they were bent on being listened to. I can imagine the zeal with which they dispatched their right-wing Christian magazines and pamphlets throughout the country. They never got lost in the post. They always arrived on time. Sometimes even before time. As if propelled by some secret benefactor, of which, alas, there were many in places of power.

Funnily enough I never heard priests or clergy talking about these Christian glossies. They did not cause a stir at church houses even when they arrived in twos and threes. Personally I was fascinated with the minds behind the publications, the editors, the writers, their mission statements, their fears, their concerns and worries for the future of this land.

I am talking about groups of Christian fundamentalists and their very active publishing machines that operated during the eighties. It seems they saw themselves as the last defenders of "Christian Western Civilisation" against what PW Botha called the "total onslaught" of communism – they were a type of religious arm of the government that cushioned apartheid.

I believe they were sincere people. Some, however, we now know sold their souls to the government of the day – knowingly or unknowingly. Their "Christian" worldview became suspiciously compliant to the political teachings of the old National Party. In their books, pamphlets and leaflets they regularly castigated the historical churches for having so-called communist leanings. Some were even co-opted into the National Security Management System (NSMS). (In fairness none went as far as their Austrian counterparts when that country was annexed to Germany in 1938. In gratitude for the anschluss Friedrich Werner, a member of the Ecclesiastical Council of the German Evangelical Church, called on all pastors to take an oath of allegiance to Hitler. Many did.)

These groups, generally the well-to-do, found themselves in a closed "Christian" comfort zone which by its nature virtually cut them off from any hope of "interpreting (or understanding) the signs of the times" (Luke 12:54-59; Matthew 16:1-4). Their literature, always well funded, tended to border on the hysterical. Much of it was too shrill to be taken seriously. An underlying fear (for them, justified) stalked the pages. But the loving all-embracing Lord of history was absent.

Some sample pamphlets or magazines sent to the clergy were as follows: *Tradition Family Property* (TFP) newsletter; critique of *The New Nation* newspaper and *Liberation Theology* by Young South Africans for Christian Civilisation (Johannesburg); *The Aida Parker Newsletter* (Auckland Park); *Signposts* (Arcadia) – both funded by the security arm of the former government; *Family Protection Scoreboard* (Arcadia); *Stand To* (Veterans for Victory, Houghton); *Gospel Defence League* (Cape Town); *Christian Mission International*, (Primrose); *The Catholic Defence League* (Silverton); *The Christian Resistance Group* of South Africa (Edenvale); and *Alliance for the Promotion of People's Rights* (Sandton).

How the tone of these publications differed from the *Kairos Document* (1986) that sensationally emerged from the experience of

235

conflict in the townships in 1985 and spoke about "the church of ordinary South Africans in the struggle" or the "church of the streets"! The apartheid state, the *Kairos Document* declared, was the enemy of God, a remark which sent painful spasms racing through government boardrooms.

In 1986 the American televangelist, Jimmy Swaggart (an archetypal right-wing Christian), visited South Africa and preached against communism, liberation movements and the ANC which he declared was a front for Moscow. One wonders who paid Jimmy's airfare. On the re-imposition of the State of Emergency in June of that year, the government broadcast his sermon on TV to bolster its policy. Ironically, even today, Jimmy Swaggart records are still to be found in many township homes.

Leaders of these Christian pressure groups might have redirected their energies to helping build bridges from their world of privatised piety to a more public moral responsibility. That would have been a service to South Africa. Some, perhaps, are already trying. Otherwise they fall into a category of Christian recently reproved by Pope John Paul II in *"The Coming of the Third Millennium"*. He criticised their "lack of discernment, which at times became even acquiescence … concerning the violation of fundamental human rights by totalitarian regimes. [He regretted] … the responsibility shared by so many Christians for grave forms of injustice and exclusion."

In January 2001 the Pope further marginalised Christian fundamentalists and even dismayed some of his more traditional followers when he declared to a weekly audience that "the voice of the prophets … echoes again and again to remind us that we must commit ourselves to liberating the oppressed and to working for justice. Without this commitment," he continued, "our worship is not pleasing to God."

But not all Christians were of a right-wing persuasion. Not all followed the same voices or experienced the same fears. Many saw the Bible in another light, a less Euro-centric light, perhaps. I hope that a story will illustrate the point.

One day in December 1984, the VMSG held a police-monitored prayer meeting at Father Photolo's house with guests representing the

Lutheran churches of Germany. It was a wonderfully prayerful occasion. The Lutheran ministers expressed a sort of spiritual astonishment at the unfamiliar Biblical texts we used for our devotion. Afterwards they explained that in the Western world, generally free from violent strife, middle class and comfortable, these texts were seldom referred to. Indeed they were redundant. Even our Biblical experts had little to say about them, they told us. Some of our texts used the word "oppression" and made reference to its consequences. This was not a word often used at prayer meetings in Europe or North America.

In fact there are at least twenty root words in the original Hebrew Bible for the word "oppression". This fact has gone unnoticed by Biblical scholars, interpreters and translators simply because they have never experienced oppression or been in contact with it. That day the Lutheran churchmen tasted that experience and their eyes were opened.

It must be said that as local church leaders we had been primed by our people's Biblically-grounded expectations of us. Those parts of the Bible where vital community aspirations were embraced and dealt with by a loving God seemed to have great appeal in those days. People of faith, in their darkest moments, legitimately expected to be comforted by a God whose very Son had known the depths of human despair. It was as simple as that. In those conditions a type of spirituality suited to our fast-changing circumstances began to emerge. Perhaps I could call it a type of situational, Biblical spirituality.

It was a time when the Exodus story of the Bible assumed huge proportions in the minds of believers. If God had liberated his people in the past He could do it again. And He would. Or would He?

The episode of Christ's agony in the garden surged into throbbing life not only for Holy Week but also for all the year round. In fact Holy Week itself became quite emotional and personal when the parallels with South Africa were delicately teased out. After all, Christ was arrested, betrayed, assaulted, mocked, imprisoned, interrogated and finally charged with treason, and sentenced to death. All this was happening in South Africa. And the Eucharist with its historical and political roots in the Passover commemorating the ancient liberation of the Jews spoke loudly to all who had ears to hear.

Christ's critical attitude to the evil and arrogance of the leaders of his time took on a new meaning for those who endured similar tyranny. The anger of Christ came alive again.

Again, the fact of Christ rising from the dead and the mighty hope it conveyed somehow kept a light at least flickering in believers' hearts. When celebrated not as a perfunctory, sanitised rite, but knowingly, with enthusiasm (Acts 2:4-13) and people-driven, then the Christ of history was present, embracing his people into vigorous new hope. I even wrote a version of the Stations of the Cross to reflect more accurately the Lord's identity and solidarity with the landless poor.

The Bible readings of Sunday worship (remember the fiercely positive attitudes of St Paul in the face of outrageous fortune) always took on fresh meaning when interpreted from the vantage point of the poor in the pews. This interpretation was probably lost on those worshipping faithful in the former white-only areas of the country. It was certainly lost to the preachers of the gospel of prosperity – whether black or white.

In ancient times God heard many prayers of outrage, of despair, of disbelief and of anger. "How long, Lord, am I to cry for help while you will not listen; to cry 'oppression!' in your ear and you will not save?" (Habakkuk 1:1-2)

And why not? These were stormy times for the people of God, for the people from Egypt. His often fiery and sometimes discouraged prophets were familiar with up-front, no-nonsense confrontations with Him. Yes, they loved him but there was a heavy price to pay. So often prophets such as Jeremiah wanted to give up and return to private life.

"Come quickly to my rescue ... save my life from these dogs," cried the Psalmist (20-21, 22) echoed thousands of years later by apartheid's prisoners of conscience.

In the late 1980s, even as the South Africa government resorted to the most extreme measures of repression, the people of God were already questioning the action of the state through the angry words of his prophet, Isaiah (3:15): "What do you mean by crushing my people, by grinding the face of the poor?" And to his people God was giving the assurance, "I am with you, do not be dismayed; I will strengthen you, I will help you" (Isaiah 41:10).

How we wished he would hurry up with the help!

And so came the 1990s. Violent resistance to threatened and imminent change went into high gear. The days of the drive-by shootings and other forms of planned death were upon us. Could Bible spirituality walk us or indeed hurry us through those frightening times? Who were the shadowy figures, "who come and go like the wind" (Habakkuk 1:11) conniving behind closed doors to keep the area and the country in a continuous state of fear and horror? I remember appealing to Ephesians 6 to describe the evil forces set free by willing human helpers. And the same verses would also provide the spiritual energy necessary to weather the onslaught – to be "strong in the Lord with His energy and strength".

With all this in mind who could have blamed the police for thinking that priests were "using the Bible to promote communism"!

It is gratifying to look back in the realisation that possibly, just possibly we were living witnesses to one of God's more dramatic interventions in human history as, through His people's resistance, He sounded the last days for apartheid.

The events of township life at the time, their lived context, lured us clergymen into a new, more flexible, pastoral, personal, Biblical and charismatic spirituality. Other prevalent local spiritualities, for example those which motivated active or silent consent to apartheid or even the theological stance of the mere bystander, would not easily have found a home in this pulsating climate.

Part Seven
Finale

Chapter 50

Apartheid is not the work of man but a creation of God – DF Malan,
former South African Prime Minister

On 27 April 1994 South Africans came out in full force to finally
dismantle this "creation of God".

Apart from church elections, Sebokeng residents Michael Mofokeng
and his wife Marie had never been invited to vote for anyone or
anything before. Now they were being asked to choose fellow blacks to
be their leaders. More than once they had questioned whether blacks
could lead blacks in any organisation, never mind a government. It was
a little frightening. They were used to whites guiding their lives, making
decisions for them – whites they knew were more educated than "us
blacks". It was therefore important to understand people's damaged self-
esteem when preparing to address them about the elections.

Some of my teachings before the elections took the form of a series
of questions gleaned from church Justice and Peace literature and
moderated to provoke reflection and dialogue in the community.

I include here some questions from these teachings: Who knows how
to vote? (A majority of hands in the congregation shot up, unlike three
positive responses in a neighbouring parish eight weeks earlier). Who
is the best or worst leader you know? Why should we all vote? (I met
at least two people before the elections who decided not to vote
because they had been born again in their churches! Jesus was
enough, they said.) I asked – if no one voted, what then? How can we
change a government if it is not doing its duty?

Will things change immediately after the elections? (No, they
replied, in contradiction to the prevalent media hype about coping
with heightened expectations.) How will we manage the transition
from an historical culture of protest against authority (in schools,
universities, police and civics) to a culture of disciplined productive
energy?

After some clarifications about fundamentalist religious political parties, I mentioned the significance of voting in honour of the memory of all those who had died in the struggle against apartheid. Finally on the penultimate Sunday before the elections as I exhorted the faithful to shed their conditioned fear of politics and enter that very arena in order to bring the values of God to political debate, a red-and-white banner was unfurled by an altar server and fixed to the pulpit front. On it were the immortal words of Psalm 127: "With the Lord we will build the house."

Which was why I had decided "to walk the last mile" as a domestic election observer with the communities I had lived with for 25 years.

On the eve of the first day of special votes (sick, aged, infirm) launching South Africa's first-ever democratic elections, a tangible sense of unfolding history resonated on all local radio talk shows. You sensed it in the excited tones of callers' conversations. I remember poring over my observer's manual and simultaneously listening to the election conversation with Radio 702's articulate Denis Beckett's phone-in guest, Eskom executive, Dawn Makhobo, recently seconded to the Independent Electoral Commission (IEC). Whites were ringing in to say that the spate of right-wing bomb blasts and killings in metropolitan areas wouldn't intimidate them. Indeed they were more than ever determined to vote. In Sebokeng I wrote the following in my diary that night (Monday, 25 April 1994):

> *Tonight an uncanny silence falls over the townships,*
> *barely concealing a profound awareness of tomorrow's*
> *events now preoccupying the minds and hearts of*
> *thousands of infirm, sickly, blind and bed-ridden*
> *residents as they finalise arrangements to be brought to*
> *the polling stations in a few hours.*
> *Nor are they aware that hundreds of whites – perhaps*
> *thousands – have fled the country in fear of political and*
> *social chaos during the coming three days. Or that those*
> *who had decided to stick it out have been stockpiling*
> *foodstuffs, leaving empty shelves in many supermarkets.*
> *Thus in some quarters, there is low-intensity exhilaration*

while in other parts of our divided human family there is
low-intensity panic-buying. Equally, tomorrow's voters
know nothing of the fact that gun shops have recently
broken all sales records. And they would be astonished to
hear that British and Portuguese airlines are rumoured
to be on standby for their citizens if necessary.

Residents, if they had heard of the above, were not a little amused
by this peculiar white alarm, aided and abetted perhaps by alarmist
newspapers.

I pondered township mood changes as I stood in the dark silent
churchyard. The mood of the community before these elections and on
the days leading up to the Vaal uprising (September 1984) were two
noticeably different moods, this one of joyful anticipation, the other of
sinister foreboding. It was always tangible. Yet September 1984 was
the beginning of the end of apartheid and led, ten years later, to these
elections.

Tuesday, 26 April 1994, was special votes day. I offered the usual
Tuesday morning Mass at Evaton as a sort of blessing on the coming
day's extraordinary happenings. Normally a faith-sharing and
healing Mass, I explained to the fifty-odd parishioners that today
would not be an extended service, as I had to leave immediately for
the polling stations.

~

At Esokwazi School I found about a thousand people in various
conditions of feebleness, sitting stoically on yellow school chairs waiting
to discover the mysteries of voting in the 20th century. The sun was far
up and the mid-morning heat was beginning to burn. I was accompanied
by Magouws Motau, a local Justice and Peace worker. Cars, vans and
lorries were arriving and depositing elderly voters at the school gates
where they were ushered in by peace monitors clad in their distinctive
orange overalls. We were the first election observers to arrive, and our
special blue caps, blue armbands and identity chains elicited enquiring
stares as we edged past elderly voters to the school building. We were
told that the voting section had been hastily changed to another room.

A harassed presiding officer, just arrived, rushed from table to table, answering questions, giving directions, answering phone calls, checking the credentials of party agents, greeting and directing us to a table where we signed a book. Finally the hall appeared ready, election officials were behind their tables, ink and X-ray equipment was in place. So too were the voting booths, strategically sited around the school hall. Buthelezi stickers were being pressed into place at the foot of ballot papers. (The ballot included photos of party leaders as well as the names of the political parties contesting the election; Chief Mangosuthu Buthelezi had brought the IFP into the elections only at the last minute, and stickers bearing his name and photo had to be added to every ballot by hand.) we had a final briefing from the presiding officer, and the doors were thrown open.

Elderly people entered timidly, eyes wide in wonderment, as they were directed to the first of five points to have their hands inked before collecting their folded and stamped ballot papers. Then the excitement began in earnest. Being a special votes day, some could not see, some could not walk, some could not hear and had difficulty expressing themselves, and the majority could not write.

Our aloof observer neutrality began to crumble, as more and more the presiding officer and election officials sought our help in aiding feeble voters as they entered the booths. Soon I was shuttling in and out of voting cubicles on a regular basis.

An official called me to assist Mrs Mathabo Nhlapo, an elderly granny, who, clutching her still-folded ballot, could not even see the cubicle ledge in front of her on which to lay her voting paper. Loosening her grip on the paper I unfolded it while at the same time checking over my shoulder to see if party agents were present to witness the operation. I asked her again, loud enough to let them hear me, who she wanted to vote for and if she could see a picture of her favourite politician's head on the long rectangular ballot paper in front of her. She grasped the paper again with renewed vigour and brought it to within centimetres of her face, carefully scrutinising each political face as she moved down the list of parties. At last she stopped abruptly, eyes riveted on Mandela. "That's him!" she exclaimed up at me with a marked sense of satisfaction.

"Can you write, grandmother?" asked a young monitor.

"No," she said and the monitor looked at me for help.

"Can you make a cross?" I asked.

"Yes," she replied and I placed the little election pencil in her shaky hand.

By now she had lost her focus on Mandela's picture so we started again. With gestures and sounds of encouragement I talked her through two meandering cross-bar strokes within the box to the right of the candidate's face. By now other agents of lesser-known parties had silently withdrawn (she wasn't searching for their party), leaving a monitor, an ANC agent and me to complete the process. I folded the ballot paper for her, shoved it into her 89-year-old hand and ushered her out of the cubicle towards the ballot box table where other elderly residents were lining up to deposit their refolded papers. All looked confused and somewhat overwhelmed by the strange procedure. Young election assistants politely but firmly kept the line moving from section to section.

Grandmother Nhlapo, having deposited her vote, turned and moved in the direction of the exit. But it was not to be. Questioned if she had voted a second time she looked up quizzically at her questioner. Thus she learned that she must once again cross a ballot paper, this time for the provincial parliament. Meanwhile I had been summoned to another booth where Paul Mokoka, a retired Bible teacher, recognised me through his thick glasses, with a smile. He needed little help. But the calls kept coming to go to other cubicles. I began to worry that if the congestion continued I'd have no time to visit other polling stations. I stayed anyway.

Early in the afternoon the first filled steel voting boxes were formally sealed. Voting stopped. The 14 election officials watched silently as the presiding officer explained the procedure. No one had a match to melt the wax seal. He asked my advice after discovering that the party agents didn't have the prescribed clips to attach the pink strips of ribbon formally binding the box lids. I told him to use his discretion. Now empty boxes were introduced, raised high for inspection and placed once again on the appointed tables. That job completed, the doors were opened and South Africa's first free election was once again under way.

My stomach continued to register a unique event in history. It was a day when adrenaline ruled.

There seemed to be a feeling in the hall that as observers, my colleagues and I were some type of election gurus sent to oversee the arrangements and management of the elections – like school inspectors from the regional DET offices! The presiding officer asked us questions expecting us to have prompt and informed answers. We couldn't help for the most part as we felt we might be infringing on the rights or interfering with the work of voting officers, party agents, or IEC monitors all of whom were milling around and hypersensitive to their own rights and duties. Our brief was to observe and nothing more.

UN observers now arrived, natives, I learned, of Holland, Ghana and Finland. I had met some of them earlier during their familiarisation trips through the townships. After introductions and a brief chat, they soon drew the presiding officer's attention to a party agent reluctant to identify himself to them. Good sense prevailed. "A National Party representative," whispered the Ghanaian observer to me, conspiratorially, as if indicating a new species (a black National Party member!) of human being.

Voting was now in full swing again and a certain rhythm was apparent. I was with the old folks in the booths for another two hours. Finally I emerged into the bright mid-afternoon sunlight, exhausted and foot weary.

At Sebokeng Hospital near the casualty department, a hall had been allocated to patients for election purposes. Monitors and election officials chatted in small groups. Youth leader and election volunteer Johnny Dlhabu burst through push doors deep in conversation with some colleague and appeared breathless – he needed to talk to me about the problems he was having regarding election procedures. Beaming, he told me that the local Vereeniging police, having been called at 4 a.m. to accompany election equipment to the townships, had only arrived at the IEC offices at 8 a.m., and that was only after repeated calls from him threatening them with some recently enacted electoral by-laws. I returned him to his regional IEC base office outside Vereeniging where he wanted to attend to the next day's election preparations.

Here I met some old acquaintances: Cosmas "Sampie" Thokoa, former Evaton altar server, YCW trialist, ex-Black Allied Workers Union chairman, Bible College graduate and PAC supporter; Tladi Kekana, son of Evaton socialite Moss (now deceased) and recently chairman of the Washington DC branch of the PAC; John Nkabane, ANC and just back from exile and studies in Cuba.

Mezwi Twala, a well-known local IFP leader, engaged some IEC staff and myself in a hurried discussion on how the IEC ought to help one of his bed-ridden party supporters to get to a voting station in Vanderbijlpark before closing time.

When Dlhabu had finished his work we returned to Sebokeng Hospital. There, Peter Skosana (now executive mayor of Sedibeng) emerged from a group. We had last met when he was a member of the DPSC at Sharpeville. At the hospital he was an ANC party agent. I went home and had a beer. I forgot to ring Sister Shelagh Mary, the bishops' anchor for the elections, about the events of the day. According to the radio, election logistics were a countrywide problem.

Chapter 51

On Wednesday, 27 April, the second day of elections, I started at Sebokeng Technical College at 9 a.m. – Dlhabu must have done a good job, as the presiding officer boasted that his election equipment arrived at 5.20 a.m. Everything was ordered and calm. I admired the courtesy of the young people who were managing the election stalls. Voters filed past in reverential awe.

There was something sacred in the air. Secular liturgy at its best!

Party political agents wore easily identifiable armbands. Usually it was the ANC and National Party. Sometimes the PAC was present. All were ready to dive at booths at the least signal of distress. A small, bemused dog wandered into the hall and accompanied his master from table to table, and appeared slightly nonplussed when his owner disappeared behind a voting booth.

There was a constant crackle and rustle of paper as sheets were torn from ballot blocks, folded and finally stamped on the outside with the election symbol. That night I wrote the following:

> *Outside, as I make my way from the school, it strikes me.*
> *That out-of-character mood of the township today –*
> *about the way people carry themselves, exchange*
> *greetings. A discernible quality accompanied by a*
> *collective lowering of voices as people find common*
> *ground, a lowering of FMs, a silencing of hooters, of*
> *subdued laughter, a lack of brashness. A sort of township*
> *retreating into low gear in order to deal with an*
> *unknown factor, everybody treading lightly, noticing one*
> *another in invisible solidarity.*
> *Township people have lived through similar defining*
> *moments in the past, especially 1976 in Soweto or 1984*

in the Vaal. But this time it lacks the tangible tension of
the morning of a mass stayaway, the lurking fear and
unpredictability of a political funeral, the quiet defiance
of a Sharpeville Day (21 March). Something completely
new is unfolding today. It's as if people own today, as if
it's theirs, and has not been imposed on them from
outside. Today they're experiencing it for the first time;
tomorrow they'll be savouring it, and after that. You
knew even the spotter planes, familiar over township skies
at times of crisis, were friendly today.

At Ubuhle Secondary School, party agents sat Sphinx-like and important in their taped-off area of the election hall observing everything and missing nothing. A former socialite, and much-travelled businessman, turned National Party agent, Ike Bikitsha, beamed an ingratiating smile of recognition in my direction. I greeted him politely. Two men in blue overalls, smiling ear to ear, danced a jig of joy as they made their way from booth to booth. The struggle, the pain had been worth it. In this great moment they were relishing it. I suggested to the presiding officer, Mr Mothae, that a few more ballot folder assistants would help process voters more quickly at that table. It worked. A former Soviet diplomat in Mozambique, now a UN observer in South Africa, leaned over to me and confided that the political scenario of South Africa at this delicate moment was similar to that of his native Russia, namely the erosion of law and order and the danger of a right-wing security forces backlash.

As I left the school I bumped into Mokete Makume, a local defence unit commander who I had come to know a couple of years earlier. We chatted about days gone by.

Thursday 28 April was the third day of elections. At Botebo-Tsebo Secondary School there were very few people voting. Most had voted the day before. I then decided to vote. A parishioner and communications student at the local technikon, Thandi Twala, stepped forward and quickly grabbed my ID, indicating that she would assist me to cast my vote. Afterwards she explained at length the state and progress of her studies.

There was something I didn't want to miss. I decided to call on a formerly all-white voting station at the Civic Centre, Vereeniging. Up to now in the townships my dominant emotion was joy. But as I approach Vereeniging a new gut emotion was resurfacing. It was a certain feeling of fear and suspicion reserved in the past for encounters with apartheid's officialdom or worse, apartheid's executors, administrators, the police or Security Branch. I passed a few armed police and soldiers loitering outside the town's municipal hall. When I entered the brightly lit hall, it looked all new, elaborate, sanitised and orderly. What a contrast with the townships.

My church collar was noted by the election staff; they must have wondered who I was and what a *predikant* might be doing involving himself in elections. Besides, he wasn't of their *kerk*.

And then at 7 p.m. I left for the Vereeniging Showgrounds with my spirits soaring to new heights. (If this continued there would be no Armageddon and time was running out for the prophets of doom!) This was my last port of call. It was the officially appointed place where counting took place. My IEC cap enabled me to be waved through the guarded gates where convoys of ballot boxes escorted by police vehicles were regularly passing.

Entering one of the vast halls I noticed a group of Afrikaner IEC monitors talking excitedly among themselves near the door. I was taken aback. I hadn't expected this. Vereeniging Afrikaners who had accepted the new order of things were an unknown quantity to me. I hovered around voyeuristically. Maybe they're excited about a rumour that the National Party was winning in the nearby Conservative Party-controlled Vanderbijlpark.

Dozens of volunteer counters were already busily seated at tables sorting out ballot sheets. Ballot papers were being unfolded and passed on to counters, who stacked them carefully, according to the party voted for – all under the beady eyes of party officials and election monitors. There must have been about one hundred and fifty counters in this hall. Nearby there were two other counting halls. The atmosphere was relaxed, though confusion was evident in some parts of the building. Trays of sandwiches were distributed among the counters. Rows of cardboard boxes dotted the hall with inscriptions

such as "Counterfoils (stubs) of Used Ballot Books and Any Partially
Used Ballot Books", "Unused National Ballot Papers" and sealed steel
boxes with "Counting Centre Reconciliation Statement for National
Ballot Papers".

I was intrigued at the sight of a National Party man patiently
explaining to an adamant ANC official why, in his opinion, a recently
opened ballot box should have been relegated to the "disputed" section
of the hall.

A more common ground for complaint among party zealots
concerned ballot papers found to be packed in two neat rows after the
witnessed opening of ballot boxes. Real consternation followed and
endless discussion between all and sundry.

I greeted Daisy Oliphant, a church leader and ANC candidate in the
area. Later she was declared a winner. Zodwa Mabaso, a church
development officer and former detainee, greeted me. She was
counting ballot papers. I talked with a Canadian Catholic Organisation
for Development and Peace official.

There were, of course, many stories from the elections, some
charming. Like the grand old granny who found out only later that it
wasn't appropriate to bring home her voting paper as a souvenir!
Another old lady adamantly insisted on voting for God – and had it
inserted manually on the voting paper. At Kalfontein farms near
Vanderbijlpark, a farmer and his wife ran the elections in their area
and allegedly instructed their illiterate employees to vote for the bald
man on the voter's sheet, who was, of course, FW de Klerk. And they
did!

These elections gripped the consciousness of the voting public. Even
small children before the elections could tell me that IEC equals
Independent Electoral Commission without in any way understanding
what each of the three words meant. They were buzz words. Fourteen-
year-olds wondered why they couldn't vote, such was their enthusiasm.

Small, apartheid-built school halls, often noisily chaotic, became the
arena where centuries of waiting ended in seconds, in some ways
profoundly anti-climactic, for the hungry voters. It was poignant. In
those moments the numbness brought on by decades of injustice,
alienation and exploitation was lifted for the first time, though not

251

forgotten. But for the present, voters were too immersed in the pains of new birth to comprehend the significance of the miracle breaking out all around them.

~

Foreign press people subsequently wrote with awe about the patience of people waiting in five-hour sun-drenched lines to cast their votes. For the moment it did not strike them that the wait for freedom too had been a long wait. That other queues too required patience, such as the monthly pension queues which are endemic to African life, and that endless pass office lines had been built into the fabric of black life.

It has been said that the overseas press, when covering Africa, suffers from a "White Mischief" or "Out of Africa" time warp. That might well be true. In our case the foreign media (and our own at times) seemed to be building up to an exciting and gory election thriller with its oft-quoted maxim "If it bleeds, it leads". Apocalyptic violence did not break out and nowhere in my wildest dreams did I expect it to. The presence of legions of locally known youthful peace monitors so noticeable in their orange bibs assured voters that these were their very own community elections.

The media had to be satisfied with reporting peace, getting to know townships and learning how to pronounce African names. This meant they had to grapple with an all-new, sometimes spiritual-sounding vocabulary such as "healing a nation," "journey to oneness", "fractured land seeking reconciliation", and "miracle".

Had they heard of the hijack of the car of election observer Sister Aideen Mcintyre on the morning of the elections in Evaton, it would probably have made headlines across the globe.

About six hundred years before Christ, the prophet Habakkuk was heard to remark:

> *Look and pay attention;*
> *Be amazed and astounded,*
> *For I am going to do in your own days*
> *Something that you would not believe if you*
> *Were told it.*
>
> (Habbakuk 1:5)

More recently Chief Albert Luthuli contextualised it: "Somewhere ahead there beckons a civilisation which will take its place in the parade of God's history with other great human syntheses: Chinese, Egyptian, Jewish, European. It will not necessarily be all black but it will be African."

Chapter 52

One of the outstanding human victories of the century – Inauguration
Day, 10 May 1994

On 9 May 1994 I organised *"Sekhafothini"* (worker's lunch box)
lunches for ten happy church Justice and Peace workers. We were
heading for Pretoria next day. It was inauguration time and we wanted
to be part of a significant moment in the history of the human family
here on the southern tip of Africa, in the cradle of human history.

For decades people had been imprisoned, tortured, degraded, hunted,
resettled, abandoned, declared invisible, and assassinated inside and
outside prisons all in the pursuit of this moment.

On the morning of 10 May, restrained excitement marked the
atmosphere of the townships as the hours approached the great event.
Many were prepared to go to Ellis Park Stadium where for R10 they'd
see the swearing-in ceremony on a giant TV screen, followed by
international soccer during which the new president would make a
personal appearance.

Departing Sebokeng at 7 a.m., we (Michael Ramorau, Magouws
Motau, Teboho Khumalo, Sabata Thato, Doctor Malinga, Matshediso
Khumalo, Mamorena Mohlaloka, Madimakatso Molahloa and Anna
Mokaene and myself) followed a deserted M1 freeway, passing under
bridge after bridge guarded by SADF troops.

In Pretoria with almost no traffic in sight it was easy to find our
allotted parking area. From being guardian of the old order, Pretoria
today was hosting an event celebrating the death of its own recent
history. Not many cities of the world do that. My stomach jolted for the
first time that day when a white policeman, a little embarrassed,
presented us with New South African flags as we left the parking area.
Was it a peace offering, I thought, a symbol of newfound good will?
Apartheid's police were not noted for gentle gestures of loving

fellowship. We smiled uncertainly as we accepted the flags with a little wonderment, perhaps even puzzlement too. Within our faith system we knew prodigal sons and daughters had their place too.

Soon we were shuttled in waiting buses through the recently cordoned-off areas of the city to the wide-open lawns in front of government buildings.

Disembarking, we were swept up by a wave of humanity, all moving in the same direction, as if to a friendly match between two star teams. But everyone knew it was much more.

Hawkers and vendors lined the route vying for our attention as they flashed in front of us New South African flags, souvenir key rings, T-shirts, scarves and a host of other Mandelabilia. "Viva, my peanuts!" shouted a peanut seller. Pretoria, dour capital of a former police state, today gushed joy, excitement and hope in a new, very different, political dispensation. A sort of "new Jerusalem".

Entering the hallowed grounds of the Union Buildings must have come as a positive emotional jolt to any former non-voter who ever had to suffer for his or her political convictions. Was there a touch of the Promised Land in the air? Had Mandela reached the promised land whereas Moses only glimpsed it?

Today activists would have thought of all those who had suffered and died in the struggle to make this day possible for the crowds now converging on the area. Some wept quietly for their friends who had died so that today could happen. Their joy was tinged with loneliness. But they knew the deceased were there in spirit.

Meanwhile up beyond at the Union Buildings, assembling around the inauguration stage, veteran ANC politicians and guerrillas nudged one another and in whispered, knowing tones asked if this was really happening. Was it real? Wasn't it worth it? If only Oliver [Tambo] had seen this, if only Chris [Hani] had been here today … had lived to see what he had died for.

We found our way to a suitable place in a fast-filling natural amphitheatre. A huge TV screen at the far right-hand corner of the grounds kept us in touch with the national and international VIP arrivals at the hidden-from-view area of the inauguration. Thabo Mbeki was cheered by the crowds; FW de Klerk barely so, Yasser Arafat certainly, but Fidel Castro, cigarless, received the loudest welcome so far.

When the president-elect alighted from his official car the cheering assumed roaring intensity sustained by a sea of multi-coloured New South African flags. And when a white general, for a fleeting moment, was seen saluting Mandela, millions of black hearts missed a beat. A new patriotism was being born.

By now the Botha Lawns in front of the Union Buildings were comfortably full and we were sitting on the grass, picnic style. We had arrived. I was glad I came to Pretoria. I wanted so much to feel our history happening, to taste its rich positive flavour, to absorb its emotional fallout, to savour its rainbow spirituality, to experience the results of struggle, prayer and sacrifice – surely a significant moment of grace.

For some time now a hushed silence accompanied the formalities on the inauguration platform. The new President of South Africa had taken the oath of office and had acknowledged a huge emotional ovation. Moments later President Mandela had stepped forward to deliver his historic and carefully inclusive speech of reconciliation, setting the tone for future months among his followers and reassuring whites now facing the prospect of diminishing power and privilege. That night I wrote about the day's experiences:

> *It was barely audible at first – the sound that slowly caught people's attention, forcing them to turn and search the skies to the rear of the multitude. A collective intake of breath, of incomprehension, slowly giving way to comprehension, recognition and then wild prolonged jubilation as military aircraft emerged from behind the Voortrekker Monument and in tight formations droned into the valley of Pretoria, streaming smoke trails of the new flag's six colours, a symbol of the new "rainbow nation". The 40 000-strong crowd was still madly waving flags at the friendly blue skies as more formations of combat helicopters towing the New South African flag passed over in salute of the nation's first real president.*

256

In these never-to-be-forgotten moments the excitement of today's celebration shifts into even higher, supercharged gear as 19 million new-born voters tremble and cheer and cry and embrace and dance and sing in a spontaneous outpouring of joy. Social ecstasy. It is unbelievable; that infectious wave of collective emotion gaining strength as recognition breaks through that these machines of war, until lately symbols of oppression, are now symbols of friendship. It is the day's most tangible, dramatic evidence of the transfer of power. A "terrible beauty" is born. Exhilaration deepens as it dawns on South Africa's newest patriots that this Military, this air force, is their very own and no longer the oppressive instrument of an alien power. It's overwhelming. "Viva South African Defence Force, Viva!" cheers a matronly ANC supporter. People wipe away tears. I do not bother. I let them be. It is that kind of day. I wonder what the white pilots see, feel and experience as they pass over the city.
"I've never seen a miracle like this before!" shouts Malinga over the din, hyperventilating with excitement. "The Old Man is a Messiah!" cries Matshediso, tears flowing freely in a sea of joyous humanity. A fitting climax, a consecration, a fulfilment, an awesome homecoming written across the southern skies.

The rest of this slowly unfolding rite of passage is etched into history. And when President Nelson Rolihlahla Mandela left for his first engagement at Ellis Park Stadium the music and cultural entertainment was in full booming swing. Popular comedian and MC, Joe "S'Good S'Nice" Mafela, reduced inauguration fever to more manageable levels and had the crowd eating out of his hand with his catchy slogan, "Shine, South Africa shine!" repeated regularly with other equally catchy responses from a delirious audience. We joined in the singing and the swinging with appropriate abandon.

There are times when, through some deep inner surge of intuition, one is acutely aware of history being made. This was one of those times.

Chapter 53

The presence of troops here is not aggravating the situation. I regard them as people who want peace. It is only an evildoer who would be afraid of the police because they are going to be a clamp on him. The State of Emergency has improved the position in the townships
Last mayor of Lekoa, Esau Mahlatsi in *Leadership*, Vol. Six 1987

This book could end here, at the point when a former boxer was made president of South Africa after 27 years of imprisonment, a fitting end to a long journey. Then the TRC intervened. It criticised the freedom movements for not controlling sufficiently their followers during the street wars of the 1980s. At the same time the TRC criticised the churches nationally for their lack of commitment to the struggle against apartheid.

In June 1997 the churches of the traditionally black areas of the southern tip of the Gauteng Province (Vaal Triangle) made an unusual submission to the TRC. The TRC was surprised. No other regional grouping of churches had addressed the TRC before. Our submission (see Appendix 6), which was tabled on behalf of the Gauteng Council of Churches (Vaal) by Reverend Gift Moerane, was significant in that the churches as a body asked pardon for not raising their voices sufficiently in the townships to curb the excesses of youth activists, especially those allied to the liberation movements. It outlined what the churches had tried to do during the last decade of apartheid in the region. This book attempts to describe some of that.

A list of recommendations were also made to the TRC. The TRC responded by appealing to the churches of the Vaal Triangle to become instruments of healing and reconciliation in the area.

The churches accepted this challenge. They knew that Christ had, among his disciples, followers from different political camps. Matthew, who was a tax collector and had collaborated with the system – the

Roman Empire in his case, perhaps believing in a policy of accommodation or even that you could change the system from within, an option often put forward today. Or could it be because he had a wife and children to look after?

Simon the Zealot, on the other hand was a tunnel-vision, anti-government revolutionary bent on the violent overthrow of the illegitimate government of the day. Each in his own way found Christ. Or perhaps more accurately Christ's love found them. Surely, I thought, this applies to former councillors too.

Are black town councillors elected under the former government still to be regarded as social outcasts in the black community? It is a question that worries many, not least the councillors themselves. I believe it is appropriate to raise the question at this juncture, as a sort of closure to this period of South African history.

~

The Lekoa Town Council (Vaal) during the revolt of the 1980s was viewed in two ways, as were other black municipal councils throughout the country. On the one hand it was perceived as a "perpetrator" of government policy for blacks, and, on the other, as a body of elected representatives of the people trying to do a difficult job which would, some hoped, eventually lead to greater black autonomy and, ultimately, to liberation.

There is something timeless in the dilemma in which the councils unexpectedly found themselves. How unaware and unprepared they were to cope with shuddering social change.Every country in flux seems to contain people and groups who fail to decode the signs of the times – or decode the signs of the times in a peculiarly flawed way, such that they are overtaken, even swallowed up by events. This was the fate of many town councillors fighting a rearguard action seen as favouring the old order. For a rare insight into the minds of former councillors read their submission to the TRC in Appendix 7.

The following is the author's interview with a former councillor who preferred to remain anonymous:

Interviewer: Esau Mahlatsi was elected to the Lekoa Town Council in 1977 and subsequently elected as chairman and mayor of Lekoa in 1983. Did the deceased ever talk about alleged corruption among his fellow councillors? If so what was the corruption?

Councillor: I don't remember.

Interviewer: Mr Mahlatsi was quoted as saying that he would resign from the council only if his constituents in Zone 12 asked him to do so. Do you have any comment on this?

Councillor: People who were anti-councillor asked the councillors to resign. They were not his constituents. What would have happened thereafter? Who would have run the township?

Interviewer: Did the councillors ever feel that the white administration board was using them?

Councillor: No.

Interviewer: "*Masole* (soldiers of) *a Mahlatsi*". How did the council feel about this description of the controversial "*kitskonstabels*" of the 1980s? (Kitskonstabels, literally "instant police" in Afrikaans or "Blue bottles", were trained by senior Security Branch officers near Cape Town. They were similar to municipal police or "Greenbeans" or "*Amatshaka*" who were black auxiliaries hurriedly trained and set up on Rhodesian lines and similar to the Black and Tans in Ireland in the 1920s. Their purpose was to remove all opposition to the government and to create the appearance of black on black violence for the international media.)

Councillor: They were not very happy with it. However that's how the people chose to describe them. They (the "*kitskonstabels*") were doing their duty.

Interviewer: Why in your opinion did the residents of the Vaal Triangle dislike the Lekoa Town Council so much?

Councillor: It was not everyone but a select few who thought councillors were exonerated from payment of service charges. These select few did not want to be associated with whites.

Interviewer: In hindsight, would it have been better for the councillors to have resigned earlier?

Councillor: It would not have helped, as I believe something else would have cropped up for which they, the councillors, would still be blamed. The councillors were helping the community.

Interviewer: According to the evidence of the first Delmas Treason Trial the Mahlatsi family accumulated many properties during the time the mayor was chairman of the Lekoa Council. Could you comment on this?

Councillor: The family had properties before they came into the council. Unfortunately they were also on the trade committee and this committee did the tendering.

Interviewer: What was the attitude of the administration board officials to the churches during the 1980s?

Councillor: They were not against religious institutions. However this can best be answered by the administration board.

Interviewer: What frightening experiences did you or your family have during that time?

Councillor: The killing of councillors was terrifying. When my house was surrounded and attacked by a mob we as a family did not respond or react but knelt down and prayed. Soon after the crowd moved away. To be separated from your loved ones while staying at the administration board, Sebokeng, was a bad experience.

Interviewer: How can former councillors help to build reconciliation and healing in South Africa?

Councillor: Nobody will take their word. They are still regarded as enemies of the people. The councillors too need healing.

Interviewer: Why was the former State President, PW Botha, offered the freedom of the Vaal Triangle townships?

Councillor: State President PW Botha was invited by the council to visit the Vaal Triangle in 1987. He was to come and tell the people that the council was recognised by the government. Also to plead for calm and stability in the places where the riots had started – riots that were spreading throughout the country. The late councillor, Esau Mahlatsi, made the invitation. Although Mr Botha did come, his government did not do anything for the councillors. Mr Botha did not even send condolences to the families of those councillors who lost their lives.

Interviewer: Is there anything else you would like to add?

Councillor: The present councillors are worse than the former councillors. They must now deliver to the very people just like formerly. They are finding it very difficult and at times are asking how it should be done.

Services must be paid for, though not all are willing to do this. We are now back to square one. Soon you will hear the councillors being called to resign again. In the past councillors were working for the people. The former councillors planned many things that are being done now, e.g. the shopping complex in Zone 10 and the road near the railway. The stadium was planned and should have been completed by now. If there are people to be compensated for their losses it is the councillors.

Epilogue

My somewhat monastic training for the priesthood did not equip me for parish work, foreign parish work, foreign parish work in an abnormal society, or indeed in a country undergoing revolutionary change. For that I blame nobody.

However I have to say that the long, drawn-out demise of apartheid played havoc with my traditional spirituality, that is, the tested ways I was taught to manage my daily life with God in His world.

In my nicely ordered northern-hemisphere seminary education of 30 years ago, the God of the unexpected was never mentioned, never talked about, never even thought about. The God-in-other-cultures, or the God-of-great-changing-circumstances, remained confined to the pages of the Bible. I don't apportion blame here either. I was, after all, an ordinary average product of my own ordinary average Euro-centric background.

In the townships we lived by a life-rhythm not of our making. It was a rhythm mostly dictated by circumstances, by a people under attack and in the throes of desperation.

Here God – the God of surprises acted outside our inherited categories and seminary-taught frameworks. It wasn't easy to see him or to hear him in the situations we met. So often we struggled to find his roving mischievous will. His nudge came at the most unsuitable of times. His nod came in the most unlikely places. At least we thought so.

Reaching beyond the boundaries of the local church communities to the broader community of the townships – a new field, I might add – was probably the biggest single challenge clergy had to face in the Vaal Triangle and elsewhere during the 1980s. Indeed there were times when church leaders were hurled into the fast lane of social involvement. Some did not see this as suitably religious activity.

Certainly it was unsettling when a new (Emergency) ministry or service was thrust upon you, demanding almost instant response under the focused eye of the public.

Mediating peace and change with the police and municipal authorities under extremely volatile conditions, whether on the streets of Sharpeville or Sebokeng, was not what churchmen were trained to do in their schools of education and formation. Looking back, some elements of these church interventions were similar to what happened in the so-called "velvet revolution" in the former communist countries of Eastern Europe.

Yes, shepherding a flock through a maze of frequently unpredictable happenings in a rolling revolution was different and daunting. Being swept up by the urgency of the moment at one of these flashpoint occasions often left me yearning for the more familiar rhythm of day-to-day church life. But how could we silently observe a world in convulsions from the security of our manses, presbyteries and religious houses? Surely the church had been called not only to bind up wounds but also to obstruct evil?

We were untrained and unqualified for managing the fallout from an uprising. Of course not everyone called it by that name. Archbishop Denis Hurley referred to what he called "crisis ministry" when he said:

> *It is not enough just to preach to people during a crisis.*
> *The Catholic Church's (and other churches') response to*
> *last year's unrest in the Vaal black townships is an*
> *example of crisis ministry. During the unrest, priests*
> *worked closely with the people, often acting as their*
> *representatives.*
>
> *Ecunews* Jan/Feb 1985

It is interesting to compare these perceptions of Christian service with those of Professor Tjaart van der Walt in his report on the role of the churches in the Vaal Triangle. After even-handedly discussing the different theological positions of churches ("me and Jesus" called the vertical stance, and "me and my neighbour" called the horizontal stance), Van der Walt said that the VMSG was "characteristic of the horizontal stance ... with very clear signs of certain undercurrents, e.g.

of black theology, the theology of liberation and even the theology of revolution." I have often wondered who or what situations helped him to draw these conclusions. What theological criteria did he use? Certainly the mainstream historical churches supported their clergy in the Vaal townships at the time. Gravely, he warned the churches: "Shoemaker, stick to your last." These experiences left their mark on the individual clergyman, and in the public domain "created waves" in the area of Christian witness.

This book draws attention to the extraordinary inter-church co-operation during those days. I would like to think that the local churches' stance was drawn from their own particular calling. It was a calling that at the time drew inspiration from the unconditional compassion of the Good Samaritan and applied it to a real-life situation in South Africa, a movement of solidarity based on an understanding of God as "the one who sees the misery, hears the cries and knows the suffering" (Ex. 3:7) of the victims of oppression. Apartheid – or any other evil system – is not what Christ had in mind when he said, "I have come that you may have life, and have it abundantly"(Jn 10:10). I believe ours was a sort of reflective response to the presence of God in a situation of modern urban, low-intensity civil war.

Remarkably, no black right-wing vigilante groups linked to the administration board sprang up, as was the case in other townships. This must have been due to the influence of the former town councillors and very much to their credit.

No political-ideological clashes took place in the Vaal Triangle in the early more dramatic years of the upheaval. This was due to the influence of the VMSG, who at numerous meetings cautioned against such clashes. When they surfaced we quickly snuffed them out.

The English-speaking media worked closely with the churches during the troubles of the 1980s. Both parties were mutually helpful to each other. The churches supplied much of their information while the press agreed to publish what the clergy requested. Those newspapers with black journalists were clearly the best informed. The who's who of black journalists were all there. *The Star's* Maud Motanyane, Themba Khumalo, Phil Mtimkhulu, Revelation Ntoula and

Peter Honey were there. *The Sowetan* had Charles Mogale, Len Maseko, Thami Mazwai, Nkopane Makobane, Joshua Raboroko (now deceased) and of course the ever-present Len Kumalo. The *Rand Daily Mail* had in place Robert Tshabalala, Montshiwa Moroke, Rich Mkondo and photographer Tony Naidoo. *City Press* had Sinnah Kunene and Khulu Sibiya. Finally the *Sunday Mirror* had Ruth Bhengu, John Qwelane and Themba Molefe on the spot. The nation is indebted to them and their editors for the magnificent contribution they made to the liberation struggle as it went into its final days in the Vaal Triangle – this in spite of crushing censorship laws controlling their profession. The foreign networks also played their part in telling it like it was. Unfortunately we South Africans were never allowed to see their reports from the battlefield.

Yes indeed, these were times of soaring joy and plummeting pessimism, fierce times, bitter times, times of death, of awakening, times for talking and times to stop talking, times of joy, of sweat, of tears, of fear, of anxiety and stress, of expectation, regression and recovery again. Every variety of emotion had its moment.

Now new times are upon us: times for confessing, for reparation, for forgiving, for receiving forgiveness, for listening and hearing one another's stories, for healing the wounds and memories of the past. Patriotic South Africans are already doing this. There are signs of hope for a country in transformation.

Appendices

Appendix 1

The founding members of the Vaal Ministers Solidarity Group (VSMG) were Luther Mateza (Presbyterian), Ben Photolo (Anglican), Edward Lennon (Catholic), Geoff Moselane (Anglican), Lord McCamel (McCamel Church of God), Lucas Bambezela (Catholic), Ben Marutle (Methodist), Herbert Koaho (NGK), Washington Malumbazo (Presbyterian Church in Africa), Gerry Dabula (African Methodist Episcopal Church), Peter Lenkoe (Anglican), Patrick Noonan (Catholic).

Appendix 1a

(1982) Among those who attended the first meeting of this Action Committee were Michael Kgaka (Zone 14), Dorcas Ralitsela (Zone 7), Gcina Malindi (Zone 13), Thabiso Ratsomo (Zone 13), "Chippa" Motubatsi (Zone 7), Esau Ralitsela (Zone 7), Sekoati Mokoena (Boipatong), Elizabeth Letanta (Zone 13), Simon Nkoli (Zone 14), Edith Connie Lethlake (Zone 7) and Bavumile Vilakazi (Zone 3).

Appendix 1b

19 February 1984. Speakers included David Mphuthi, Hlabeng Matlole, Lekgwakgwa Ramakhula and Modise Mthombeni. Popular songs provided the cement for bonding the diverse audience: "Siyaya e Pitori" (We are marching to Pretoria); "Siyaya e Houtkop" (We are marching to Houtkop Administration Board); "Hlanganani Bazali" (Parents unite); "Hlanganani Basebenzi" ("Workers unite"); "Senzeni na?" (What have we done?); "Nkosi Sikelel' iAfrika" (God bless Africa). A further meeting is held at the house of Petrus Mokoena (Evaton Ratepayers Association). This includes the Zone 7 committee and people from the Evaton Ratepayers Association, including the chairperson Mr Caswell Kgabi, and others such as April Sefako Mokoena and "Chippa" Motubatsi. Also present were Mphuthi, Lekgwakgwa Ramakhula, Esau Ralitsela, Dorcas Ralitsela, Edith Connie Lethlake and Elizabeth Letanta.

Appendix 1c

Sunday, 26 August 1984. This morning at St Francis Xavier Catholic Church, Small Farms, in Evaton, the Evaton Ratepayers Association meets under Petrus Mokoena to discuss the issue of land acquired in Evaton on which the administration board wants to build. Edith Connie Lethlake (Vaal Organisation of Women) and Rina Mokoena address the meeting. Gcina Malindi of the Vaal Youth Congress (steering committee) also addresses the audience. The strategy is that those at this and a subsequent meeting will join forces because of similar political interests.

Appendix 1d

Meeting at Bophelong, Sunday, 2 September 1984, attended by a large crowd including VCA members and local leaders such as Johnny Motete, Mbongo, an elderly activist Jeremiah Tsholo (78), Chairman of the Committee of 10, Toto Mbongo, Sello Hlanyane, Bonani Mafa, Stompie Mokgele (Navy), Vicks Thafane, Mokula and others. Members of Lekoa Town Council had been invited but their presence triggered off anger. After an address by Ma Mogotsi someone switched off the lights and chaos followed even out onto the streets.

Appendix 1e

Talks on a Sharpeville street – Wednesday, 5 September 1984. The residents' delegation consists of Father Ben Photolo (Anglican) who, I was later informed, had been called from his parish at Evaton since Moselane is incapacitated, Lydia "Malebone" Makume, a local ambulance driver, Mongezi Radebe (later to be detained after the stayaway on 2 November 1984), Tshepo Photolo son of Father Photolo, and Aupa Mantsoe Ramokhoase.

Appendix 1f

A meeting (arising from the previous "car bonnet" negotiations), Sebokeng, Saturday, 8 September 1984. Present: Reverend Geoff Moselane (Anglican Sharpeville); Lydia Makume (Sharpeville); Joyce Mokhesi (Sharpeville); Mongezi Radebe (Sharpeville); Litau Litau (Zone 14, Sebokeng); Davidson Mokoena (Zone 14, Sebokeng); Walter Mbathe (Zone 14, Sebokeng); Reverend Lucas Bambezela (Catholic Sebokeng); a Mr Seretide (Taxi association, Zone 13, Sebokeng); Mrs Khumalo (Zone 13, Sebokeng); Canon Ben Photolo (Anglican Evaton); Tshepo Photolo (Evaton); Lord McCamel (McCamel Church of God, Evaton).

Appendix 1g

Vaal Ministers Solidarity Group emergency relief fund:

South African Council of Churches	R	6 600
South African Catholic Bishops Conference	R	2 800
Catholic Diocese of Johannesburg	R	3 000
Ministers of Independent Churches	R	20
Emmanuel Catholic Church, Sebokeng	R	12
AME Church, Sharpeville	R	50
Don Mashinini, Evaton	R	200
Sebokeng and Evaton taxi owners	R	720
Sancta Maria Convent, Vanderbijlpark	R	100
Kgotsong NG Kerk, Sharpeville	R	30
ZCC: Leboa Comb. School, Sharpeville	R	35
Methodist Church, Phelandaba, Sharpeville	R	10
St Luke's Methodist Church, Sharpeville	R	12
Ikaneleng Bokamoso, Sharpeville	R	114,32
Collected by resident, Sharpeville	R	14,36
Catholic Community, barrage	R	1,70
Individual donations, Sharpeville	R	7,80
Mr Molefe, Sharpeville	R	200
Catholic groups from overseas	R	944,43

Nyolohelo Catholic Church, Sebokeng ....R   15
Vereeniging and Vanderbijlpark inspectors.................................R   280
Orange-Vaal African Chamber of Commerce ....R   760
Principals and teachers, Vereeniging circuit ....R   856
Our Lady of Fatima Catholic Church, Sharpeville ....R   23,44
St Joseph Catholic Church, Boipatong ....R   31,35
Majakathata Taxi Association, Vaal Triangle ....R   200
Sharpeville teachers and principals ....R   80
St Stephen's Methodist Church, Sharpeville ....R   15
Anonymous ....R   70
Secular Franciscans ....R   805
Franciscans ....R   600
St Vincent de Paul, Dundee, Scotland ....R   317
Total..R 18 925,20

This money has been disbursed among approximately 68 families who lost a
loved one in the period September 1984 to January 1985 in the riots in the Vaal
Triangle. The Vaal Ministers Solidarity Group takes this opportunity to
expressing their deep appreciation and profound thanks to all who gave so
generously.

Vaal Ministers Solidarity Group
July 1985

Appendix 2
Those who died in the Vaal Triangle from 2 September 1984 to 1 January
1985. Ages have been given where possible.

> *Killing by shooting formed the overwhelming proportion of all*
> *deaths at the hands of the South African police* – Truth and
> Reconciliation Commission, 1998

This list of the deceased was compiled in the heat of the moment by the Vaal
Ministers Solidarity Group. As the number rose, the black community-based
newspapers and other interested parties were informed.

Sharpeville: House
1. Frank Mmutle Machobane (22)   1334
2. Thusi David Tota (30)   S/136
3. William Sanku Ramatlakane (23)   5069
4. Abel Koboekae (45)   2965
5. Ezekiel Morosi Pule (26)   S/281
6. Joseph Mahlomola Malieha (13)   S.874
7. Joseph Magwagwa Motaung (23)   S/1174
8. Maud Nzunga (7 months)   3818
9. Lucas Mokua (34)   8416

10. Alex Mabaso (52)	S/7
11. Prosper Dywili (21)	8779
12. Khuzwayo Jacob Dlamini	7487
13. Maria Mvala (26)	6503
14. Martha Ndabambi (58)	8878
15. Lemell Isolene (16)	2180
16. Mafa Thulo (22)	S/1182
17. Joseph Mahlomola Mphutlane	S/696 (Buried Ficksburg)
18. Godfrey Mpondo (7)	3342

My informal investigations in Sharpeville produced the following figures of the 18 residents (not outsiders as alleged by the government) who died violently between September and December 1984. Seven were married, one was engaged, three were under 13, four over 40 years, 13 were killed by the police, one by the municipal police (Mpondo), one by a crowd (Dlamini), three were believed to have been killed by tear gas (Ndabambi, Koboekae and Nzunga). Francis Tahleho Korotsoane disappeared in police custody in unexplained circumstances in early September 1984. A case was opened at the time.

Boipatong: House
1. Isaac Ngakane (57)	323 Ngqika Street
2. Isaac Selalale (24)	393 Hlubi Street
3. Solomon Ntsundu (30)	1551 Malebogo Street
4. Edwin Mentor	Bereng Street (Burial Thaba Nchu)

Bophelong
1. Eliah Phalane (21)	486 Phalane Street
2. Reuben Twala (19)	168 Tsolo Street
3. Johannes Mthimkhulu	Address unknown

Sebokeng: House
1. Lawrence Pekeur	13750	Zone 11
2. Caesar Motjeane	13064	Zone 11
3. Abram Mabokoane	13349	Zone 11
4. Enoch Makhubu	4768	Zone 12
5. Elizabeth Sellane (44)	2891	Zone 13
6. Petros Mokgatla (17)	3669	Zone 13
7. Stephenson Lebeoane (14)	2466	Zone 13
8. Stephen Mangayi (20)	2969	Zone 13
9. Joseph Sithole (23)	3737	Zone 13
10. Elias Phele (31)	1407	Zone 13
11. Jacob Moleleki (17)	1090	Zone 13
12. Johannes C. Chakane	17078	Zone 14
13. Moses Malelane	19063	Zone 14
14. Isaac Mohese (21)	19236	Zone 14
15. Solomon Mnqwevu (33)	17588	Zone 14
16. Maria Mlangeni (42)	18800	Zone 14
17. Alex-Maria Skaledi (35)	18801	Zone 14
18. David Mashole (19)	18804	Zone 14

19. Moses Melenyane (16)	19063 Zone	14
20. Anna Moshwaduwa	18289 Zone	14
21. Isaac Mokoena (21)	18039 Zone	14
22. Joseph Mbele	11202 Zone	7B
23. Alinah Mnyanda	9486 Zone	7B
24. Michael Zondo	9618 Zone	7B
25. Phineas Matipidi	12956 Zone	7B
26. Nicholas Mgondwa (10)	11484 Zone	7B

Evaton [vp1]- Small Farms House

1. Isaac Mohlabadie (32)	1277
2. William Shange (16)	980 Adams Road
3. William Molaba (16)	460 Evaton
4. Dingaan Mofolo (14)	1495 Togo Road
5. Patrick Grabe	2810 Evaton
6. Frans Tsibolane (19)	13/5 Small Farms
7. Solomon Zamisa	75-8 Small Farms
8. Nathaniel Qokokoane	2051 Evaton
9. Trypina Buang	1753 Adams Road, Evaton
10. Isaac Matshoba	1517 Togo Road, Evaton
11. Edward Tshabalala	Evaton
12. Christopher Khumalo	26/6 Small Farms
13. Johannes Tsele	5 Canner Street, Evaton
14. Julia Maduna (37)	1st Avenue, Evaton
15. Agnes Mokoena	1821 Adams Road, Evaton
16. Abram Mofokeng (35)	192 Adams Road, Evaton
17. Martinus Ntelele (24)	268 Adams Road, Evaton
18. David Matsholo (18)	1837 Glasgow Road, Evaton
19. Piet Motaung (13)	6/2 Adams Road, Evaton
20. Leburu "Dutch" Lipoko	Adams Road, Evaton
21. Blair Gordon (3 weeks)	Walkerville

Appendix 3

This is the original text of the document sent to Washington by the International Freedom Foundation from their South African branch:

Salaminah Borephe

In 1975 I joined SASO (South African Students Organisation), the student organisation which was operating at Black schools, because they said that they would help get us better education. All their meetings were held through the Student Christian Movement at our school. After I had joined they told us that SASO was a branch of the ANC.

In 1976 we were fighting Afrikaans at our schools, but we at Jordan High School were not doing Afrikaans. So we influenced other students from other schools. We assaulted our teachers and burned cars. When the police and school inspectors asked us why we were fighting because we did not do maths in Afrikaans we told them that we were fighting for our Black brothers and sisters.

We used to hold meetings at school for the students. The easy way to get the students was through SCM (Students Christian Movement). We pretended to

271

be having the service but in fact we were told by our leaders about communism. After the services we sang freedom songs. At the meetings we tried to get other students to fight against Afrikaans as well. Some of them said that they would rather be educated, and wanted to go to school. Because our leaders told us that we must burn the schools if the students wanted to go to school, we burnt down some of the schools in the area. Our leaders told us that White people had told them to tell us to burn down schools. Our leaders in SASO also told us that the communists would set us free from slavery.

In 1977 SASO was banned, and we looked for another organisation. We were told that SASO was banned because it told the truth.

In 1979 I joined COSAS (Congress of the South African Students). This was seen by the students as a continuation of SASO, and had the same leadership. We were told by our leaders in COSAS that COSAS was the youth wing of the ANC. Because Afrikaans was removed from the schools, but we saw nothing getting better, we were told that we must continue the struggle.

In COSAS we were told how to make petrol bombs. We were told by the Church Ministers how good communism was, and they promised us a better education in other countries which were ruled by the communists. That was the thing that made me to join these organisations. The Anglican Ministers taught us in the Catholic churches how to make petrol bombs, and told us that the communists would kill the Whites to set the Blacks Free. We were told that the communists were Black people from central Africa and they taught us that Samora Machel from Mozambique and Dos Santos from Angola, and Mugabe and Nkomo from Zimbabwe were heroes and would liberate us. Once they took us to a meeting in a large hall in Johannesburg where there were a lot of White people. There they explained what COSAS was, and told us how to make petrol bombs. We were not allowed to discuss things, but were given lectures. We were told that Mandela was our leader, and that he was in jail because he fought for Blacks.

There was much hatred planted in us towards the White people, but especially towards Afrikaans speaking people. We were told not to listen to Afrikaans speaking people because they were liars.

In 1983 a COSAS meeting was called. When we arrived at church there were lots of weapons. The Minister told us that the Russians had sent the weapons and that the children from 16 to 18 must take a gun. The leaders took one first. They were all AK-47s. The guns that were left over were given to the COSAS members. The Minister told us that they would teach us how to use the guns because everybody was asking. He told us that the guns were to kill White people, but we never killed White people, only Blacks. He then told us that we must always try and get more guns, and that we must kill the policemen to get their guns.

In 1984 the residents of Lekoa were told by the community councillors that the rent was to go up by R5,00. We members of COSAS and United Democratic Front were not pleased about the matter. We organised a leaders' meeting. We wanted to have the solution of this matter. Then the other Reverend of Anglican in Sharpeville together with Reverend Marchemel and

272

the other from Sebokeng Anglican were there with us as they were our leaders. They told us that all community councillors must die on the 3rd September 1984, if they did not want to listen to the people. On Friday pamphlets were distributed where people were told that they must not go to work, and all schools should be closed, and all the shops. That was supposed to happen on Monday. But on Saturday the Community councillors also distributed their pamphlets saying to the people that they can go to work and to school. On Monday people were confused, some went to work and when they returned they were assaulted, others were even killed. Some of the residents who went to work were burnt with petrol.

On Sunday 2nd September there was a meeting of the residents at the Roman Catholic Churches in Zone 12, at Evaton and at Sharpeville. The Ministers told the people to kill the community councillors the following day because they did not want to listen to the residents. On Monday morning at about 5.30 a.m. we were already at the streets stoning cars and busses. We told other people who wanted to go to work to return home. At about 8 a.m. we went to the community councillors' homes. The person we wanted more than others was the Mayor Mr Mahlatsi. Firstly we went to Mr C Matshiane's home because he was the newest of them all, at that time we were at Zone 11. At first when we arrived he was not there. Then we went to the Mayor's home but he escaped with a car. We tried to run after him but it was in vain. Then we found his new car in the yard. We started by smashing the windows of the house and of the car. After that we burned the whole house together with the new car. After that we went to the shop centre and burned all the shops, but before burning them we took all the things out of the shops and took them home. After burning the shops we send some of the students to go to Mr Motshiane's home and check if he's not yet back. They came quickly and told us that he was there. Then we went to his home. Before getting to his yard there was other coming from Evaton, Zone 3 and 7? There were such a great number of them that one could not count. We waited for them and when they arrived we went together to Mr Motshiane's house. He locked himself in the house together with one of his Friends. The wife and children were not there. So the young boys climbed on top of the house to remove the roof. The others smashed the windows. The friend tried to escape. He got out of the house and tried to go to the street. The boys caught him and burned him with a petrol bomb. Mr Motshiane also came out and was hacked by knives and pangas. He died there in the street. Then we wanted to go to the Lekoa offices and burn them. But when we tried to go out of the location we were confronted by the police. At that stage we saw that they are going to shoot us. I can say here that from that morning all we did we did it freely because there were no police inside the location. They were standing outside the location, others were moving with a helicopter above us. We ran away and went back to Zone 12 to finish off the shops. The other three died this way. Mr Dlamini was necklaced, in Sharpeville. Mr Diphoko was shot while running to the police helicopter. The other one was hacked to death with knifes and pangas. Two weeks after that there were no food in the locations. We had to buy brown bread at R1,50 a loaf and white bread R2,00 a loaf. While we were members of COSAS we were told that the town councillors were sell-outs and must be killed. They always used the bible to tell us why we must murder the councillors. They would say that Mandela was like Moses who had come to set us free. Because the police were outside the townships, we were told that they were too scared to come into our areas because we were so strong. We were also told to kill the policemen. Some COSAS members had guns to do this. They told us that we had to be prepared to die for the struggle.

These organisations use children from ages 12 to 18. The children at these ages become easily influenced. We were told to burn the schools because they said communists would come and build better schools for the Blacks. They said we must get rid of the White men. South Africa will then be called Azania. When I wanted to go to University, the leaders in COSAS were not happy. They said that we should wait and go to university in Moscow.

In October 1984 I got converted. I gave my life to the Lord Jesus. I went to the police to tell them about my case because it was then that I realised how bad I was. I went there not expecting to come back because what I did what was against the law. I know that now I should be behind bars. But by the grace of God they did not lock me inside. I think the Lord saw my heart that I really repented and cried over my sins. I think the Lord saw my heart and touched their hearts that they did not put me in jail. Before I got converted I used to have nightmares. I couldn't sleep at night. Every time I will see pictures of those people who were burning and hear them cry in my ears. I was so depressed I did not know what to do. It was after meeting with the Lord Jesus that it disappeared.

Appendix 4

Some church interventions during the struggle for liberation
"Political" funerals, prayer meetings with social themes, regular services and Masses for detainees, raising awareness through posters, pamphlets, sermons, visits to imprisoned activists, international public statements, distribution of awareness building magazines such as *Learn and Teach*, youth dramatisations on the killings of 1976 performed annually in churches on June 16 when all other demonstrations or commemorations were banned, training of trade unionists, leadership courses for community workers, use of church premises for public meetings, Detainees' Parents Support Committee activities and monitoring government actions in the townships by local and overseas activists, public religious processions in defiance of emergency regulations, constant promotion of the relevance of church social teaching.

Appendix 5

Following is a list of those who died in the massacre at Boipatong. seventy-four were charged for the Boipatong murders of which 16 were finally convicted.

Name	Street
1. Richard Jim Nzimeni (40)	194 Senqu
2. Maleshwane A Letsoko (34)	194 Senqu
3. Pheto Andries Letsoko (36)	194 Senqu
4. Mbolawa Michael Msibi (15)	625 Bapedi
5. Violet Nozinja Radebe (48)	625 Bapedi
6. Maria Mofokeng (26)	85 Bapedi
7 Elizabeth Khaile (19)	85 Bapedi
8. Sibusiso Msibi (8)	25 Bapedi
9. Ronika Phale (15)	757 Hlubi
10. Modiehi Elizabeth Moloi (14)	765 Hlubi
11. Ntombifikile Nonjoli (7)	765 Hlubi
12. Memi Martha Nonjoli (45)	765 Hlubi
13. Maphathi Linah Manyika (48)	734 Bafokeng
14. Matilda Hlubi (13)	722 Bafokeng
15. Mpho Julia Mgcina (39)	696 Bafokeng
16. Magete Andries Manyika (52)	734 Bafokeng
17. Lubenyo Flora Moshope (69)	761 Lekoa
18. Lindiwe Julia Latha (13)	46 Slovo Park
19. Toli Samuel Ngcukutu (47)	46 Slovo Park
20. Madidjane J. Khoza(40)	4 Slovo Park
21. Aaron Mathope (9 Months)	109 Slovo Park
22. Simon N. Ramoeletsi (53)	153 Slovo Park
23. Maria Ramoeletsi (Serathi) (53)	153 Slovo Park
24. Nomvula Jemina Latha (17)	46 Slovo Park
25. Agnes Malindi (4/6 months)	23 Slovo Park
26. Konu Liza Mias (48)	31 Slovo Park
27. Mamatshidiso R. Mathope (43)	109 Slovo Park
28. Mohlopheki J. Mbatha	133 Slovo Park
29. Poppie Mbatha (5)	133 Slovo Park
30. Bafana Benjamin Genu	1411 Ngwenya
31. Mtuli Mnyila (32)	4204 (Kwamasiza Hostel)
32. Phenduka Zephrid Sibisi (42)	1090 Barolong
33. Maria Dlamini	1109 Barolong
34. Mantsali P. Dlamini	1109 Barolong
35. Modise P. Sebolai (30)	121 Bakwena
36. Modise P. Sebolai (50)	666 Moshoeshoe
37. Dikeledi Anna Debolai (52)	666 Moshoeshoe
38. Litefo Nellie Kubu (70)	1183 Moshoeshoe
39. Sampie Solomon Mosoetsa (27)	666 Moshoeshoe
40. Khabonina Maria Mlangeni (30)	238 Thaba-Bosiu
41. Mmatebesi Aletta Moeti (24)	104 Majola
42. Mamosenyehi B. Lerobane (61)	45 Majola
43. Elizabeth Francinah Ndimane (74)	1401 Bereng
44. Matseliso Flora Msomi (51)	11548 (Ex. Zone 11 Sebokeng)
45 Benjamin Mosoetsa (47)	762 Sebokeng

Appendix 6

Submissions by the Gauteng Council of Churches (the Vaal region) to the TRC post- hearing meeting, held at the Sebokeng College of Education, 21 June 1997.

1. Introductory remarks: Thanks to members of the TRC for the noble course that you have jointly undertaken of healing the wounds suffered by our society during the apartheid era.

2. Theological rationale: The SACC, through her former Regional Council of Churches, got involved actively in the battlefield against apartheid. The South African Government during that period of apartheid had a theology of its own; we chose to call it "State Theology". "State theology" was simply the theological justification of the then status quo with its racism and totalitarianism. The status quo reduces the poor to passivity, obedience and apathy. "State Theology" misused theological concepts and biblical texts for its own political purposes. Because of this gross violation of the "Will of God" by which people should live, the ecumenical and prophetic church was left with no other option but to intervene prophetically and become the voice of the voiceless. It had to interpret the Bible in the context of the situation prevailing at the time. We chose to obey God rather than men (Acts 3:29). We engaged in defiance campaigns. On the other hand, the State appealed to the conscience of Christians in the name of "Law and Order" to accept the use of "violence" as a God-given duty, with the primary aim of maintaining the status quo of oppression. The Church could not allow people to be sacrificed for the sake of unjust laws. Our true Christian faith commits us to work for true reconciliation and genuine peace. We pointed out to the apartheid regime that there could be no true reconciliation and no genuine peace without justice. In the 1980s, South Africa reached a decisive moment in its history. A fundamental assessment was taking place concerning the basic structures of its apartheid order. The Church pressed on to make structural change possible and sustainable.

How did we assist in this role?

We promoted our campaigns and provided sanctuary for internal refugees as well as providing material for families of political detainees and prisoners. Agencies such as NAMDA (National Medical Doctors Association), LHR (Lawyers for Human Rights) and DPSC (Detainees' Parents Support Committee) worked closely with us in this challenging task. Much support came from the oppressed masses and their organisations.

Vaal Chairperson, it will not be easy for any person who has not worked in this area to tell exactly what the situation has been like during those years of oppression. The Council of Churches is one of the sources that can provide the TRC with information which could assist sub-committees operating within the TRC structure.

1. During the period of the "total-strategy" (PW Botha's anti-communist clarion call), this area became one of the targeted places. This system worked from the late 70s and became very sophisticated, roughly from the early 80s until the early 90s. This period involved the application of destabilisation tactics in a fairly generalised and indiscriminate manner.

   There was direct military action i.e. "Operation Palmiet". This operation took place in 1984 during the height of the Vaal rent boycott. This phase gave way to another period from the late part of 1985 until the National Peace Accord. This phase can be described as a phase of intensified and more selective destabilisation confined to particular places like Sebokeng, Boipatong and Sharpeville. There was also a substantial increase in activity by the apartheid government-sponsored dissident groups – secret assassins, the Eagle clubs (WHAM) and organised criminals.

   On the other hand, members of the security forces employed dirty tricks against the community. One of their major efforts made was to coerce people to act as State witnesses in political trials. Young and old people were bought to sell out their leaders. And criminals from Kwa Madala at ISCOR compound (Vanderbijlpark) allegedly worked with some members of the police. In the broader community these operations were characterised by mass indiscriminate killings which became part of the everyday life of the community in the Vaal. Perpetrators were not brought to court.

2. An incident of history that cannot go without mentioning is the massacre of Sharpeville residents on 21 March 1960. This event has left an indelible mark in the minds of people. Another event that freezes the blood is the Sebokeng night vigil massacre at Nangalembe's house (Zone 7), where about thirty-eight mourners were shot dead whilst praying.

   Our then field workers informed the police at Sebokeng police station in advance about the looming tension around that area and the possibility of attack at night. Although the security forces were cognisant of this case, no intensified deployment of police was made as a preventative measure. From that period up to the Boipatong massacre, peace never reigned in the Vaal area. Therefore, one of the great tasks before us is to bring together the broader Vaal Township residents and former Kwa Madala residents in pursuit of building peace and reconciliation.

3. As the church we apologise nevertheless for the times when we were silent in the face of violations of human rights carried out by government forces, structures or those aligned with them. We also apologise for our silence in not sufficiently condemning the violations of human rights carried out either as revenge attacks or in the name of the struggle. We furthermore offer our services as ministers of healing to victims and perpetrators from whatever quarter they come. For us the past hearings have been a transforming experience. Those TRC hearings were like starting a new journey of discovery that opened up new avenues of hope. This is the reason why we have come

4. Recommendations: On the strength of our experience in working and in discussions with community members and leadership, we trust that this document will find support in this sitting of the TRC today. Now we wish to make our recommendations for reparation.

We recommend that:

a) Children who lost their parents through these acts of terror should receive urgent assistance for their welfare and education.

b) Destroyed properties be rebuilt without discrimination as to the political alignment of their owners.

c) That graves of the victims of 1960, 1984 and 1992 be built and properly fenced up and memorial stones be erected at these sites. Furthermore, we believe that a memorial stone should be erected to the memory of all who died in the struggle for justice over the years. Among these we mention our own field worker, Saul Tsotetsi

d) That religious bodies together with the reparations and human rights committees should identify a day of mourning for this community. During the mass burials people did not have time to mourn. This is part of the process of healing and reconciliation.

e) That a memorial park be built which would include, among other things, a museum where the history of the struggle for freedom is depicted. A building or buildings where training would be offered in various skills should also be considered.

f) We as a church offer to continue with the process of reaching out to bring healing and reconciliation to all groups. In this context we notice that very little progress has been made in the area of bridging the gap between black and white in this area. We commit ourselves to work in this area as well as in bringing the various disparate groups in the township together.

g) We commit ourselves to work towards a genuine consensus among all in the Vaal.

h) That the government agrees on a special day with the National Body of Churches to have contrition and cleansing services throughout the nation. We already had one in Sebokeng hostel led by the Council of Churches and one organised by Khulumani Support Group at Nyolohelo Catholic Church at Zone 12.

i) A request to the government to embark on a job creation project.

j) That professional and trauma counselling be provided for all who have been affected by the trouble in the Vaal.

k) On rehabilitation of society, we need to focus on disarming particularly young people. This issue in the Vaal remains a central point in our attempt at building peace and reconciliation. There won't be peace while young people are so heavily armed and continue with revenge killings, as is the case particularly in Sharpeville.

l) The Council of Churches in the Vaal has already structured itself to monitor that recommendations put forward today are carried out.

m) In 1991, the church in this area was put on trial by the then Lekoa Town Council, town clerk Mr Louw. Allegations were made by the town clerk on behalf of the entire Council that we were (terrorists) carrying AK-47s. This occurred when the clergy marched to the Council offices to hand over a memorandum. We were arrested, charged and sentenced to three years' suspended sentence. We therefore, in the spirit of reconciliation request that the criminal record placed on our heads be removed. We felt severely ill treated by the unjust apartheid regime.

n) People like Father Geoff Moselane, Rev Lord MacCamel and the rest of the then Delmas trialists should be offered an apology from those who were persecuting them.
o) We encourage all those who were involved in acts which violated the human rights of others to come forward and ask forgiveness. Gauteng Council of Churches (Vaal region) June 1997

Appendix 7

In the following pages councillors give a brief account of their side of the story. There is something plaintive, sad and poignant in their voices. A sense of being caught on the wrong side of history. Much remains to be said. May I take this opportunity of thanking them for allowing me to use their submission to the TRC.

Former Lekoa Town Council submission to the Truth and Reconciliation Commission, August 1996

We were councillors elected into office after the collapse of the advisory board system in 1977. Service charges were increasing almost yearly before we came into office. People were not happy and by 1984 their cup of dissatisfaction was filled to the brim.

An increase (in rent and services) was mooted that an amount may be added after the budget showed a deficit. This increase was never implemented, but, unbeknownst to the councillors, the people had taken a decision to do away with the councillors.

On 3 September 1984, mobs broke into bottle stores and looted them. Some friendly residents warned some councillors to be aware, as they were the next targets. Some unfortunate councillors were not warned. Those who were warned took to their heels with whatever they could lay their hands on. Life was important.

On 4 September 1984 all hell broke out. Property was destroyed, houses were burned down and belongings were destroyed by fire or carried away by the very people who elected us. Some of our colleagues were found at home brutally killed, namely, Mr Jacob Dlamini at Sharpeville, Mr Chakane at Sebokeng and Mr Motjeane also at Sebokeng. The wife of Mr Dlamini was so traumatised that she became insane and subsequently died. The wife of Mr Chakane is also insane though still alive. Mrs Motjeane is not healthy following her husband's death. These men had children who must be brought up. After these riots, which spread throughout the country, the councillors were left with nothing. Some houses were built in Zone 10 to accommodate them but they had to buy them. What with?

The children of the councillors feared to go to school because of the obnoxious tag attached to their parents. Most of the councillors never got work since, and are now not in a good state of health.

As ex-councillors, where do we belong, as it seems the people and the government do not want us? We are aware apartheid is a costly commodity but why at the expense of the councillors? Why? Why? Why?

Suggestions: We feel that concessions should be given to these ex-councillors to be exempted from taxation and medical expenses; bursaries should be granted to the children who still attend schools or universities. The ex-councillors should be given proper accommodation. Alternatively, the houses built for them in Zone 10 should be given to them as compensation. The rest we leave to our government to know what to do about those who suffered and are still suffering.

Areas of healing: People have to be counselled about the needs of a community and accept the fact that we all must pay for services.how can this be accomplished?

The president or his nominee must meet the former councillors and hear what they have to say and get it from the horse's mouth. Meeting the people at ground level and making them aware that although the government wishes to help them they must play their part.

List of former councillors:

MM Mkhiwane	P Mahlatsi	**Killed on 2 May 1992**
JD Ramagole	ML Ramotshidisi	EC Mahlatsi
S Mofokeng	Reverend Ne Ttladi	
BM Nzandai	V Ndijshwa	**Deceased:**
C Cindi	M Shale	T Mosala
Ms M Phosisi	P Mphulanyane	A Dlamini
N Mokati	J Tshabalala	S Tshabalala
P Radebe		S Mathlare
J Motshele	**Killed during riots:**	S Motsoahole
S Kodisang	J Dlamini	
PS Mofokeng	JC Chakane	
ND Mpondo	S Motjeane	
A Sekobane		

Appendix 8

The towns

Sebokeng has a population of more than half a million people. The town was established in 1965 when 18 772 houses were built on the site of the present township. The word Sebokeng means "the gathering of the peoples". The township is characterised by many different cultures and languages. It is situated on the Golden Highway about 65 km south of Johannesburg and 20 km north of Vanderbijlpark. Sebokeng residents work all over the Gauteng area and have access to two universities, a technikon, a teachers training college, technical colleges and more than one hundred schools. During the seventies and eighties Sebokeng was the administrative headquarters for the six townships of Bophelong, Boipatong, Sharpeville, Zamdela, Refengkhotso and Evaton. Under this authority the Lekoa Town Council (a grouping of "elected" black business people) functioned. It threatened to raise tariffs for rents and services in 1984 and this sparked off violent protests and a ten-year rent boycott in the black areas of the Vaal Triangle. Protracted negotiations between black trade unions, the white Vaal Chamber of Commerce and Industry, white representatives of the Orange-Vaal Administration Board, the black Lekoa Town Council and the churches failed to end the historic boycott. The Vaal Civic Association was launched in Sebokeng. Half of the population lives in informal settlements, which are progressively being eliminated. Huge single-men hostels with a total of 19 504 beds are situated just outside the township and some of the serious violence of the eighties and nineties was linked to these hostels. With the new government the housing landscape is changing for the better.

Boipatong has 27 000 residents. It was established in 1953 when 1 880 houses were built here to supply labour to the Iscor steelworks at Vanderbijlpark nearby. The name Boipatong means "the place of refuge" or "hiding place". It has two high schools and four primary schools. Like other townships under the Lekoa Town Council, Boipatong was involved in the long rent boycott of the eighties that followed the uprising of 1984. Boipatong became world news in 1992 because of the massacre of its residents by hostel dwellers from Iscor's Kwa Madala hostel. It was this tragedy that stalled negotiations that were to lead to a new South Africa

Bophelong's population is 14 000. Bophelong was established in 1955 when 1406 houses were built in the area. Its name suggests "life", "liveliness" or "vitality". It is another formerly segregated black residential area providing the work force for Iscor steelworks.

During the apartheid era, housing development was suspended because government policy decreed that Africans should not enjoy permanent residence in urban South Africa, and partly on account of fears that a proposed highway would cut through the township. But towards the end of 1986 – the highest point ever in state security activity – the State President PW Botha announced that black townships would not be moved unless it was absolutely necessary. It was from here the first shots that fuelled the uprising of September 1984 were fired.

Sharpeville has a population of 65 000.The Union Steel Corporation, a scrap metal company, started in Vereeniging in 1911 and spawned Top Location about ten years later. Top Location, popularly called Topville, was a fenced-in permit-controlled migrant settlement with a Sophiatown-type personality adjoining the area today known as Duncanville. Adelaide Tambo, wife of former ANC leader Oliver Tambo, was once removed from Top Location.

Between the forties and late fifties the residents were moved to the new township of Sharpeville. People of mixed blood were sent to Rust-Ter-Vaal, and Indians to Roshnee. The township is named after a mayor of neighbouring Vereeniging called John Sharpe.

The original Sharpeville was administered and policed by Vereeniging Town Council, which ruthlessly suppressed all political activity. The Pan-Africanist

Congress, however, found Sharpeville a fertile political breeding ground when in 1960 they mobilised for the Anti-Pass Campaign. This led to the infamous Sharpeville massacre of 69 residents in that year. It was a watershed moment in South African history that propelled black resistance into armed struggle. Sharpeville was also part of the ten-year rent boycott that started in the Vaal Triangle in 1984. The signing into law of the new constitution took place at Sharpeville's George Thabe Stadium on 10 December 1996, when a constitutional assembly mural was unveiled by the President, Nelson Mandela. On the same day, Cyril Ramaphosa, chairperson of the constitutional assembly said, "At Sharpeville, in Vereeniging, both powerful symbols of past relationships between South Africans, we are making a break with the past, a break with the pain, a break with betrayal. We are starting a new chapter."

Vereeniging has a population of 80 000. This town – the name means "unification" – was founded in 1892 on the banks of the Vaal River, south of Johannesburg. It is situated in one of the busiest industrial areas in the country. Coal found in 1867 stimulated the establishment of Vereeniging, a formerly white town. Factories in the area produce liquid fuels, chemicals, building materials, agricultural implements and plastics. The Treaty of Vereeniging, ending the Anglo-Boer war of 1899-1902 was signed here at the turn of the century. At the signing of the new constitution into law, in December 1996, in nearby Sharpeville, the chairperson of the constitutional assembly, Cyril Ramaphosa said: "At Vereeniging in 1902 a treaty between the British and the Boers effectively disenfranchised the black majority."

Vanderbijlpark has a population of 68 000 and was established at the outbreak of World War Two. Named after its founder the famous scientist, Dr HJ van der Bijl, it is the hub of the iron, steel (Iscor) and metallurgical industries in South Africa. Like Vereeniging, it is situated on the Vaal River about 80 km south of Johannesburg. Formerly a whites only town it was until recently managed by the Conservative Party. Dr Carel de Wet, MP for Vanderbijlpark and later South African ambassador in London, said at the time of the Sharpeville massacre in 1960: "It is a matter of concern to me that only one person was killed." Its Iscor hostel called Kwa Madala became world news in 1992 when the inhabitants attacked the residents of Boipatong, a black township close by.

Evaton has a population of between 198 000 and 270 000. Sometimes called the dark city because it was for so long without electricity in the past, Evaton is situated north of Sebokeng on the Golden Highway.
The town which is one hundred years old was sanctioned by President Kruger as compensation to Africans who had supported him in the Anglo-Boer War. The famous Evaton bus boycott or Azikhwelwa of the fifties was largely spearheaded by the ANC Youth League, which had defected to the Pan-Africanist Congress in 1949. The "Russians", a group of Basotho gangsters who terrorised the townships of the Vaal Triangle, became famous for their

opposition to the boycott. It was one of the few townships where Africans retained property rights during apartheid. Evaton always had its own administration, culminating in the establishment of the ill-fated Evaton Town Council. Given its rich cultural and social life, Evaton is truly the Sophiatown of the Vaal Triangle. It was a participant in the boycotts, mass stayaways and resistance strikes of the eighties.

Appendix 9
Abbreviations used in text

AME	African Methodist Episcopal Church
ANC	African National Congress
AYU	Azanian Youth Unity
AZAPO	Azanian People's Organisation
CIS	Crime Intelligence Service
CODESA	Congress for a Democratic South Africa
COSAS	Congress of South African Students
DET	Department of Education & Training
DPSC	Detainees' Parents Support Committee
HF	Holy Family
IEC	Independent Electoral Commission
IFF	International Freedom Foundation
IFP	Inkatha Freedom Party
MK	Umkonto We Sizwe
MSHR	Missionary Sisters of The Holy Rosary
NGK	Nederlandse Gereformeerde Kerk
NSMS	National Security Management System
OFM	Order of Friars Minor
OP	Order of Preachers
OVAB	Orange Vaal Administration Board
PAC	Pan-Africanist Congress
RSM	Religious Sisters of Mercy
SACBC	South African Catholic Bishops' Conference
SACC	South African Council of Churches
SADF	South African Defence Force
SAP	South African Police
SASO	South African Students' Organisation
SCA	Sharpeville Civic Association
SCA	Sowetan Civic Association
SCM	Students Christian Movement
SFSC	Security Forces Support Committee
SYC	Sharpeville Youth Congress
TRC	Truth and Reconciliation Commission
UDF	United Democratic Front

VASCO	Vaal Students Congress
VCA	Vaal Civic Association
VIC	Vaal Information Centre
VMSG	Vaal Ministers Solidarity Group
VWO	Vaal Women's Organisation
YCW	Young Christian Workers

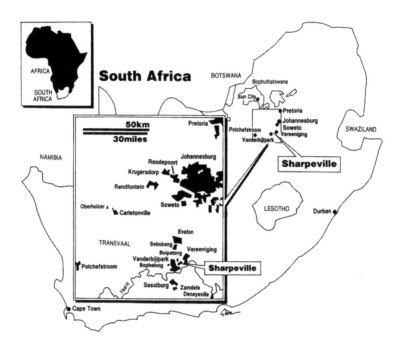

From *The Sharpeville Six* by Prakash Diar (McClelland & Stewart, 1990)

285